NO HARD FEELINGS

'A must-read that topples the idea that emotions don't belong
in the workplace, *No Hard Feelings* offers a path towards a
future I want to work in: an emotionally expressive, yet
respectful (and high-performing!) workplace.'
Susan Cain, author of *Quiet* and Co-founder of Quiet Revolution

'*No Hard Feelings* is one of the most original, insightful, and
laugh-out-loud funny business books I've read in a long time. It will
transform the way you think about the role of feelings in the workplace.'
Cal Newport, author of *Deep Work* and *Digital Minimalism*

'*No Hard Feelings* is both a charming, sparkling read and a clear-eyed
roadmap to harnessing the things that make us most human into tools
that will make you more productive, effective, and happier at work.
A must read for every leader and every aspiring leader.'
Laszlo Bock, CEO of Humu and author of *Work Rules!*

'*No Hard Feelings* dispels the myth that there's no place for
emotions at work. You can't communicate clearly unless you're
aware of your own emotions, and the emotions you're sparking
in others. You can't build productive relationships at work if
you're showing up like a robot. This book will help you build
the emotional discipline you need to succeed.'
Kim Scott, author of *Radical Candor*

'If you've ever thought it's best to check your emotions at the office
door, this book will change your mind. It's full of lively illustrations
and practical examples to show how you can harness emotions
to become more creative, collaborative, and productive.'
Adam Grant, author of *Originals, Give and Take,*
and *Option B* with Sheryl Sandberg

'Warm, witty, and wise, *No Hard Feelings* is the missing manual
for reconciling emotions with professionalism intelligently.'
Chip Conley, Strategic Advisor at Airbnb and author of *Wisdom at Work*

About the Authors

Liz Fosslien is a marketing and design consultant whose clients include Salesforce, Ernst & Young, and the Stanford d.School. Liz most recently served as the creative director for Parliament, a firm that facilitates collaboration between Fortune 500 executives, entrepreneurs, and bestselling business book authors. Before that, she worked on branding and product at Genius, and ran statistical analyses at the aptly named Analysis Group. Liz is also an illustrator (she drew everything in this book!) and chart-maker whose personal projects have been featured by *The Economist*, NPR, *The Financial Times*, the *Freakonomics* blog, and CNN. She has a BA in mathematical economics from Pomona College.

Mollie West Duffy is an organizational designer at global innovation firm IDEO. Mollie formerly worked as a research associate for Nitin Nohria, the dean of Harvard Business School, and Michael E. Porter, a renowned strategy professor. She's written for *Fast Company, Quartz, Stanford Social Innovation Review, Entrepreneur, Quiet Revolution*, and other digital outlets. She has a BA in organizational behavior from Brown University and an MFA in design from Parsons School of Design. She's taught at Stanford and Parsons. She lives in Brooklyn with her husband.

NO
HARD
FEELINGS

Emotions at Work
(and How They Help Us Succeed)

Liz Fosslien and Mollie West Duffy

BUSINESS

PENGUIN BUSINESS

UK | USA | Canada | Ireland | Australia
India | New Zealand | South Africa

Penguin Business is part of the Penguin Random House group of companies
whose addresses can be found at global.penguinrandomhouse.com.

First published in the United States of America by Portfolio/Penguin,
an imprint of Penguin Random House LLC 2019
First published in Great Britain by Penguin Business 2019
003

Book design by Cassandra Garruzzo
Typeset by Jouve (UK), Milton Keynes
Printed in China by Printer Toppan Leefung Printing Limited

A CIP catalogue record for this book is available from the British Library

ISBN: 978–0–241–32870–5

www.greenpenguin.co.uk

MIX
Paper from
responsible sources
FSC® C018179

Penguin Random House is committed to a
sustainable future for our business, our readers
and our planet. This book is made from Forest
Stewardship Council® certified paper.

To our families, with the greatest emotion of all: love.

CONTENTS

A DAY AT THE OFFICE

CHAPTER 1

The Future Is Emotional

W hen Howard Schultz returned to lead Starbucks in 2008 after an eight-year hiatus, he cried. Not alone—hidden in a bathroom stall or locked in his corner office—but in front of the entire company.

Daily sales figures were falling by double digits. The two CEOs who preceded Schultz had grown the company at breakneck speed, but when the recession hit in 2007, the foundations of this hastily constructed empire began to wobble.

Ahead of his return, Schultz spent nights in bed staring at the ceiling, worrying about what he would say on his first day back as CEO. He desperately wanted to reassure tens of thousands of employees that their livelihoods were not in jeopardy. But boosting morale wasn't just a strategic move; he felt personally responsible for the well-being of the people who worked at Starbucks. Schultz, who had grown up poor and watched his parents struggle to make ends meet, knew how much they depended on their jobs.

When he walked onstage, he realized his employees needed to see vulnerability from the person they were trusting to fix their problems. The truth was, he felt distraught about the direction the business had taken while he was gone, and they deserved to know that. Schultz chose to lift a mask that few employees—much less CEOs—remove in front of their coworkers. Setting aside formality, he let tears roll down his cheeks.

Crying can sometimes seem manipulative or calculated. But Schultz had the emotional intelligence to pair this moment of vulnerability with a reassuring follow-up: he laid out his plan for a comeback and then invited feedback from workers. That month, Schultz was flooded with more than five thousand appreciative emails. And by 2010, the tide had turned: Starbucks' stock price was higher than ever.

Most of us vastly underestimate the size and scope of the emotional needs we bring to the office. Beyond the leader-employee relationship, emotional dynamics affect our motivation, health, communication, decision making, and more. Yet most of us ignore those emotions. Why is it that when we think of professionalism, we immediately jump to the idea that we should suppress everything we feel?

This is a book from two friends who each had to learn, somewhat painfully, the importance of acknowledging emotion at work. When we[1] started our first jobs, we thought professionals did not fail, did not fuss, and certainly did not feel. But we soon realized this view is unrealistic and stands in the way of our sense of fulfillment, and ultimately our success.

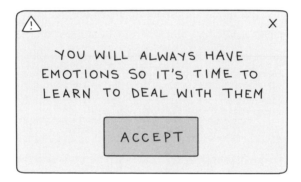

As a young analyst at an economic consulting firm, Liz had gotten the job she thought she always wanted. But long nights of staring at depositions under fluorescent lights left her increasingly depressed and anxious. Liz finally quit, with no backup plan. She took a job at Starbucks to pay the bills

[1] **A note about "we":** this book is written by two authors. You will see first person plural for the majority of the book, except when we're telling a story, and then we'll switch into the first person and denote it by labeling the section with *Liz* or *Mollie*.

and started researching why she had been so unhappy and what she could have done to improve her mood.

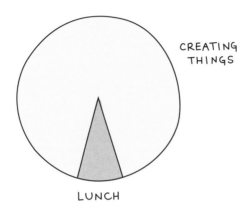

WHAT WE THOUGHT WORK WOULD BE

CREATING THINGS

LUNCH

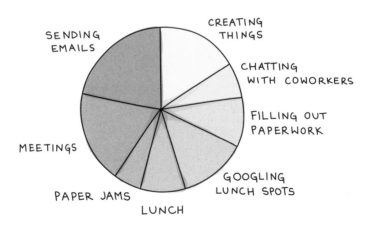

WHAT WORK IS

SENDING EMAILS

CREATING THINGS

CHATTING WITH COWORKERS

FILLING OUT PAPERWORK

MEETINGS

GOOGLING LUNCH SPOTS

PAPER JAMS

LUNCH

Meanwhile, Mollie was working in a stressful job as a product manager for a start-up. She woke up one morning and realized the area above her right eye was completely numb. When the sensation didn't go away after a few days, Mollie went to a doctor. The diagnosis? Anxiety. The numbness was caused by the tension Mollie held in her shoulders and neck. In that moment, Mollie realized she needed a different job. She wanted to work in an office where she didn't have to bite down high levels of fear, anxiety, and frustration until they caused her physical pain.

But Mollie couldn't quit right away, and it took six months for her to find a new job. As she looked, she started reading about emotion, culture, and the workplace because she knew what it felt like to be stuck in an unhealthy work situation. Liz continued to do the same. Our goal was to better understand our feelings: When are they useful and when are they just noise? Can we mold them to change how we experience work? We're guessing you opened this book looking for answers to similar questions.

Our shared story began in 2014 when a mutual friend set us up on a platonic blind date. We bonded immediately: we're both introverts, and we both have an irreverent sense of humor, need to wear sleep masks to get a good night's rest, and enjoy taking on creative side projects. By then, we were each working in New York; Liz had decided to move from the West Coast to take a job at Genius, a (then early-stage) music-media company, and Mollie was in grad school.

When we met, our shared interest in the myriad ways emotion affects work led us to start coauthoring illustrated articles on the topic. But we soon hit a stumbling block: we had never worked closely together before, which led to miscommunication. Mollie felt that Liz was obsessing over details that no one else would notice, whereas Liz felt that Mollie was moving too fast. Our email exchanges became more and more tense, and our projects soon stalled. Hoping to save our personal and professional relationship, we scheduled a dinner to discuss our issues in person.

It was hard! Neither one of us wanted to say anything for fear of making the other person feel bad. But our differences went deeper than our perennial coffee vs. tea debate and needed to be brought out into the light.

And to do that, we had to overcome our instinct to pretend feelings didn't matter.

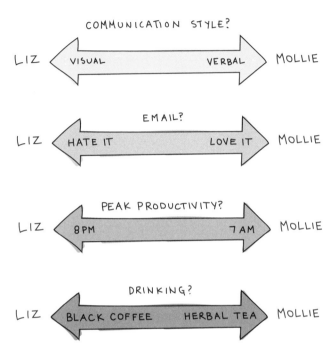

Had we not already been researching emotions at work, we probably wouldn't have given so much credence to our feelings—and we'd never have noticed that building trust always preceded our best creative teamwork. But since we were paying attention, we noticed how much emotion affected every part of our collaboration *and* the rest of our professional lives, like decision making and employee-manager communication.

That's because the future of work is emotional. No scripts exist for our most difficult professional interactions. When you hear the phrase "emotion at work," you might think of career milestones: job interviews, salary negotiations, and annual reviews. But you've probably felt just as intensely about day-to-day, seemingly mundane events. You're thrilled to receive a 🖐️ from the CEO in response to your Slack comment, you're infuriated when a colleague interrupts you for the fifth time, and you fret over whether you need to immediately reply to a work email that appears in your inbox on a Saturday evening.

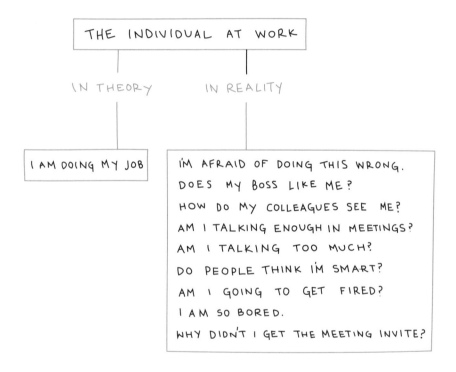

The forces that compel us to ignore our emotions at work must be combatted. Modern work requires an ability to effectively harness emotion—but most of us have never learned how to do this in our professional lives. As we start to recognize the importance of soft skills, we're left wondering: Is it possible to be *too* soft? How much emotion can we express before we come across as unprofessional? What if our "authentic self" is overwhelmed and anxious—should we be open about these feelings? How does who we are (for example, our gender,[2] race, or age) affect the answers to these questions?

Suppression and avoidance might seem to be the easiest answers. "Let's go back to checking our emotions at the door." But this attitude is counterproductive. Humans are emotional creatures, regardless of circumstance. By ignoring our feelings at work, we overlook important data and risk making preventable mistakes. We send emails that cause unnecessary anxiety, we fail to find work meaningful, and we burn out.

We're guessing you've heard of emotional intelligence (EQ), the ability to recognize and understand both how you and how those around you feel. You

2 **Note:** Though recent research treats gender as nonbinary, most studies focus solely on differences between males and females. We discuss biological differences in a binary context but acknowledge this leaves some individuals out and hope they are included in future research. When we talk about differences between male and female emotion and communication styles, we refer to gender as a nonbiological role.

might even know that EQ is a better predictor of success in the workplace than IQ. But real achievement at work requires going one step beyond emotional intelligence: you need to learn to be reasonably emotional. This means matching how you communicate your feelings to the specific situation. To do that, you need emotional fluency—the capacity to productively sense emotion, and to know how and when to translate what you feel into healthy action.

A friend of ours recently lamented, "I need to give my team difficult feedback, but I have no idea how to start the conversation." When we join a company, we receive extensive training about how to schedule meetings and fill out expense reports. But no one tells us what to do if we're upset with a coworker or how to bounce back from a botched meeting with our boss.

HOUSE OF REALISTIC WORK HORRORS

1 ACCIDENTAL REPLY ALL
2 LOGIN PROBLEMS
3 HORRIBLE TRAFFIC
4 BORED TO DEATH
5 14-HOUR WORK DAY
6 "CAN WE CHAT?"
7 WORK BFF QUITS
8 MEDDLING COWORKERS
9 VISIBLY SICK COLLEAGUE
   WHO WON'T GO HOME

Two major changes necessitate a deep understanding of emotion at work. The first is how much we interact with our colleagues. Today, the top skills employers seek are the ability to work on a team and the capacity to communicate verbally with others. As *The Economist* stated, "In modern business, collaboration is next to godliness." But the downside to more collaboration is more conflict. We can all relate to Elaine's famous *Seinfeld* line, "I had to take a sick day. I'm so sick of these people." The second change is our relationship with our jobs. We work more than ever, we place a premium on meaningful work, and we increasingly let what we do define who we are. These shifts influence everything from our health to our motivation to our decision making.

Although emotion at work is not a new topic, we usually hear about on-the-job feelings as enemies that need to be wrangled into submission. That's how we used to approach our feelings at work, too. Now we know that our feelings can be guideposts, and we try to learn from them and express them effectively. We want you to start looking at emotion as something that can be treated with care and affection. After all, you bring your feelings to work every day.

We created the Seven New Rules of Emotion at Work to serve as a guide for how and when to rely on your feelings. Success depends on learning how to let emotion into the workplace without letting it run wild. By confronting our envy, we learn what drives us. By accepting our anxiety, we can reframe

NEW RULES OF EMOTION AT WORK

BE LESS PASSIONATE ABOUT YOUR JOB

INSPIRE YOURSELF

EMOTION IS PART OF THE EQUATION

PSYCHOLOGICAL SAFETY FIRST

YOUR FEELINGS AREN'T FACTS

EMOTIONAL CULTURE CASCADES FROM YOU

BE SELECTIVELY VULNERABLE

it as excitement and become more successful. By learning how emotions affect our decisions, we create a fairer and more welcoming workplace. In other words, this book will teach you how to take hold of and examine your emotions—which, yes, sometimes means keeping a healthy distance from them. By the time you finish this book, you'll understand *why* you might feel something and you'll know what to do with that feeling.

Effectively processing what you feel gives you the power to do more than bring your whole self to work: it enables you to bring your *best* self to work. By "best self" we don't mean "perfect self." Your best self might still become hotheaded, seethe with envy, or cry out of sheer frustration. But your best self knows which of these feelings contain important signals and which are just noise. Your best self knows how to learn from and talk about these emotions, without *becoming* emotional. Your best self is authentic, without bulldozing over other people's feelings.

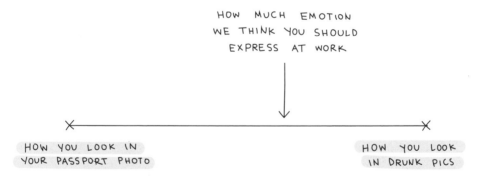

In each chapter, we'll look at how emotion affects one of seven central aspects of work: health, motivation, decision making, teamwork, communication, culture, and leadership. Our goal is not to provide you with a one-size-fits-all regimen. After all, this is impossible: each workplace is different, and every person brings unique contexts and experiences to the office. Instead, we outline general frameworks with which you can better identify, interpret, and apply the power of emotion to different situations. In each chapter, we also list small, practical changes you can make starting today.

We wrote this book for anyone who has felt alone, bored, frustrated, overwhelmed, or insecure at work. We'll provide tips for those who want to stop getting stuck in unhealthy patterns and for managers looking to build a successful team and culture. We've tried to write a book that addresses as many on-the-job experiences as possible (including those of remote workers, introverts, and minority professionals) without trying to speak *for* any group or individual. While we (Liz and Mollie) have different work experiences and styles, we are both white American women in our early thirties. We understand the difficulties, for example, of being women in tech, but we *don't* know how it feels to be nonwhite in an otherwise all-white office. As you'll see, in

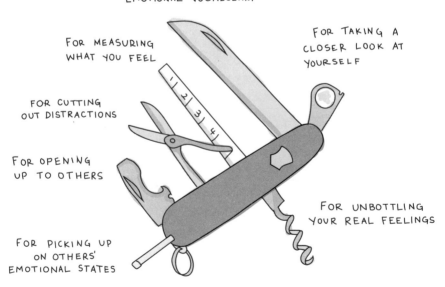

A SWISS ARMY KNIFE FOR EMOTIONS

FOR SHARPENING YOUR
EMOTIONAL VOCABULARY

FOR MEASURING
WHAT YOU FEEL

FOR TAKING A
CLOSER LOOK AT
YOURSELF

FOR CUTTING
OUT DISTRACTIONS

FOR OPENING
UP TO OTHERS

FOR UNBOTTLING
YOUR REAL FEELINGS

FOR PICKING UP
ON OTHERS'
EMOTIONAL STATES

some sections, we'll point you to additional resources written by people who can better describe and offer advice for certain workplace experiences.

If you've ever chewed your fingernails before an impending presentation, been so frustrated you ended up staring at the same spreadsheet for an entire afternoon, or wished you could just turn everything off and be a robot for a couple days, we've been there too. And we're here to help.

Liz AND Mollie

PS: To help you make the skills in this book actionable, we've created an emotional tendencies assessment. See page 247 for a flash version or take the full assessment on our website at lizandmollie.com/assessment.

CHAPTER 2

Health

Be less passionate about your job:

Why taking a chill pill makes you healthier

H

ow many of these statements apply to you?

- You get anxious if you haven't checked your work email for ten minutes
- When your friends ask you how you've been, you start detailing a minor work inconvenience
- Later, you dream about said inconvenience
- You obsess about work during dinner, at the gym, and when you're trying to fall asleep
- Your mood depends almost completely on how work is going

If you answered "a lot," it might be time to take Drake's advice: "You need to get done, done, done, done at work."

Caring too much about a job is unhelpful and unhealthy. It makes small problems seem exceptional and throwaway remarks feel appalling. And it's not only leaders or women or Virgos who care too much: it's possible to be overly attached to any job at any level. That's why we came up with the first new rule of emotion at work: *Be less passionate about your job.*

Caring *less* offers a solution to a lot of anguish. You don't hyperventilate before a big presentation. You're not frustrated to tears by incompetent team-mates. You actually put your phone away on date night, and you're not haunted by work FOMO[3] as you backpack through Machu Picchu.

---

3 Fear of missing out. Now you don't need to have FOMO about FOMO.

AFFLICTIONS OF THE MODERN WORKPLACE

THIRD-DEGREE
BURNOUT

DIARRHEMAIL

JOINT-PROPOSAL
PAIN

EXTENSION
HEADACHE

"Be less passionate about your job" doesn't mean "stop caring about work." It means care *more* about yourself. It means carve out time for the people you love, for exercise, and for a guilt-free vacation. It means remind yourself that few people look back at their lives and wish they had stayed at the office until 10:00 P.M.

It would be hard to teach yourself to care less without first getting to the root of the problem. *Why* have we become work martyrs?

1. We think the only way to succeed is to never stop working. We fear even briefly disconnecting will derail our careers.
2. We believe happiness is the result of professional achievement—not the other way around. "Life will be amazing once I get promoted," we tell ourselves. "When I'm making millions, this will all be worth it."

THE 7 DEADLY WORK STRESSORS

SCOPE CREEP

OBSESSING ABOUT EMAIL ON VACATION

THE INFORMATION FIREHOSE

YESTERDAY!
TOMORROW!

UNPREDICTABLE SCHEDULES

SLEEP DEPRIVATION

SOCIAL ISOLATION

UNREALISTIC DEADLINES

In this chapter, we'll put these beliefs under a microscope. We'll show you that each is more myth than gospel, even though sometimes you *will* have to work insane hours or for a boss who emails you 24–7.

ALL WORK, NO PLAY

In 1996, Steelcase, a large office furniture manufacturer, installed a four by six foot glass display in the lobby of its Manhattan headquarters. Inside the display case was a colony of harvester ants meant to show how "Ants live to work, and work to live."

Unfortunately for Steelcase, the public wasn't thrilled with the analogy. *The Wall Street Journal* pointed out that because harvester ants live only about three or four months, Steelcase's motto should be, "You work, and then you die." But Steelcase was right: advances in technology have blurred the lines between our personal and professional lives. We're constantly accessible, which means we feel constantly accountable.

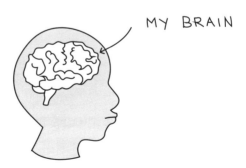

THE LEADING
CAUSE OF STRESS:

MY BRAIN

Some of you may be thinking, wait a second, this is all super dark—isn't it okay to be passionate about your job? Yes! Odds are, at points in your career, you *should* apologetically back out of dinner plans because you need to solve a problem for your boss. But chronically overworking is bad for your health and—counterintuitively—for your success. In fact, productivity starts to drop after working about fifty hours per week. Perhaps you've heard the old saying, "Work expands to fill the time available for its completion." In other words, giving yourself less time might make you more efficient.

"I wish I could go back and tell my much younger self, 'Arianna, your performance will actually improve if you can commit to not only working hard but also unplugging, recharging, and renewing yourself,'" reflects *Huffington Post* founder Arianna Huffington. So how can you emotionally detach from even the most demanding job?

How Stress Affects the Body

Did you know that the mere anticipation of an anxiety-inducing event or period can become a stressor? For example, Liz stresses about travel travails (long security lines, long delays, long flights) for weeks before she actually heads to the airport. And Mollie sometimes worries about paying down a mortgage even though she isn't even close to buying a house.

Stressors disrupt your body's balanced internal state; your stress response is your body's attempt to return to normal. To rapidly transport nutrients and oxygen to your muscles, your blood pressure and your heart and respiration rate all spike. At the same time, any processes that are less important in the short term—such as digestion, growth, and reproduction—slow down.

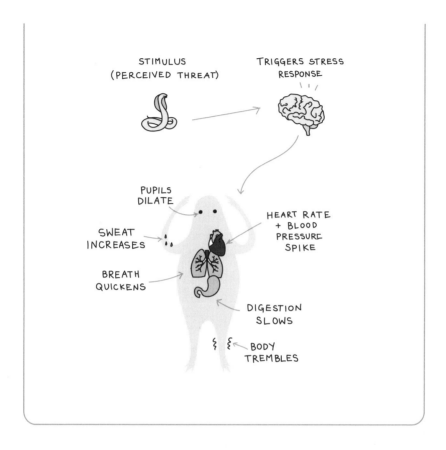

Give yourself a break

Go on vacation: Extended time off keeps us healthy and productive, especially if we have little or no contact with our colleagues while we're away. But more than half of Americans don't take all of their paid vacation. It's hard to head to a remote island when the thought of being away from your email for a day leaves you wracked with guilt. Liz used to fear even asking for vacation because she thought her bosses might view her as unreliable. Managers, how you talk about vacation matters. A lot. The majority of employees say their managers communicate nothing, negative messages, or mixed mes-

A TOURIST'S MAP OF PARIS

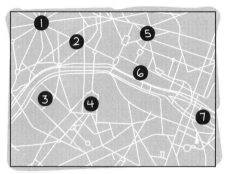

1 ARC DE TRIOMPHE
2 CHAMPS-ÉLYSÉES
3 EIFFEL TOWER
4 LES INVALIDES
5 OPERA
6 LOUVRE
7 NOTRE-DAME

A WORKAHOLIC'S MAP OF PARIS

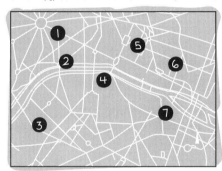

1 EMPLOYER'S PARIS OFFICES
2 CAFE WITH AMPLE OUTLETS
3 NO PHONE SERVICE HERE!
4 FREE WI-FI (GOOD COFFEE)
5 GREAT QUIET SPOT FOR CALLS
6 FREE WI-FI (BAD COFFEE)
7 FANCY RESTAURANT WHERE
YOU CAN APPEASE YOUR PARTNER

sages about taking vacation; with a little more encouragement, almost everyone would use more vacation time. For those of you whose managers *do* discourage taking a vacation, the next few paragraphs will be helpful.

Take a night off: Scheduling leisure time throughout the workweek is just as important as taking vacation—and often easier to swing. When the Boston Consulting Group instituted a predictable time off (PTO) policy that gave each member of a six-person team one weeknight off a week, employees became happier, more relaxed, and less likely to quit. Team members also learned to be more mindful of one another's well-being. "Even if we were working hard," noted one consultant, "we were still looking out for each other to make sure that people were not getting burned out."

TRUE OR FALSE: THIS COUNTS AS A REAL VACATION

Getting a night off also gives you a chance to catch up on sleep. When they haven't gotten enough rest, surgeons slip and drivers crash. Sleep deprivation also makes us gloomy and anxious; if we've been up too long, we start to perceive friendly-looking faces as menacing. So when you haven't slept well, we recommend taking this sound advice from Mollie's mom: "You're not allowed to make judgments on your life when you're short on sleep."

Block off a day: One day every week, Liz does not let herself schedule meetings, calls, or even social events. This off day lets her catch up on her work, so the rest of the week doesn't feel quite as hassled. If you can't block off an entire day, try blocking off a few hours for focused work.

Make room for minibreaks: Stepping away from your desk for even five minutes helps you relax—and stay focused. Danish students who were given a short break before taking a test got significantly higher scores than their peers who didn't get any time to relax. Research also suggests taking a few minutes to chitchat with your coworkers will help you de-stress faster than a solo break.

Set up an after-work ritual: Your brain will benefit from a signal that tells it, "Work is over!" Some ideas: walk or bike home (even brief periods of light exercise are good for you), meditate on your commute, listen to music, read a magazine, or lift weights (some studies show weight training boosts your mood more than cardio). Cal Newport, author of *Deep Work*, ends each day by transcribing any loose notes into a master task list, shutting his computer, and then saying the phrase, "Schedule shutdown, complete." "Here's my rule," he writes. "After I've uttered the magic phrase, if a work-related worry pops to mind, I always answer it with the following thought process: I said the termination phrase."

Chiseling out time for yourself is the easiest and first step toward detaching from your workaholic identity. But that's usually easier said than done: you're emotionally attached to that self because you've spent a lot of time together! To fully cut ties, try these additional mind-set shifts.

Don't extend the logic of the workplace into your time off

Many people are overly enthusiastic about optimizing free time. Stop falling into the type-A trap of compulsively making your hobbies more work than work. If you love to play piano, don't force yourself to practice for thirty minutes at precisely 8:00 P.M. every weeknight and then beat yourself up when you miss a day. Studies show when we mathematize our experiences—by tracking our steps or measuring miles hiked—we don't enjoy them as much.

... *BREATHEINBREATHEOUT FOCUS ONYOURINNERZEN...*

OLIVIA FITS IN A FULL MEDITATION
SESSION BY LISTENING TO IT AT 3X

Get comfortable with being rigorously unproductive once in a while. Being at rest for a time is not the same as wasting time: when you cut yourself a little slack, you'll be more focused and creative when you get back to work. Dedicate a weekend every few months to a short getaway. Make Saturday a no-chores and no-errands day. If you're an extremely type-A person, schedule social events that give you "permission" to step away from work.

Cultivate personal relationships outside of your job

"I love my job," Beyoncé told *GQ* in an interview, "but it's more than that: I need it." We now feel our work reflects who we are and look to our jobs to give us meaning and purpose. In a recent survey conducted by *The New York Times*,

Americans valued "having a fulfilling job" over "being married," "being religious," "being a good neighbor," "being involved in the community," "having a lot of friends," and "having enough time for yourself."

The busier we are, the more important we feel. We consider ourselves tougher and more dedicated than our lazier colleagues. Work provides us with a sense of purpose and can offer instant gratification in the form of praise, raises, and promotions. But the more we tie who we are to what we do, the more we emotionally attach to our jobs. We put constant pressure on ourselves to always be our best and then feel exhausted when we fail to live up to this unrealistic standard. And when we depend on our bosses for validation, the smallest bit of critical feedback starts to feel like a rejection of our entire selves.

Personal relationships help you maintain a healthy emotional distance from your job—and keep you happy. Sociologists who tracked the day-to-day fluctuations in people's emotions found that workers are happiest and least stressed on weekends. Nothing revolutionary there. But! The same pattern held true for unemployed people. Turns out that what makes us happy is not just free time, but when our free time aligns with our friends' free time. In other words, spending time with the people we care about makes us happy. "That social network, that each of you have each other's back, that they're there for you and you're there for them . . . That's a precious, precious resource," explains Christina Maslach, a leading researcher of burnout.

Burnout

Burnout is more than occasionally feeling tired or bored. According to psychologist Christina Maslach, these are the top three signs of burnout:

- Emotional exhaustion: You feel chronically drained. You have trouble sleeping and constantly get head colds.
- Depersonalization: You've become cynical and callous toward your colleagues. Small things (chewing, loud typing, spelling errors) irritate you more than they used to.
- Lethargy: You feel ineffective and disconnected from the projects you used to find fun; you're just going through the motions.

Burnout is serious, but there are some steps you can take to undo its effects. The first is to figure out why you might be feeling so down and then think of what you can do to fix the issue.

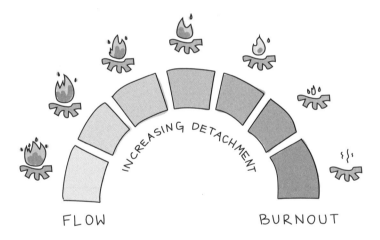

FLOW   BURNOUT

If you have an erratic boss, can you move to a different team? If you never receive any recognition at work, can you try gently outlining your accomplishments when you next meet with your manager? If you're stuck in the same routine, can you learn something new, start exercising, or sign up for an event you'd normally never attend? Talking with your loved ones, getting more sleep, and working on your mental health (by spending time in nature or meditating) can also help. But if the root cause of your burnout is a job that makes you miserable, it might be time to look for a new position.

Stop overestimating your importance

Have you ever gotten sick and been surprised to find your office didn't come to a crashing halt while you were out? Though it's nice to be necessary, your colleagues will almost always be fine without you for a few hours (or days). In most jobs, work is never done, which means there's never a perfect time to go on vacation or head home for the day. Too many of us agree with the statement, "No one else at my company can do the work while I'm away."

I CAN'T GO ON VACATION! THIS WHOLE
OPERATION WILL FALL APART!!

Focus less on your own importance and more on those around you. Compassion helps us become resilient: it improves our immune response, reduces our stress levels, and is associated with the pleasure networks in our brains. One way to practice compassion is to ask a colleague, "What's on your mind and how can I help?" Of course, if you consistently put someone else's needs ahead of your own, you'll eventually be utterly drained and resentful. Make sure you're aware of your emotional limits to avoid compassion fatigue.

Fall out of love with your phone

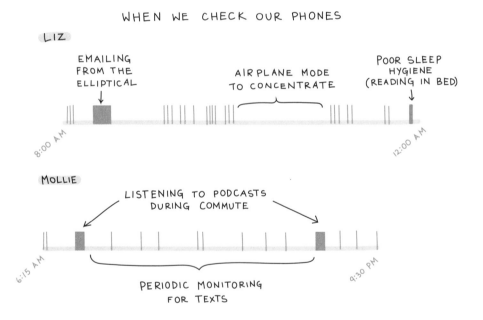

WHEN WE CHECK OUR PHONES

LIZ

EMAILING FROM THE ELLIPTICAL

AIRPLANE MODE TO CONCENTRATE

POOR SLEEP HYGIENE (READING IN BED)

8:00 AM

12:00 AM

MOLLIE

LISTENING TO PODCASTS DURING COMMUTE

6:15 AM

9:30 PM

PERIODIC MONITORING FOR TEXTS

"People are all insane and talking on machines and twittering and twottering. All that. I'm here looking for peace and quiet," lamented the late Maurice Sendak, author of *Where the Wild Things Are*. We could all do with less "twottering": too many of us are controlled by a constant stream of notifications that leaves us

THERE'S GREAT WI-FI IN THE MEDITATION ROOM

stressed, distracted, and frustrated. The average person checks her smartphone twice as much as she thinks she does. In fact, we're so phone addicted that nine out of ten of us experience phantom vibrations, which is when you feel your phone vibrate in your pocket . . . only to realize it's not even there.

If you want to have more energy, limit your email, social media, and messaging usage. Every ping is a distraction (Who is it from? What did they say?), and constantly having to shift your attention to and from your phone can make you feel tired and unfocused.

MOLLIE: I try not to check work email after dinner, otherwise I dream about work; these are not good dreams. When I really need to concentrate, I'll put my phone on "do not disturb." I also love writing on planes and trains without wi-fi—no digital distractions!

Suggestions to help you establish digital boundaries:

- **Touch email once.** When you open an email, you must respond to it immediately. Liz used to read all her emails first thing in the morning and, in an effort to get right to work, would then mark them all as unread with a plan to respond later in the day. That meant she spent the morning obsessively thinking about all the emails waiting in her inbox instead of focusing on her work.

- **If you're in a leadership role, set an example.** After she had children, TV writer and producer Shonda Rhimes changed her work email signature to read, "Please Note: I will not engage in work emails after 7:00 P.M. or on weekends. IF I AM YOUR BOSS, MAY I SUGGEST: PUT DOWN YOUR PHONE." Dan Calista, CEO of the consulting firm Vynamic (whose motto is "Life is short. Work healthy."), created an email policy called zzzMail. Employees cannot send one another emails on weeknights after 10:00 P.M., on weekends, or during holidays.

THE POSITIVITY PARADOX

Aside from devoting our time and mental energy to work, we often unconsciously hand over something far more precious—our self-worth. You may have high hopes for that enormous raise, prestigious promotion, or swanky new job, but your excitement will almost always be less intense and less lasting than you predict. Researchers find that your impact bias, the gap between what you think you will feel and what you actually end up feeling, often leads you to "miswant": you pine for futures that don't end up making you very happy. "I think you are out of your mind if you keep taking jobs that you don't like because you think it will look good on your résumé. Isn't that a little like saving up sex for your old age?" asks Warren Buffett.

Goals are great, and a raise or a promotion *will* feel amazing in the moment. But promotions are usually not the keys to a happily ever after. It's time to shed the unhealthy habit of glorifying the future to justify a miserable

present. "The direct pursuit of happiness is a recipe for an unhappy life," writes psychologist Donald Campbell. Constant happiness is unattainable (or at least we have yet to experience it personally). We usually describe ourselves as "happy" when we get more than we already had or when we find out we are a little better off than those around us. Neither of these are permanent states. Contentedness, on the other hand, can be more emotionally stable. The most content people craft their ups *and* downs into redemption stories: something bad happened, but something good resulted.

So how can you be more content now, in your less-than-perfect work life? In this section, we'll look at ways to feel better in the moment.

Stop feeling bad about feeling bad

Our jobs can put a lot of pressure on us to radiate happiness and positivity. The values of many companies explicitly encourage employees to be positive:

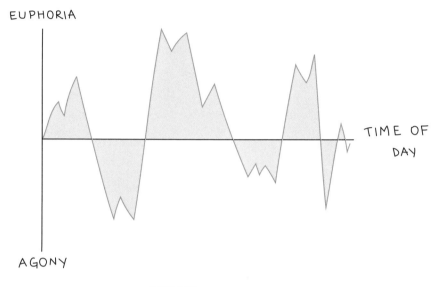

EUPHORIA

TIME OF
DAY

AGONY

$$AS\ LONG\ AS\ \int_{MORNING}^{EVENING} MOOD(s)d(s)>0\ \text{YOU'RE DOING OK!}$$

- Tiffany & Co.—*Focus on the positive*
- Kellogg's—*Promote a positive, energizing, optimistic, and fun environment*
- Zappos—*Build a Positive Team and Family Spirit*

The pressure to be perky is so great that the National Labor Review Board ruled employers cannot force employees to always be cheerful (we're guessing a lot of employees sulked in satisfaction after the ruling). But the nature of work is to experience setbacks and to show up when you're needed, even if you don't feel like it. So stop blaming yourself for not feeling happy all the time. A better version of the familiar adage "Grin and bear it" may be: "Sometimes you have to bear it, but you shouldn't force yourself to grin."

When we try to suppress our sadness, disappointment, or anger, we are more likely to feel those same emotions. A survey that asked people to rate how strongly they agreed with statements such as "I tell myself I shouldn't be feeling the way that I'm feeling" revealed that those who felt bad about feeling bad had lower well-being than their more self-accepting peers. "How we approach our own negative emotional reactions is really important," explains University of Toronto assistant professor Brett Ford. "People who accept these emotions without judging or trying to change them are able to cope with their stress more successfully."

LIZ: Last year a close friend's sister moved to a new city and initially felt overwhelmed and depressed. In an effort to cheer her up, my friend began to end each of their conversations with an upbeat "Be happy!" After a few weeks of this, his sister told him that the phrase was making her feel worse. "I'm going through a big change and I'm going to feel sad sometimes," she said. "And that's okay. Stop telling me to only be happy." The next time they spoke, my friend ended the conversation with, "Feel feelings!"

RX PRESCRIPTION

STOP FEELING
BAD ABOUT
FEELING BAD

Another reason to cut yourself some slack: a little pessimism can go a long way. Liz will often convince herself the worst is going to happen (e.g., she'll flub an important client presentation or bomb a test), but this anxiety motivates her to work harder. Researchers differentiate between strategic optimists and defensive pessimists (like Liz): strategic optimists envision best possible outcomes and try to make them happen whereas defensive pessimists tend to focus on what could go wrong and then work hard to avoid those situations. In studies, these groups perform equally well *except* when defensive pessimists are forced to cheer up.

You can also try a technique called reappraisal. The physical experience of stress or anxiety—a faster heartbeat and higher levels of stress hormones—is almost identical to our body's response to excitement. Harvard Business School professor Alison Wood Brooks found that people who take advantage of this similarity by reframing their stress as excitement (for example, by saying "I am excited" out loud) perform better. As psychologist William James writes, "The greatest weapon against stress is our ability to choose one thought over another."

"I'M STRESSED"   "I'M EXCITED"

Confide in a few people, but don't vent

Talking to a trusted colleague when you're upset can be cathartic; when nurses who are frustrated with patients or doctors can share their frustrations with one another in private staff rooms, they are better able to handle stress. One of our friends who worked as a social worker told us she would often admit to her colleagues, "I'm having a horrible day." This openness allowed her to discuss *why* she was upset, which helped her process her anger or sadness and prevented her from projecting those feelings onto her patients.

But it's possible to get mired in your woes. Chronic venting, when you rehash the same problems without trying to understand or solve them, makes you and the people listening to you feel worse. Women might be especially susceptible to the downsides of venting because they are often socialized to handle problems by talking about them. Psychologist Amanda Rose found that although revisiting issues and focusing on negative feelings strengthened female friendships, it also left both women feeling more anxious and depressed.

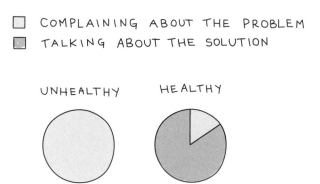

When you're upset, it feels good to run to someone in your support network, the group of people who will immediately take your side (your mom or your best friend, for example). But if you talk to *only* these people, you sabotage your ability to learn from or fix the problem. Make sure you also confide in your challenge network, the people who will tell you hard truths and push you to resolve the issue.

Get a clear picture of what you need to do

This tip is less about cultivating contentedness and more about blocking unnecessary stressors. Uncertainty feels bad. When you're confused about what you're supposed to be working on, you become wracked with guilt and anxiety. And at work, feeling unsure often turns into feeling unnecessary. You start to fear for your job. You pull late nights at the office trying to do everything, but with no real sense of accomplishment or relief. Research by Berkeley professor Morten Hansen shows that a quarter of us are often unable to focus because of a lack of direction from our bosses.

You will feel a lot better about leaving at a reasonable hour or taking vacation if you know you're doing a good job (in fact, high performers take almost twice as much vacation as their colleagues). And the first step to feeling confident is to figure out your boss's priorities. "Working on the right thing is probably more important than working hard," notes Flickr cofounder Caterina Fake.

How can you ask for guidance without looking incompetent? If you're not sure whether the launch email or report draft is more pressing, don't tell your boss you're confused. Instead, create a list of the big items on your plate and rank them in order of importance. Then take this list to your manager and ask her to confirm your prioritization. You can say something like, "Here's what I'm working on this week. Is there anything you would like me to prioritize differently?" (And managers, a great question to

UNCERTAINTY

CERTAINTY

ask at the end of every meeting or one-on-one is, "Did you get everything you needed today?")

Another way to avoid uncertainty: as you field requests, always ask "When do you need this by?" Then create a to-do list and make sure every item you add is specific and can be checked off. For example, "Finish the presentation" is vague. Instead, write "Finish writing the introduction for the presentation."

Focus on the here and now

Harvard psychologists Matthew Killingsworth and Daniel Gilbert estimate we spend only half our time focused on the present. Why does that matter? We're happiest when we live in the moment, no matter what we're working on. In a study of more than five thousand people, Killingsworth and Gilbert found that a wandering mind is usually an unhappy mind.

When our minds wander toward the past or the future, they often end up ruminating. Rumination differs from healthy reflection, when we analyze specific elements of a problem to better understand it. Say you email your coworker edits to her draft and don't get an immediate response. Rumination occurs when you jump to thoughts like "she thinks I'm dumb" or "my edits are always bad."

You can learn to bring your mind back to the present and stop ruminating. The first step to feeling better is to notice your cognitive distortions, or the dirty tricks your brain plays on you. Psychologist Martin Seligman identified the "three Ps" we tend to focus on after a negative event:

- Personalization: thinking that the event is all your fault
- Pervasiveness: thinking that the event is going to ruin every aspect of your life
- Permanence: thinking you are going to feel like this (e.g., bad) forever

PERSONALIZATION
THE GHOST OF ACTIONS PAST

PERVASIVENESS
THE GHOST OF ACTIONS PRESENT

PERMANENCE
THE GHOST OF ACTIONS FUTURE

Don't give the Ps a chance! If you find yourself pessimistically obsessing, reframe your thoughts. Here are some ideas:

- Personalization: Instead of immediately thinking, "I'm the reason we lost the client," try to look at what happened more objectively. On any project, issues will come up that are beyond your control. Own up to your mistakes, but don't needlessly blame everything on yourself.
- Pervasiveness: If you realize after a meeting you had a stain on your blouse, try not to become consumed with anxiety. A tiny mistake is unlikely to start a chain reaction that ends in complete disaster.
- Permanence: The words *always* and *never* are usually indications your self-reflection has turned self-destructive. Say your boss isn't happy with a one-pager you created. Instead of thinking, "I'll never be a good designer," focus on the single event: "This wasn't my best work, but I can learn more skills and improve."

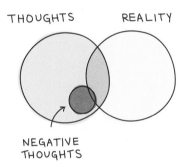

Another way to stop yourself from ruminating is through social distancing, when you try to look at your situation through someone else's eyes. Ask yourself, "What advice would I give to a friend who felt similarly?" This question forces you to step outside negative thinking patterns.

Lastly, remember your thoughts are simply that: thoughts. Acknowledge them, but recognize they are not inevitable truths (even if they *feel* true).

Let go of what you can't control

Stressors fall into two categories: those you can do something about (the withins) and those beyond your control (the beyonds). If you're anxious because of withins—unanswered emails in your inbox or an impending deadline—the easiest way to feel better is to complete the thing that is stressing you out. "Nothing diminishes anxiety faster than action," notes the American painter and writer Walter Anderson.

How do you stop stressing about the things you *can't* control? First, you have to be diligent about recognizing what you can't control. If you feel responsible for the beyonds, you'll never be able to confidently say you've done enough and relax.

> LIZ: A few weeks ahead of a two-hundred-person event I was organizing, I felt overwhelmed. One of the attendees was a career coach. Noticing I sounded stressed on a call, she asked me, "When will you know that you have done enough?" The answer seemed obvious: "When I feel the event has gone well." She laughed. "How much of the event do you think you can control? I bet it's less than 30 percent. What if a speaker gets sick or the caterer doesn't show up or it rains heavily during the planned patio lunch?
>
> 'Enough' has to be a metric that is within your control. For example, 'By the end of the week, I'll have sent the program designs to the printer.' 'Enough' can't be 'When I feel good,' because feeling good is a moving target."

Psychologist Nick Wignall schedules five to fifteen minutes every day to write down all his anxieties. He then highlights everything that is (1) an actual problem, (2) urgent (it must be done in the next day or two), and (3) within his control. Nick would *not* highlight a hypothetical worry like, "What if I get sick before the big client meeting next week?" He *would* highlight "I forgot to reply to Christine's email." For each highlighted problem, Nick sets a reminder to complete the next smallest step he can take (e.g., "Respond to Christine's email tomorrow at 9:00 A.M.").

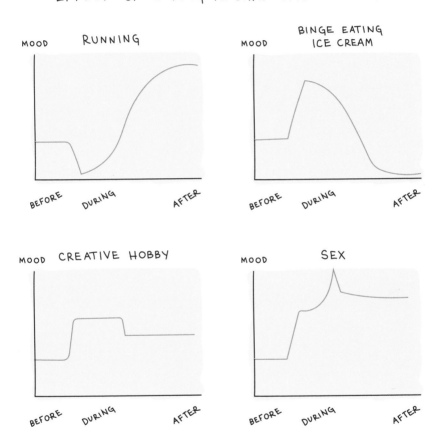

TAKEAWAYS

1. Take the break you can, whether it's a vacation, a day off, or a mini-break.

2. Make time to be rigorously unproductive, see friends and family, and step away from your email and phone.

3. Stop feeling bad about feeling bad. Reframe your stress as motivation or excitement.

4. Prevent rumination by viewing your thoughts as simply thoughts, not as inevitable truths. Stay in the present and take care of the things within your control.

CHAPTER 3

Motivation

Inspire yourself:

Why you're stuck and how to get moving

MUNCH'S I'M SO FRUSTRATED
I COULD SCREAM

I n 2001, managers at Best Buy were extremely skeptical about a radical new program HR had just announced. "I actually felt pretty scared about the people on my team and what would happen to our business results," recalled a senior supervisor named Beth. The new program was based on an internal survey about workplace motivation that had been sent out two years earlier. Employees had overwhelmingly supported one statement: "Trust me with my time. Trust me to do my job and I will deliver results and be a happier employee to boot."

The survey results had led Best Buy to run a pilot program that allowed roughly three hundred employees to choose their work hours from a set of schedules (9-to-5 could become 8-to-4, for example). The employees in the pilot program were much happier *and* worked harder when given more freedom. Now, despite concerns from management, the Results-Only Work Environment (ROWE) program—which let employees "run free like unicorns"—was about to be rolled out to the entire company. Here are the thirteen guideposts for ROWE:

1. People at all levels stop doing any activity that is a waste of their time, the customer's time, or the company's time.
2. Employees have the freedom to work any way they want.
3. Every day feels like Saturday.
4. People have an unlimited amount of "paid time off" as long as the work gets done.
5. Work isn't a place you go—it's something you do.
6. Arriving at the workplace at 2:00 P.M. is not considered coming in late. Leaving the workplace at 2:00 P.M. is not considered leaving early.

7. Nobody talks about how many hours they work.
8. Every meeting is optional.
9. It's okay to grocery shop on a Wednesday morning, catch a movie on a Tuesday afternoon, or take a nap on a Thursday afternoon.
10. There are no work schedules.
11. Nobody feels guilty, overworked, or stressed-out.
12. There aren't any last-minute fire drills.
13. There is no judgment about how you spend your time.

"You can imagine the shitstorm we created," noted Jody Thompson, an HR employee who led the shift to ROWE. Beth, the skeptical manager mentioned earlier, worried: "I just couldn't understand how I could let them do whatever they wanted whenever they wanted. How in the world would work get done?"

WHY AREN'T YOU MOTIVATED?

Motivation is a mess of chicken-and-egg relationships. Have you stopped making progress because you're bored, or are you bored because you stopped making progress? Are you unmotivated because your work seems pointless, or does your work feel pointless because you're unmotivated?

If you've previously read about motivation you're probably familiar with this depressing statistic: only 15 percent of workers feel engaged at work. That means most of us come into the office each day struggling to dredge up the desire to do, well, anything. But motivation isn't something that happens once and then you're done. Finding reasons to get up every morning and to do your job well is a dynamic, ongoing process. That's why this chapter is devoted to the second new rule of emotion at work: *Inspire yourself.*

In this chapter, we're going to disassemble all the elements of your job (and your mind-set) so you can look at them with new eyes. We'll show you

WORKWEEK FORECAST WHEN
YOU'RE NOT MOTIVATED

WORKWEEK FORECAST WHEN
YOU'RE MOTIVATED

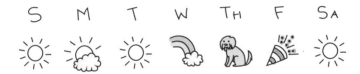

how your emotions create and sustain motivation and pinpoint the four main reasons why you might be lacking motivation: (1) you have no control over your work; (2) you don't find what you do meaningful; (3) you've stopped viewing work as a place to learn; and (4) you don't like your coworkers. These are thorny problems, so this chapter might feel more prescriptive than others.

You don't have autonomy

"Ain't no feeling like being free," sing Destiny's Child. It's one thing to choose to work on a project but an entirely different thing to *have* to work on a project. Sometimes we don't even realize our lack of freedom is bringing us down, so we call it something else. Across a series of nine experiments, people who said they wanted power turned down promotions to jobs that gave them a lot of influence and instead picked jobs that gave them a lot of freedom.

HOW TO MOTIVATE YOURSELF WHEN NOTHING ELSE IS WORKING

MAKE A CUP
OF COFFEE

LOOK AT
YOUR BILLS

PUT ON
UPBEAT MUSIC

BE INSPIRED
BY BEYONCÉ

Of course, few jobs will let us do whatever we want, whenever we want. But the more decisions we get to make for ourselves, the better we feel and the harder we work. When Walmart began offering flex shifts, which gave employees the ability to make their own schedules, absenteeism and turnover both dropped. And back at Best Buy, ROWE was an enormous success despite initial concerns.[4] Young workers chose to start later so they could fit in a morning workout and avoid rush hour. Employees with children left earlier

---

4 In a controversial move, Best Buy's new CEO decided to stop ROWE in 2013 (despite estimates that ROWE saved Best Buy $2.2 million over three years). Many believe the program was eliminated due to pressure on the new leadership to look tough.

to attend after-school activities. Morale and productivity shot up. Voluntary turnover dropped. "I couldn't have been more wrong," admitted Beth, the supervisor who had expressed reservations. In the first year of ROWE, her team became twice as productive and her lowest performer suddenly excelled. "Giving [my lowest performer] ownership of how she spends her time has done wonders. I can only wonder how many other 'low performers' out there have the same potential."

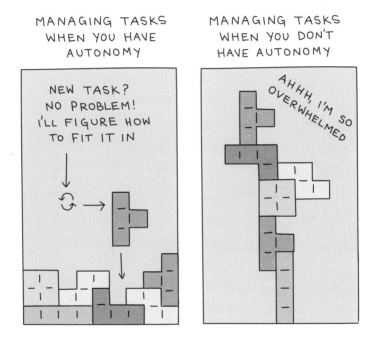

But what if you work for a micromanager or a company that won't be rolling out ROWE anytime soon? "Ask yourself: 'Is there one small thing within my own realm I can do differently tomorrow?' The answer is almost always yes," Daniel Pink, author of *Drive*, advised us. Although it can be challenging, it's possible, even in constrained professional situations, to create moments of freedom and inspiration. Find a half hour to read up on something you're curious about. Walk around the block between your afternoon meetings. Grab a few coworkers and head to the coffee shop on the corner for a quick break. "You can usually carve out a little slice of sovereignty even if you don't have total control of your schedule," Daniel Pink told us. "And something is better than nothing. Taking two ten- or fifteen-minute breaks in the afternoon is doable for most people."

Motivation and the Brain

Say you finish giving a presentation and your boss asks, "Why are you wasting my life?" (Jeff Bezos once said this to an engineer.) The next time you're asked to present, you might lack motivation as your habenula—the part of the brain that stopped our ancestors from eating poisonous berries by reminding them how bad mistakes feel—reduces the amount of the neurotransmitter dopamine in the brain.

Dopamine, which helps control your brain's reward and pleasure centers, lies at the intersection of motivation and action and is released when we seek a reward. Dopamine levels in our brains vary the most when we aren't sure if we'll be rewarded. Playing slot machines and checking our email, for example, are so addictive because they don't guarantee a specific outcome—we keep coming back for the chance to win or receive an interesting message. Studies of roulette players recorded an equal amount of activity in dopamine-rich brain regions when gamblers lost money with a miserable near-miss as when they won.

WE'RE
DEFINITELY
GETTING
A REWARD!

COOL

OK

DOPAMINE

THERE'S A 50%
CHANCE WE'LL
GET A REWARD!

OMG

DID SOMEONE
SAY WE MIGHT
GET A REWARD?

WHOA

DOPAMINE

LIZ: If you want to get really crazy about staying motivated, set up a variable reward system for yourself. I created a habit of focusing on a single task (no checking Reddit or email!!) by pressing a random number generator button every time I successfully concentrated for an hour. If the generator (which was set to pop out a number between 0 and 10) gave me a 2, 3, 4, or 7, I allowed myself to eat a bowl of ice cream (cookie dough!) after lunch that day.

- **Ask your manager to define outcomes rather than processes.** Members of teams who are able to create their own processes are more motivated. Ask if your team can decide how to get to the end result; Liz's design clients often give her a clear description of what they want and when they need it but then let her figure out how to get it done.
- **Focus on small wins.** Crossing something as small as "Answer Caitlin's email" off a to-do list energizes us. Harvard Business School professor Teresa Amabile calls this the progress principle: even ordinary, incremental progress makes us happier and more engaged with our work. (But remind yourself how your small goals connect to a larger purpose; losing sight of the bigger picture saps motivation.)
- **Ask open-ended questions.** Employees at IDEO start brainstorms with, "How might we . . . ?" "How" asks employees to be descriptive, "might" suggests there are good answers, but not a single correct answer, and "we" signals inclusivity and teamwork.
- **If you're a manager, hold office hours.** Office hours are an opportunity for your reports to come to you with questions. Instead of constantly monitoring their work, give them the chance to problem solve and reach out when they need help.

You don't find your work meaningful

"It's not that I'm lazy," explains Peter in the movie *Office Space*. "It's that I just don't care." It's hard to motivate ourselves to do something when that something feels pointless. Just ask behavioral economist Dan Ariely, who had research participants assemble LEGO toys. While Ariely saved the toys from one group, he dismantled the other group's toys right before their eyes.

Participants in the first group made an average of eleven toys. The second group stopped after just seven. "People want to feel like they're contributing," notes Ariely. "They want a sense of purpose, a sense that work itself has an impact."

THE LITTLE ENGINE THAT LITERALLY COULDN'T EVEN

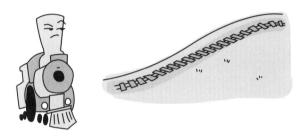

BUT *WHY* SHOULD I GO UP THE HILL?

"It used to perplex me when I read about people who liked what they did so much that there was nothing they'd rather do," writes venture capitalist Paul Graham. "The fact is, almost anyone would rather, at any given moment, float about in the Caribbean, or have sex, or eat some delicious food than work on hard problems." A job won't always align perfectly with what we love to do, but there are ways to make our least favorite tasks bearable if we remind ourselves of the people our work affects. In a survey of more than two million people, social workers, surgeons, and clergy members reported the highest job meaning, even though their work is not usually associated with frequent lighthearted and happy moments.

How often do you remind yourself who you're helping by drafting a tedious email or cleaning a data set? Understanding the broader impact of our work makes us more productive—and helps us get through particularly dreary days. Even brief interactions with the people who benefit from our work make a big difference (Google calls these "magic moments"). Wharton professor Adam Grant arranged for workers at the university's scholarship fund-raising call center to meet with a few scholarship recipients. Though the meeting lasted only five minutes, the workers learned how much their efforts had changed the recipients' lives. A month later, the callers who spoke with the scholarship recipients had raised almost twice as much as those who did not.

LIZ: My favorite "magic moment" story comes from Maurice Sendak, who wrote and illustrated *Where the Wild Things Are*. One day, Sendak received a letter with a charming little drawing on it from a boy named Jim. In return, Sendak drew a Wild Thing on a card and sent it to the boy. A few weeks later, he received a letter from Jim's mother that said, "Jim loved your card so much he ate it." "That to me was one of the highest compliments I've ever received," Sendak recalled. "He saw it, he loved it, he ate it."

THAT ONE APPEARS TO BE JOB CRAFTING

Because there are no absolutes, our mind-set matters—a lot. If your goal is to inspire yourself, reframing how you view your work can change how meaningful you find it. Yale professor Amy Wrzesniewski found you can actively shift your work toward the things you enjoy through a process called job crafting. There are baristas who see handing out a morning latte as brightening someone's day and graphic designers who feel their greeting cards have enabled more happy birthdays than they'll ever be able to count. These are both examples of job crafting. Paquita Williams, a conductor for New York City's MTA subway system, views herself as a caretaker for her passengers. When a power outage stopped Williams's train underground, she walked through the subway cars cracking jokes to make passengers feel better.

How to find the parts of your job that could become meaningful:

- **Follow fun.** "My main focus in life is surrounding myself with interesting and fun people and curating my environment to be maximally fun," writes MIT Media Lab Director Joi Ito. Take note of the moments that bring you lightness to help you uncover the parts of your job you find most meaningful.
- **Talk to your manager about how to get more engaging work.** After a long period of feeling bored at a past job, Kate Earle, former chief learning officer at Quiet Revolution, decided to leave. Kate told us it never occurred to her to ask her boss for more engaging work. In retrospect, having an open conversation about her role and responsibilities might have helped Kate enjoy her work more.
- **Connect your work to a compelling purpose.** When a SpaceX employee who worked on the company's manufacturing floor was asked, "What is your job?" his response was: "The mission of SpaceX is to colonize Mars. In order to colonize Mars, we need to build reusable rockets because it will otherwise be unaffordable for humans

to travel to Mars and back. My job is to help design the steering system that enables our rockets to land back on earth. You'll know if I've succeeded if our rockets land on our platform in the Atlantic after launch." He could have simply said, "I assemble parts."

- **Invest in positive relationships.** Relationships can help increase a sense of meaning. Offer to mentor a newer or younger colleague or plan an event that helps people get to know one another.

You've stopped viewing work as a place to learn

LIZ: The day I quit my job as an economic consultant, I walked to the Starbucks I visited every afternoon and applied to be a barista. I wanted some sort of income while I figured out what to do next, but I didn't expect to learn much more than how to make a cappuccino.

Instead, I learned that every aspect of a Starbucks store is designed. The music and lighting change depending on the time of day. The pastries are laid out according to strict guidelines. The tables are round to ensure solo coffee drinkers don't feel lonely (there are no obviously empty seats at a round table). I suddenly had so many questions: Which beverage has the highest profit margin? (The Frappuccino; it's mostly ice.) Why are baristas not allowed to wear cologne or perfume? (Coffee absorbs odors; this is also why Starbucks banned smoking in the late 1980s, long before any other establishment did.) What is the most popular item on the secret menu? (The Nutella drink: espresso, steamed milk, chocolate syrup, hazelnut syrup, and caramel drizzle.)

Working at Starbucks sparked my interest in design and motivated me to teach myself how to use Photoshop and Illustrator. Customers spent so much money on coffee! But more than that, they loved the brand.

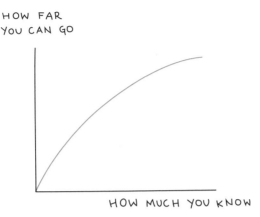

If you feel unmotivated at your job, it's time for some tough love: you've probably given up on learning.

> MOLLIE: A former colleague had moved to a new job in a new industry every year for seven years. Soon enough, she wanted to leave the job we shared. When I asked her what she was looking for, she said she wanted work that addressed all of her passions. She also admitted that she got bored easily. I realized she wasn't viewing her job as an opportunity to learn something new. If you cultivate a sense of curiosity and keep an open mind, you can find something you are interested in within any job.

"There is only one way to learn," writes Paulo Coelho in *The Alchemist.* "It's through action." Push yourself to learn something new about your company, its products, or your coworkers. If you need to be scared into taking action, no problem: technological advances necessitate continuous learning.

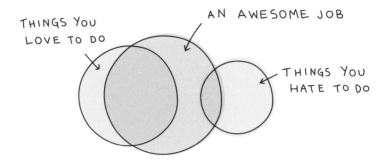

THINGS YOU
LOVE TO DO

AN AWESOME JOB

THINGS YOU
HATE TO DO

The World Economic Forum predicts more than half of children will work in jobs that do not yet exist; even the most talented engineer will one day need to code in a language that has not yet been written. In today's workplace, continuing to learn isn't optional—it's a necessity. Author Seth Godin explains, "The opportunity to level up is largely driven by you, by what you choose to absorb, by who you choose to learn from."

Boredom

In 2016, Frédéric Desnard attempted to sue his former employer for giving him so little to do that his boredom left him severely depressed. Though the court threw the case out, Desnard's claim isn't too crazy to anyone who has counted down the minutes until they could leave the office. When faced with the choice of doing nothing or receiving painful electric shocks, the average person shocked themselves five times. One man was so desperate not to be alone with his thoughts that he gave himself nearly two hundred shocks.

But boredom can motivate us by signaling that a more rewarding activity might exist. Brief periods of boredom may

help our wandering minds tap into memories and begin connecting ideas. When people lie in fMRI machines and wait for a task, their brains show increased activity in regions associated with memory and imagination. Warren Buffett and Bill Gates famously schedule time to simply sit and think. So next time you're bored, see where your mind takes you!

Learning by doing is the best way to discover work you find meaningful. The advice to "follow your passion" assumes you *know* your passion (and that you can easily make a living pursuing it). Pinpointing what you love to do without working is like trying to choose a spouse based only on their Tinder profile. "'Always produce' will discover your life's work the way water, with the aid of gravity, finds the hole in your roof," writes Paul Graham.

If you're feeling anxious, learning something new might be a more effective way of counteracting stress than simply relaxing. Niki Lustig, head of Learning and Development at GitHub, received the following email message from an employee who enrolled in a personal development class using the company-sponsored learning and development benefit: "Using what I learned from the course I had taken, I wrote a script that is going to simplify an otherwise horrifically convoluted process . . . I can't even begin to tell you how cool it was to see . . . how this is going to help the team as it continues to grow." And it turns out that excellence is a bigger motivator than even money; baseball players are often willing to take a pay cut in order to be on a winning team.

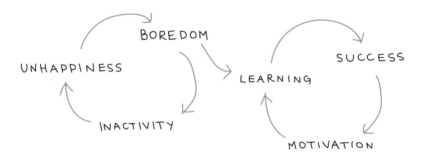

If you want to care more about something, put time and effort into it. This is called the IKEA effect: people who put together IKEA furniture are willing to pay more for their own self-constructed furniture than for identical pre-assembled furniture. They value their self-constructed furniture more because it reminds them of their competence. Additionally, praise about our performance feels good, which motivates us to become even better. Workers at an investment bank who received meaningful encouragement performed better than their peers.

Finally, delete from your memory the saying "You can't teach an old dog new tricks." It is never too late to start learning new skills. The renowned chef Julia Child began taking cooking lessons in her mid-thirties—one of her early attempts at preparing a meal ended with an exploded duck—and didn't publish her first cookbook until she was fifty-one. View your ability as something that can always be further developed. Research shows that if we view talent as fixed ("I'm not a numbers person" or "I'm not creative"), we become easily discouraged by mistakes and are less motivated to make an effort. If we instead see it as something that can we can grow, we see challenges as opportunities and try harder to solve tough problems, which both lead to higher achievement.

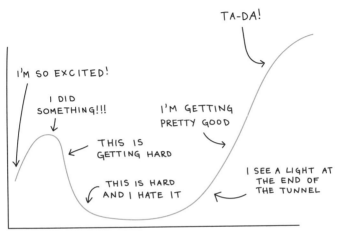

Deciding What to Learn

Too often, when we don't know what we're supposed to do, we just do nothing. There are so many options for learning that it can feel overwhelming. Should you start with gaps in your office skill set and learn Python or how to build a website? Should you plan for the future and learn Mandarin? Should you think about learning as a chance to find a mentor and learn whatever the best available mentor will teach you?

First, if your employer will help you pay for classes, take

advantage of it. You can usually use your education budget to attend conferences, pay for grad school, or (if your organization's policies allow) take up a side hobby.

But the best way to decide what to learn is to take a step back and figure out *why* you want to learn. What do you want to accomplish?

- Stay in your current industry/career, but advance your position or skills:
    o Take evening classes related to the position you want to get to
- Switch industries/careers:
    o Go to grad school
- Expand your network:
    o Attend local meet-ups and workshops
- Stay up-to-date with new developments in your field:
    o Schedule lunch-and-learns and book clubs in your office
    o Attend conferences
- Master your current job:
    o Find a mentor

How to use your emotions to help you learn:

- **Swap skills.** Schedule time with a coworker or friend to teach each other something new. For example, Liz once helped a colleague learn how to use Adobe Illustrator, and he then walked her through his top email marketing tips.
- **Take care of yourself.** Evidence suggests students who are anxious or depressed don't learn. If you feel like stress or boredom has turned

your brain to sludge, try some of our recommendations in the previous chapter on health.

- **Look for new internal opportunities.** A Southwest Airlines program called "Days in the Field" lets employees spend a day in the department of their choice. This experience gives them a better idea of where they might like to steer their Southwest career path.
- **Start a side project.** Side projects are a great way to engage a different set of muscles than those you use at work and can be one of the most rewarding ways to learn a new skill. When Liz wanted to learn coding basics, she decided to build a simple personal website from scratch. A side project is also uniquely yours—you aren't doing it for anyone else, so you'll have complete autonomy.

You don't enjoy working with your coworkers

Choice, meaning, and opportunities for learning all make work more enjoyable. But on rainy Friday mornings when we're low on sleep and irritated with our managers, research suggests our real motivation isn't a what, it's a who. People

HOW LONG FRIDAY
AFTERNOON FEELS

SO LONG!

NOT SO BAD!

WITHOUT WORK FRIENDS   WITH WORK FRIENDS

with friends at work find their jobs more satisfying and are less affected by stress. "Motivation comes from working on things we care about," notes Sheryl Sandberg. "It also comes from working with people we care about."

Not all work friends fulfill the same need. We'll cover three types: the confidant, the inspiration, and the frenemy. Understanding how and why you relate to these people will help you commit appropriate mental resources to developing workplace relationships that can quickly bolster your motivation.

The confidant

This is the work friend who will commiserate when you've had a rough conversation with your boss, rush you to the bathroom when you're about to cry, and give you honest feedback when you need it most. Confidants make us feel like we can conquer the world (or at least ace a presentation and finally ask for that raise). And they might even be the key to a more equal workforce:

CONFIDANT FRIENDSHIP MILESTONES

SENDING EACH OTHER NONWORK EMAILS

FIRST SHARED LUNCH

WAITING FOR THE OTHER PERSON SO YOU CAN LEAVE WORK TOGETHER

COVERING FOR EACH OTHER

DIVULGING YOUR WORK CRUSHES

FIRST POST-WORK HANG

FIRST WEEKEND HANG

GETTING A NEW JOB AND HIRING THE OTHER PERSON TO JOIN YOU

women in India who went to job training sessions with a friend were more successful than those who went alone.

But we're increasingly less likely to have a confidant at work. In 1985, half of Americans reported having a close work friend, but by 2004, that number had dropped to a third. Because we tend to switch jobs more frequently, we might not invest as heavily in workplace relationships. "We view co-workers as transitory ties, greeting them with arms-length civility while reserving real camaraderie for outside work," explains Adam Grant. To develop a confidant, start by building trust and sharing stories with a coworker you gravitate toward. (In more cutthroat offices, you may not be able to find a confidant. In this case, you'll have to rely on your nonwork social network for support.) Or initiate a get-together: people who provide social support to others—by organizing an office event or inviting colleagues to go to lunch—are ten times more likely to feel engaged at work as people who keep to themselves.

The inspiration

The inspiration is your platonic work crush: you don't want to be *with* them, you simply want to *be* them. This person can be either a colleague you deeply admire or a formal mentor. Mentors help improve job satisfaction, teach us how to be effective leaders, and steer us toward the right career moves. "They'll bring a field to life for you. They'll teach you how to find quality material in that field," advises economist and author Tyler Cowen. You can and should have many mentors throughout your career.

LIZ: I emailed a colleague I deeply admired when I was feeling particularly low and unsure about trying to work as a self-employed consultant. I still go back and reread her response when I want to feel motivated: "The worst thing we do is bravely step out of the mold but then stupidly use someone else's rubric to judge our own lives every day. If you're going to forge your own path, then do so without judgment. It is a beautiful thing to want something for yourself that originates from you."

The frenemy

We tend to choose friends who are similar to us—especially at work. But the more we have in common with someone, the more likely we are to compare ourselves to them. The frenemy is both our friend and our benchmark within the organization. Don't feel guilty about experiencing the occasional twinge of envy! Frenemies account for almost half of the important members of our networks.

MATISSE'S THE FRENEMY DANCE

I WAS JUST KIDDING, CAN'T YOU TAKE A JOKE?

ANYTHING YOU DO, I'VE DONE BETTER

I'D LOVE TO BUT THIS WEEK IS CRAZY

CONGRATS! I DID NOT EXPECT YOU TO GET PROMOTED!

ME ME ME ME ME

Although frenemy relationships are linked to greater stress, they also motivate us to work harder. In a study of consultants, those who had a frenemy made more of an effort to succeed and network. Leverage the positives of a love-hate relationship by partnering on an important project; you'll try harder to prove yourself and might end up with a real friendship.

. . . . .

Even the best work friendships have a dark side. Sometimes being close with our colleagues can leave us emotionally exhausted. Managing relationships we care about while giving critical feedback or rushing to meet deadlines takes effort. Talk to anyone who has worked at a startup where coworkers describe themselves as a family, and you'll inevitably hear how tiring it can be. And for every friendship, there is also someone outside the friendship. "We often only consider the impact of these relationships from the perspective of people within the friendships—i.e., Does this feel good? Do I feel connected? Do I want to show up to work? But something that can be great for people within the friendship can be really hard emotionally for outsiders, which can have negative cascading effects throughout the organization," explains Julianna Pillemer, a PhD candidate at the Wharton School. The closer the relationship between two colleagues, the more others might feel unwelcome, even if the friends aren't actively excluding anyone. When Mollie started working at a past job, everyone already seemed to be part of a clique. Mollie felt intimidated and awkward. This dynamic can prevent information sharing; we seek help from our friends, so if we feel like an outsider, we may not reach out when we should.

Taking IRL Work Relationships Online

To Facebook friend your coworker or not to Facebook friend your coworker, that is the question. People tend to fall into two categories when answering: segmentors and integrators. Segmentors draw a distinct line between their personal and professional lives. ("I'd like to add you to my professional network on LinkedIn but please never follow me on Instagram.") Integrators don't create boundaries between work and home. ("How are we not friends on Snapchat yet?")

Unfortunately for segmentors, it's becoming harder to keep coworkers out of our social media lives without hurt feelings; more than 70 percent of people like the idea of Facebook friending their colleagues, and almost half of people find it irresponsible to ignore a friend request from a coworker. Studies also show that people who withhold personal information are viewed more negatively by their colleagues. Sorry segmentors, you might just have to accept that friend request.

When we do friend our coworkers on social media, we quickly learn a lot (sometimes, too much). "Social media creates boundary transparency—where you can see the activities and relationships of coworkers outside of a work context," notes Pillemer. This can bring us closer by highlighting connections or similarities that might come up only after months of casual in-person conversation. ("We're from the same hometown!") But it can also make us even more cliquish ("We went to the same school!") or cause resentment. Say you take a week off to bike through the Italian countryside with your partner. If you post photos of the two of you clinking wine glasses under the Tuscan sun, and your team is in the midst of a particularly stressful project, they might get annoyed at you for sipping and savoring while they're pulling long hours.

Social media also makes us more aware of friendship groups, which can lead to silos. We may not even realize that two of our colleagues are close until we see them laughing together over drinks on Instagram. It's then easy to feel excluded ("Why wasn't I invited?") and be less comfortable reaching out to them the next day.

HAZARDS OF SOCIAL MEDIA

How to benefit from having friends at work:

- **Embrace small moments.** University of Michigan professor Jane E. Dutton found that high-quality connections don't require deep or vulnerable relationships. Small moments of connection full of trust and engagement can be the beginning of a meaningful relationship.
- **Prevent silos from forming.** IDEO structures all of its teams to include designers from different disciplines, so each team is cross-functional. IDEO's San Francisco office also has a ritual called Tea Time, in which people are invited to take a break from their work at 3:00 P.M. and mingle with people they don't work with directly.
- **Branch out during work events.** Studies show that work events aren't always effective at helping people make friends. "People don't mix much at mixers, and at company parties, they mostly bond with similar colleagues," says Adam Grant. To make the most of work events, talk to at least one person you don't already know.
- **Spend casual time together.** Google and Facebook plan times for employees to play games and eat meals together. At LinkedIn, co-workers get to meet one another's families on Bring Your Parents to Work Day.

To recap: motivation *can* be jump-started. You can increase your sense of autonomy, find more meaning or purpose in your work (or zero in on the parts of your job that could become meaningful), reframe work as a place of learning, or make more friends at work.

But if you've made these major changes and you still dread waking up every morning, we have one word of advice: quit. Life is too short to spend time being unmotivated for (at least) eight hours a day.

TAKEAWAYS

1. To increase your autonomy, make small changes to your schedule.
2. Job craft: shift your responsibilities toward the things you enjoy to make your work more meaningful.
3. Push yourself to acquire new skills. The more you know, the more you'll enjoy your work.
4. Invest in workplace friendships to give yourself another reason to look forward to work.

CHAPTER 4

Decision Making

Emotion is part of the equation:

Why good decisions rely on examining your emotions

LIZ: Four years ago, I was offered the position of executive editor at Genius, a (then early-stage) music-media company. After my initial "Someone wants me!" euphoria wore off, I plunged into a confused depression. Accepting the position meant I would have to move to New York in less than two weeks. At the time, I lived in a rent-controlled apartment in San Francisco, my crush had finally asked me out, and I was reasonably content at my existing job. With only three days to consider the offer, I anxiously discussed my options with friends, mentors, Uber drivers, and anyone else who would listen. In true economics-major form, I also tried to model out various scenarios and rampantly abused the phrase "opportunity cost." My exhaustive analysis led me to conclude exactly nothing. Based on the metrics I had chosen, there was no clearly superior option.

But I still had to make a decision. So, though it went against every fiber of my hyperrational background and education, I turned to my feelings. I first envisioned my life on the West Coast continuing uninterrupted. I felt a slight twinge of regret. Then I imagined what would happen if I took the job: the details of my first day, how I would get along with my coworkers, the New York abuse I would undoubtedly receive for eating a giant street pretzel. My heart beat faster—I felt excited and nervous and thrilled. I decided to accept the offer.

Over the next two years, Genius went through drastic changes, reorganizations, and an identity crisis. It was hard. Our team worked hard (often in its own unique way). We slept at the office, exchanged three-thousand-plus-word emails philosophizing about how our website mirrored samurai Japan, chose the best marketing copy via a competition called "Pitch Idol" (trophies included), and responded to GIF- and emoji-filled texts from site users at all hours of the day. Through it all, I never regretted my decision.

Though basing such a life-changing decision on my feelings seemed wildly irrational, scientific research (and my own experience!) indicates that it wasn't such an idiotic strategy after all. As we discuss in this chapter, a range of studies show that the best judgment and problem solving incorporates emotion. In fact, if emotion is entirely ignored in the decision-making equation, the results can be surprisingly harmful.

A FORK IN THE ROAD

There's a science to listening to your gut. When making decisions, we tend to think of rational analysis as straightforward and gut feelings as disingenuous. But the reason emotions get a bad reputation is that we don't know how to decode them. That's where the third new rule of emotion at work comes in: *Emotion is part of the equation*. You might eventually decide to ignore a feeling, but you should acknowledge it exists. In a lab experiment, people who reported feeling the strongest emotions (good or bad) at the moment of decision made the best investment choices—even if they didn't always *follow* their gut. Instead, they considered their emotions, thought hard about which ones might be informative, and then regulated the rest. Put differently, paying attention to *all* your feelings allows you to control them instead of the other way around.

When people talk about decision making, they tend to assume that feeling something and doing something with those feelings are the same thing: that once we open the floodgates, we'll be bowled over by the crush of our emotions.

But emotions aren't mystical signals; they're based on expertise, experi-

TYPES OF DECISIONS

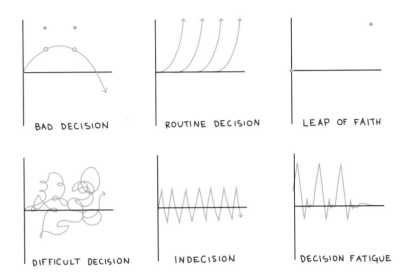

BAD DECISION

ROUTINE DECISION

LEAP OF FAITH

DIFFICULT DECISION

INDECISION

DECISION FATIGUE

ence, and rapid information processing (the psychologist William James de-scribed gut feelings as "felt knowledge"). Ever felt something in your bones that you couldn't otherwise explain to yourself? These feelings can help you narrow down and prioritize your options. Say you're applying to new jobs. If the thought of becoming a marketing associate fills you with dread, you might want to cross that off your list of potential positions. And if you feel a thrill imagining yourself as a data scientist, that's an equally important sign about what openings you should go after.

The other reason to consult your emotions when making decisions is because, well, you already are. It's impossible to make a purely logical choice. Even something as simple as choosing to put on a seat belt relies on emotional parts

YOUR GUESS MIGHT BE AS GOOD AS MINE

of the brain. It's easy to assume that "I put on a seat belt because I want to be safe" is an unemotional decision, but that choice stems from a reasonable fear of dying in an accident.

In this chapter, we'll talk about how to analyze your feelings, walk through the differences between relevant and irrelevant emotions, look at one important decision you should *not* let emotion influence, and discuss how to make the best decision based on your individual emotional tendencies.

WHAT TO KEEP AND WHAT TO TOSS

Not all feelings should be weighted equally. Trusting everything your brain throws at you without holding it up to a light is dangerous. Psychologists differentiate between *relevant* emotions and *irrelevant* emotions.

- *Relevant emotions* are directly tied to the choice you're facing. For example, if you're trying to decide whether or not to ask for a promotion and the idea of *not* asking fills you with regret, that feeling is a relevant emotion. These emotions can be useful guides for picking one option over another.
- *Irrelevant emotions* are unrelated to the decision at hand, but they like to stick their tentacles into your reasoning. Say Liz stubs her toe or gets a speeding ticket. She'll get upset and might suddenly decide her colleagues' ideas are all bad.

I WANT WHAT'S BEST FOR YOU!

RELEVANT EMOTIONS

DO WHAT FEELS GOOD RIGHT NOW!

IRRELEVANT EMOTIONS

A good rule of thumb: keep relevant emotions, toss irrelevant emotions. When you're making a decision, ask yourself, "How do I feel?" Label your emotions and then categorize each as relevant or irrelevant. If you feel anxious, think carefully about whether the decision is making you anxious or if your nerves stem, for example, from a big presentation you have to give later in the day. The ability to separate between these two buckets sets you up for decision-making success.

> MOLLIE: There are so many times when I make decisions based on how I'm feeling in the moment (tired, hungry) rather than how I think I'll feel in the future depending on what decision I make. For example, I often have a hard time motivating myself to go out to after-work drinks with my colleagues. When I get the invitation for drinks, I always want to go. But by the time 6:00 P.M. rolls around, I am usually tired and hungry. These irrelevant emotions make me want to head home to (1) eat dinner (I like to eat dinner at the grandmotherly time of 6:30) and (2) get some introvert catnip (aka alone time). But I know that if I do go out, I will feel happier and more connected to my colleagues. I have to remember to let my relevant emotions (feeling happier in the future) not fall prey to my irrelevant emotions.

Relevant emotions

Think of relevant emotions as your internal navigation system. When you imagine what would happen if you picked one option over another, that image is marked with a positive or negative feeling. For example, Liz felt a thrill when she thought about moving to New York. This emotional signal indicated it might be a good choice.

Relevant emotions are a common

SETTINGS FOR GOOD
DECISION MAKING

‹ EMOTIONS	
ENVY	ON
ANTICIPATION	ON
GENERAL DOOM AND GLOOM	OFF
CAFFEINE-INDUCED EUPHORIA	OFF
MAJOR FOMO	ON

currency that let us compare apples and oranges. Sometimes you'll have to pick between options that can't be neatly compared (e.g., should I go to law school or become a yoga instructor?). In these situations, how each choice makes you feel can help when your pros-and-cons list falls short.

Relevant emotions also tend to last longer than irrelevant emotions, so if you still feel the same thing a few hours or days later, that's a good indication it's a relevant emotion. Here are some common relevant emotions and how to think through them (some emotions can be both relevant *and* irrelevant, but the ones we're listing here are most commonly one or the other):

Anticipation

What it's trying to tell you: If one option makes you feel particularly energized and excited, that might be a signal you should more heavily consider it. That said, start tracking whether or not your anticipation is a good indicator. Psychologist Daniel Kahneman recommends keeping a decision journal: when you're faced with a choice, write down exactly what you expect to happen and why that scenario makes you feel eager. This will help you evaluate if your anticipation was accurate—and give you feedback on how to treat your emotions when you make future decisions.

Anxiety

What it's trying to tell you: There's good news about anxiety: you'll be most anxious about a decision when you're trying to pick between good choices. Psychologists call this the win-win paradox (neuroscientists refer to it as "neural correlates of First World problems"). We're not trying to cheapen your stress—a difficult choice is a difficult choice—but hopefully this helps you look on the bright side.

In order to harness anxiety in a helpful way, you have to understand where it's coming from. "Anxiety is the fear of more fear. It is rooted in the need to control the things around us to keep our reality known and safe," explains executive coach Justin Milano. One good way to tell the difference between

HOKUSAI'S WAVE OF ANXIETY

fear and anxiety: fear is momentary, whereas anxiety often lasts for days or months.

The first step is to identify what you're trying to control. Milano suggests asking yourself, "What expectation, idea, or outcome are you attached to? A specific investor? A specific client? A certain type of product working?" Once we've uncovered our attachments, we can use our anxieties in a more productive way. "The healthy thing to do is acknowledge the attachment to a certain outcome, soften your grip on it, and use your creativity to design a new path based on reality," says Milano. For example, Mollie used to feel anxious about making her clients happy, but she has learned that the desire driving this anxiety is to feel useful. She now proactively asks her clients, "What can I do to be more helpful?"

Milano developed a five-question exercise to help you discover what your anxieties are telling you and learn how to make them productive.

1. What's the anxiety?
2. Where do you feel it in your body?
3. What is the desire being mirrored? What is the desire underneath that anxiety?

4. Once you discover the desire, do you choose to act on it?

5. If so, what are the creative action steps?

This exercise will help you move from reacting based on fear to reacting based on problem solving and creativity.

Regret

What it's trying to tell you: Try picking the option you think will minimize regret. Psychologists Daniel Kahneman and Amos Tversky found that of all emotions, people try hardest to avoid regret. "When people asked Amos how he made the big decisions in his life, he often told them that his strategy was to imagine what he would come to regret, after he had chosen some option, and to choose the option that would make him feel the least regret," writes Michael Lewis in the book *The Undoing Project.* "Danny, for his part, personified regret. Danny would resist a change to his airline reservations, even when the change made his life a lot easier, because he imagined the regret he would feel if the change led to some disaster."

MOLLIE: I often use this tactic to make decisions. Before I went to grad school, I asked myself, "In ten years, will I feel more regret if I haven't gone to grad school or if I have gone?" It also helps with relationships. I've asked friends, "Will you feel more regret in a year if you're still with this guy or if you've broken up with him?" This works because it forces us to try to picture where we'd like to be in the future, and in our visualization, look to see: Will I be using my grad degree? Will this guy keep making me happy?

Though we tend to be drawn to the status quo, research shows change might make us happier. In an experiment, *Freakonomics* author Steven Levitt invited people who were on the fence about a major life decision (like quitting a job or ending a relationship) to let a coin toss determine their fate. Heads meant make a change. Tails meant stick with the status quo. Six months after the coin toss, people who got heads—who made a change—were happier. "People may be excessively cautious when facing life-changing choices," writes Levitt.

Envy

What it's trying to tell you: "When you envy someone, you learn that he or she has something you wish you had," Gretchen Rubin, author of *The Happiness Project*, told us. "When I was considering switching from law to writing, I noticed that when I read about alumni in my school's magazine who had great law careers, I felt a mild interest; when I read about people who had great writing careers, I became sick with envy."

WHAT DOES IT MEAN IF I'M MOST ENVIOUS OF MY CAT?

Envy reveals your values—if you're honest with yourself. Most of us are ashamed when we're envious, often because it implies the other person is better at something than we are. As researcher Tanya Menon points out, it takes courage to say, "I'm envious of Jane because I'm completely inadequate relative to her at this job." Next time you covet what someone else has, don't perform all kinds of mental gymnastics to convince yourself you feel nothing. Admitting your envy might be a sign that you need to improve or make a change.

Irrelevant emotions

We never make choices in an emotional vacuum. Even something as small as finding a coin in a copying machine can affect our mood, and then our decisions. But when we become aware that our feelings are unrelated to a decision, we're quickly able to discount them. The simplest way to prevent irrelevant emotions from marauding through your life is to let time pass before making a decision. Think of it as screening for unwanted visitors.

OK BEFORE YOU ANSWER, ASK
YOURSELF IF YOUR GROUCHINESS
IS RELEVANT OR IRRELEVANT

Excitement

How it affects you: Excitement makes us overly optimistic and impulsive. Excited people think they are less likely to get sick than other people and tend to spend more money (this is why casinos are filled with excitement-inducing bright lights and loud noises). Excited people also think less deeply, are more susceptible to bias, and better remember information that matches their upbeat mood. For example, if you're thrilled because you just got a big bonus, and you then sit down to evaluate a colleague, you'll remember more happy memories with her.

    How to counteract it: Excitement and anxiety are two sides of the same coin. The best way to manage both is to find ways to calm your body. Breathe in through your nose (instead of through your mouth) to better regulate emotion or go for a quick walk or run.

Sadness

How it affects you: When we're sad, we see the glass as half empty. Emotional funks make us overestimate the chances of something bad happening to us. We set lower expectations for ourselves and are more likely to pick the option that gives us something now instead of tomorrow. But feeling down in the dumps can also make us more likely to take the time to carefully think through a decision. And that's useful—to a point. Sadness predisposes us to rumination, which can make us get stuck in an infinite loop of analysis that leaves us unable to pick an option and feel good about it.

How to counteract it: Gratitude has the opposite effect of sadness. If you're not able to simply regulate your sadness away, list three things you're grateful for. To really boost your mood, write and personally deliver a gratitude letter to someone you've never thanked for his or her kindness. Compared to other happiness interventions, this simple act provides the biggest and longest boost to happiness, with benefits lasting more than a month.

UNDERAPPRECIATED REASONS TO EXPRESS GRATITUDE

DESK CHAIR IS THE PERFECT HEIGHT

2-WEEK-OLD MANICURE STILL LOOKS GREAT

A/V WORKS ON THE FIRST TRY

ELEVATOR OPENS RIGHT AWAY

Anger

How it affects you: Anger makes us hot-headed. We pick long shots over safe bets, rely more on stereotypes, and are less willing to listen to advice. And if you're Warren Buffett, your anger costs you $100 billion. In 1964, Berkshire Hathaway was a struggling textile manufacturer. Buffett, already a well-off investor, knew the company was in trouble but still thought its shares were underpriced. He bought into Berkshire expecting to soon sell his stake back to then CEO Seabury Stanton for a quick profit. But when Stanton offered him less than they had initially agreed on, Buffett saw red. Instead of accepting a slightly smaller profit, he launched a yearlong takeover campaign, buying more and more shares until he had the right to fire Stanton. Because of this "monumentally stupid decision," Buffett spent the next two decades pouring money into the failing textile company—before giving up. If he had spent the money on a better investment, Berkshire Hathaway could have been worth $100 billion more than it is today.

How to counteract it: Slow down and take a deep breath to prevent yourself from making a rash decision. And don't be so quick to shrug off advice. Researchers had people watch one of two videos before asking them to perform

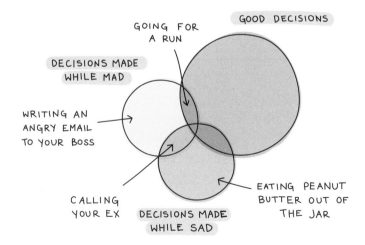

a mental estimation task: a calming *National Geographic* special that portrayed fish at the Great Barrier Reef or an anger-inducing clip from the movie *My Bodyguard* that showed a young man being bullied. People who watched the first accepted useful tips to help them make a guess, whereas people who watched the second were distrustful of advice; three-fourths of *My Bodyguard* viewers ignored useful tips—and then made worse guesses.

Stress

How it affects you: Stress seems to affect men and women's decision-making behavior differently. Where men make riskier choices under duress, women tend to choose the low-risk option.

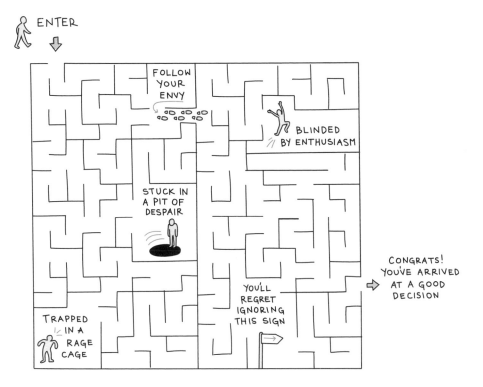

How to counteract it: No sudden movements! "When you are stressed," writes psychologist Therese Huston, "You usually want to move quickly from 'What am I going to do?' to 'At least I'm doing something.'" Gender differences also point to the benefit of diverse teams. Researcher Nichole Lighthall explains, "It might be better to have more gender diversity on important decisions because men and women offer differing perspectives. Being more cautious and taking the time to make a decision will often be the right choice."

HIRING

One giant caveat to our rule "emotion is part of the equation": you should *never* rely on your gut when hiring. Right now, emotion plays far too much of a role in the interview process. More than three-fourths of people involved in the hiring process at law, financial, and consulting firms admit they base their decisions on gut feelings ("It's like dating," explained a banker, as if dating is never a hot mess). We're also quick to judge: studies show interviews are effectively over after the first ten seconds. Once interviewers make their initial assessment, they use the ensuing conversation simply to confirm it. The problem with relying on emotion in hiring decisions is that we end up hiring people who make us feel good.

Why shouldn't we hire people who make us feel good? It's because the spark we feel while talking to someone has little to do with whether or not they're the best person for (or even able to do) the job. We see people who are similar or familiar to us as better than those who are not. ("You're from Atlanta? *I'm* from Atlanta!") So when we hire based on our feelings, "like hires like hires like hires like," Patty McCord, who led HR at Netflix for fourteen years, told us. And, in fact, the best predictor of how positively candidates will be perceived is how similar they are to the interviewer. In this section,

SINCE YOU HAVE:

A HUMAN BRAIN
AFFECTED BY BIAS

YOU'LL PROBABLY LIKE:

<   >

THIS GUY WHO LOOKS LIKE YOU!	THIS GUY WHO GREW UP NEAR YOU!	THIS WOMAN WHO ALSO LOVES NPR!	THIS GUY WHO TOLD A FUNNY JOKE!
ADD TO CART	ADD TO CART	ADD TO CART	ADD TO CART

we'll look at why following your feelings when hiring leads to poor decisions and how to hire for skills instead.

It's not breaking news that we hold biases against certain groups that cause unintentional and implicit discrimination. Women have a harder time entering stereotypically masculine fields, whereas men will often not even apply for stereotypically feminine roles. (One recruiting ad tried to combat this with the slogan "Are you man enough to be a nurse?") Women of color can face even greater difficulties. Black women feel more pressure to continually prove themselves, and Latina women who act assertively risk being viewed by their coworkers as "too emotional" or "crazy." Bias creates a self-fulfilling prophecy: if you think a candidate is going to fail—and your gestures indicate this expectation—you condemn the candidate to fail. Minority employees whose bosses think poorly of minorities perform much worse than they do while working for unbiased managers. And black men often feel compelled to work longer hours as a way to counteract stereotypes that they have a poor work ethic.

Unfortunately, turning off emotion is impossible: it will play a role in the interview process whether you want it to or not. Still, there's a lot you can do to curb bias. The best way is to clearly outline what missing skills your team needs to succeed and then objectively test if a candidate can do those things. "When you start by defining the problem, you're more open to different ways of solving it," Patty McCord told us. Blind evaluations, where a candidate's race, gender, or background is concealed, force evaluators to look only at skill level—and often lead to a more diverse set of hires. Orchestras famously reduced gender bias by asking musicians to audition behind a curtain. After implementing a blind submission process, *The Daily Show* hired more women and minorities.

WE HAVE TO HIRE THIS CANDIDATE!

Always conduct a structured interview: start by writing a list of questions and then create a scale by which you can assess responses fairly. Google's qDroid, an internal tool, lets interviewers select the job and skills they're screening for and then sends them relevant questions. Examples include, "Tell me about a time your behavior had a positive impact on your team" and "Tell me about a time when you effectively managed your team to achieve a goal. What did your approach look like?" Ask each candidate the same set of questions; if you don't standardize the interview process, you can't objectively compare answers.

Score each response immediately and compare them horizontally. Memory is unreliable, so after an interview, you will most vividly remember recent, emotional, and entertaining answers. That means if you wait until the end of an interview to score a candidate's answers, you rely on polluted judgment. When you sit down to compare candidates, look at and rank all the responses to the first question. Then look at and rank all the responses to the second question, and so on. This prevents you from focusing on a single candidate for too long, which is when bias creeps in. You might also be surprised:

IN THEORY

HIRING IS THE MOST IMPORTANT THING AND I WILL MAKE INTERVIEWING A PRIORITY

IN REALITY

OH CRAP! I HAVE TO INTERVIEW A CANDIDATE IN TWO MINUTES

the person you thought was the front-runner may have given an amazing answer to one question but given only lackluster responses to everything else.

We'll leave you with a final warning of what happens when you don't rely on structured interviews. Yale professor Jason Dana and his colleagues asked two groups of students to predict their classmates' GPAs. One group had access only to past grades and current course lists, whereas the other was also allowed to conduct interviews. The students who interviewed their classmates were significantly worse at predicting future GPA. Even scarier, most didn't notice that some interviewees had been instructed to give random and sometimes nonsensical responses.

How to reduce biased decisions in the hiring process:

- **Prepare.** Make sure you understand what skills and attributes you're looking for in a candidate. If you're pulled in to interview someone last minute (unfortunately, this happens a lot), ask the hiring manager to give you a copy of the job description and a few example questions.
- **Remove names from résumés when screening.** When researchers submitted identical résumés to businesses, those with white-sounding first and last names received 50 percent more responses than those with African American–sounding names, an effect that hasn't diminished since the first such study was done in 1989.
- **Ask for work samples.** Give candidates a typical problem they might face in the role or an issue you're currently working on. Then ask them to write out a basic overview of the methodology they would use to solve it. Work samples tend to be the best predictors of how someone will perform on the job—significantly better than interviews, education level, and even experience—and make it easier for evaluators to judge candidates based on skills.
- **Don't try to "break the streak."** Even the order in which we inter-

view candidates can affect how we perceive their competence. As interviewers, we tend to believe there should be an equal number of strong and weak applicants. If we talk to five outstanding people in a row, we'll assume the sixth candidate is less likely to be good, just to break the streak.

- **Make interviewers give each candidate a numerical likability score.** Quantifying your personal feelings about candidates makes it easier to control for them.
- **Make hiring a group decision.** Keep evaluations objective and insist hiring decisions be made by a group (not a single manager).

Negotiating

Some of our biggest decisions revolve around salaries, promotions, and project assignments. But before we enter these negotiations, we go through an internal tug-of-war. Sometimes these inner debates are straightforward ("I need to ask for extended leave because my dad is sick"), but they can also be drawn out and exhausting. ("Should I put my name in for a promotion? Who am I to ask for anything?") Our inner pessimists can compromise our ability to negotiate effectively—or convince us not to negotiate at all. You think about asking for a raise and then immediately concoct a list of reasons why you shouldn't: The company is going through a rough period. Your colleagues have also worked hard. Your boss will be offended you asked. Left unresolved, this inner turmoil might mean you make weak first offers, respond too quickly to counteroffers, and settle for less than your confident colleagues. So before you go into a negotiation, come to an inner consensus on what you want.

Next, understand your negotiation style—and how your gender or culture may have shaped it. Minorities tend to ask for less during salary negotiations, and women agree to take on more projects than their male colleagues. If you're susceptible to self-doubt, imagine you're negotiating on behalf of someone you care about. In a lab experiment, women who negotiated for themselves asked for $7,000 less than men. But when they negotiated for a friend, they demanded just as much money as the men did. It might also help to have an "if-then" plan ready: "If the other side offers me less than I want, then I will restate my reasons and ask if there are non-salary-based benefits."

MOLLIE: This might be the most lucrative advice we will give you: If you're asking for more money (either for your starting salary in a new job or for a raise at your existing job), try this magic line: "I don't want my salary to be a distraction to me while I'm in this role." I have used this sentence to successfully raise my starting salary at several jobs. By saying you don't want your salary to be a distraction (i.e., distractingly low), you are stating a fact that both you and the other person believe to be true. You are having empathy for both yourself and the other party. They also don't want you to be distracted.

WHAT TO BRING TO A NEGOTIATION

AN INNER CONSENSUS

CURIOSITY

AN IDEA OF WHAT THE OTHER SIDE WANTS

AN AMULET FOR PROTECTION

A DECISION-MAKING CHECKLIST

Checklists save lives: after pilots and surgeons started using checklists to make sure they weren't skipping important steps, accidents, infection rates, and deaths all declined. In this section, we've put together a "manage your mind" checklist. We obviously can't map out the perfect series of steps for each unique decision you'll face, but checking off the boxes for these basic steps will help you prevent easy-to-make mistakes.

First, to anyone whose nightly ritual is to mentally flip through all the terrible decisions you've made, listen up: life is filled with uncertainty. You might still be wrong even with the right process in place. You can accurately predict that a coin flip is equally likely to be heads or tails, but you'll never be able to say with complete certainty that it *will* be heads. So don't be overly hard on yourself if things don't turn out perfectly.

INDECISION JEOPARDY

GOOGLE SEARCHES I THOUGHT WOULD HELP	THINGS I SHOULD BE DOING INSTEAD OF WORRYING	POTENTIALLY CRIPPLING REGRETS	PEOPLE WHO HAVE LISTENED TO ME OBSESS	OUTLANDISH WORST-CASE SCENARIOS
$200	$200	$200	$200	$200
$400	$400	$400	$400	$400
$600	$600	$600	$600	$600
$800	$800	$800	$800	$800
$1,000	$1,000	$1,000	$1,000	$1,000

✓ **Write out your options.** If you've written down only two things, take a moment to see if you can introduce an additional alternative. Choices usually aren't binary. When you limit your decision to yes or no, or A or B, you make the stakes much higher than they might actually be. So if you've listed "Stay at my current job" and "Take the new job," think about whether you could broaden your menu by adding something like "Stay at my current job and ask for a promotion."

✓ **List everything you're feeling.** Are you irritated? Afraid? Craving caffeine?

✓ **Regulate or counteract each irrelevant emotion.**

✓ **Link the remaining relevant emotions to specific options.** Notice if a feeling is tied to a single choice. Are you most excited when you imagine yourself picking option A? Are you afraid you'll regret choosing option B?

✓ **Ask what, not why.** Compare "Why are you afraid?" to "What are you afraid of?" You can easily answer the first question with a self-pitying platitude ("Because I never try anything new"), but the second forces you to address your specific feelings about the decision at hand. "Why questions draw us to our limitations; what questions help us see our potential. Why questions stir up negative emotions; what questions keep us curious," writes psychologist Tasha Eurich.

✓ **Figure out your decision-making tendency.** Which of the following better describes you?

1. You like to gather as much information about your options as you can before picking one. Even if you find something that meets your requirements, you feel compelled to keep looking just in case. You want to pick the best possible option.

2. You have a general idea of what you want, and once you find a reasonably suitable option, you pick it and move on. "Good enough," you think.

If you picked 1, you're a maximizer. If you picked 2, you're a satisficer. Satisficers are usually happier with their decisions, even when maximizers end up with objectively better options. For example, maximizers tend to find jobs that pay more, but they are less likely to be happy with their choice because they get weighed down by complicated, inconclusive second-guessing.

A MAXIMIZER'S PROCESS

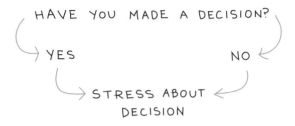

Maximizers, here are some strategies to help you get unstuck:

- **Narrow down your choices tournament-style:**
    - o Divide your options into equal piles (for example, if you have six options, make three piles of two).
    - o Pick the best option from each pile.
    - o Put the winners into a new pile.
    - o Pick the best option from the pile of winners.

- **Arbitrarily limit the number of choices you consider.** Say you're deciding where to go to lunch. You can tell yourself you'll look at only three places, instead of thirty. "'Good enough' is almost always good enough," advises Barry Schwartz, author of *The Paradox of Choice.*
- **Don't rush through the final decision.** Going back and forth between two options isn't all bad. When you're faced with a novel decision, anxiety or indecision might just be your brain's way of slowing you down so it has enough time to more accurately weigh the evidence for or against each option.

SYMPATHY CARDS FOR MAXIMIZERS

SORRY

OUR THOUGHTS
ARE WITH YOU

DEEPEST
SYMPATHIES

YOU HAD TO
PICK SOMETHING
COOL OVER
SOMETHING
ELSE COOL

AS YOUR
THOUGHTS
ARE WITH YOUR
NEXT BEST
OPTION

IN THIS TIME
OF INDECISION

✓ **Run your thinking by another person.** Walk a mentor, colleague, or friend through your options. Verbalizing your thought process forces

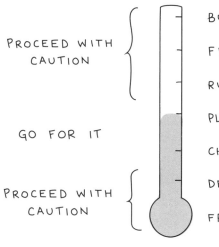

BEFORE YOU MAKE A DECISION
TAKE YOUR EMOTIONAL TEMPERATURE

PROCEED WITH
CAUTION

BOILING

FIRED UP

RUNNING HOT

PLEASANT

GO FOR IT

CHILL

DESOLATE

PROCEED WITH
CAUTION

FROZEN INSIDE

you to synthesize the information you've been collecting. The other person can also help identify biases that may be affecting your decision making.

✓ **Make a decision.** After completing the above steps, you should be able to rule out a fair number of options and be confident you made the best decision you could. And luckily, research shows that our minds work hard to help us stay content with whatever we choose— even when what actually happens is different from what we expected.

TAKEAWAYS

1. Recognize that listening to your feelings is not the same as acting on your feelings.
2. Keep relevant emotions (those related to the decision you're facing); toss irrelevant emotions (those unrelated to the decision you're facing).
3. Do not rely on emotion when deciding whether or not to hire a candidate. Use structured interviews to reduce biased hiring decisions.
4. Before an external negotiation, come to an inner consensus.

CHAPTER 5

Teams

Psychological safety first:

Why the how matters more than the who

TEAMWORK WOULD BE SO MUCH
EASIER IF I COULD DO IT BY MYSELF

*I*s my idea great or deeply dumb? our friend Lila wondered to herself, her palms starting to sweat in the middle of a team meeting. *If I say something, will people discover I'm a complete fraud?*

Lila had been on her team for only two weeks. She didn't know her new teammates well, but they both seemed hypercompetitive. Karl often talked over her, and Anna usually answered questions with an exaggerated eye roll. Lila worried they saw her as completely incompetent.

Finally, after five (or maybe ten?) minutes of internal debate, Lila went for it. As she finished her thought, Anna raised an eyebrow. Lila trailed off, filled with self-loathing. *Here comes the eye roll.* But then Anna nodded slowly. "That's really cool," she mused, sounding optimistic. Karl jumped in. "Yeah, not bad!" Relief flooded Lila's body (talk about emotional whiplash), and she smiled tentatively. Her idea *had* been pretty good.

"Why did I doubt myself so much?" Lila lamented to us over drinks in San Francisco. She stared into her half-full beer.

This brings us to the fourth new rule of emotion at work: ***Psychological safety first.*** In this chapter, we'll show you how to build a team whose members feel safe throwing out ideas, taking risks, and asking questions. We'll walk through the ways successful teams manage different types of conflict. And finally, we'll look at how you can deal with three types of particularly bad apples: jerks, dissenters, and slackers.

THE ABSENCE OF PSYCHOLOGICAL SAFETY

PSYCHOLOGICAL SAFETY

What makes a good team good? Before you answer, consider a simple experiment run by Alistair Shepherd. At the beginning of a business school pitch competition, Alistair asked participants a series of OkCupid-inspired questions. Think "Do you like horror movies?" and "Do spelling mistakes annoy you?" Based solely on the answers, Alistair accurately predicted the ranking of all eight teams—without any information about members' intelligence, experience, or leadership skills. How did he do it? The answer has to do with how each team member *felt*.

Google discovered this same elusive emotional ingredient in 2012, when a group of researchers analyzed nearly two hundred teams to figure out why some teams succeed where others fail. The results were surprising: individual team members' tenure, seniority, and extraversion didn't seem to affect team performance. "We had lots of data, but there was nothing showing that a mix of specific personality types or skills or backgrounds made any difference," recalled Abeer Dubey, a manager in Google's People Analytics division. "The 'who' part of the equation didn't seem to matter." What mattered was the "how": the best teams were those whose members respected one another's ideas. People on these teams had **psychological safety**: they felt they could suggest ideas, admit mistakes, and take risks without being embarrassed by the group. *To find out if your team is psychologically safe, see our flash assessment on page 247.*

Success depends on psychological safety. At Google, members of teams with high levels of psychological safety were less likely to leave their jobs, brought in more revenue, and were rated effective twice as often by executives. MIT researchers who studied team performance came to the same conclusion: simply grouping smart people together doesn't guarantee a smart team. Online and off, the best teams discuss ideas frequently, do not let one person dominate the conversation, and are sensitive to one another's feelings.

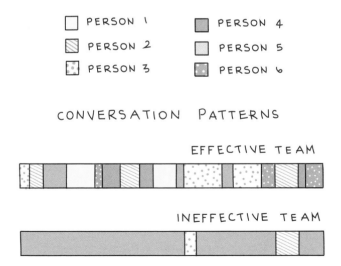

Alistair Shepherd asked about horror movies and spelling mistakes because he was looking for groups that were tolerant of differing perspectives. And Lila worried so much about speaking up because she didn't feel a sense of psychological safety.

Everyone screws up. Say Mollie admits a mistake and Liz responds by making her feel even worse than she already does. The next time Mollie needs help she might be reluctant to say anything, *even if* the long-term consequences of not asking for help will feel much worse than being embarrassed by Liz. This dynamic is present even in medicine, where mistakes can be fatal. In a simulation, teams of doctors and nurses were asked to treat a "sick" mannequin. The groups were randomly assigned an expert who either belittled team members by claiming they "wouldn't last a week" or treated them neutrally. The results? "Scary," wrote the lead researcher. The teams with a rude expert made grave mistakes: they misdiagnosed the patient, didn't resuscitate or ventilate appropriately, and prescribed the wrong medications.

Psychological safety matters even more when it comes to building diverse teams. There is an unambiguous and meaningful benefit to having people from different backgrounds on your team *only when* psychological safety exists. It's

CAN YOU STOP REFERRING TO ALL
MY QUESTIONS AS ELEMENTARY?

easy to see why. Say you have one marketing analyst and nine engineers on a team. In the absence of psychological safety, the analyst will think twice before he speaks for fear he will get savaged by the engineers. When you make the environment safe, he'll use his uniqueness as a skill instead of a hindrance. Every person on a team knows something that no one else knows. That's why teams exist: you need more than one person's set of ideas and skills to solve a problem. If you don't let people speak up, or you make them feel stupid when they do, you limit your team's chances of pulling off something magical.

Psychological safety also helps your team get to burstiness, when group members build on one another's ideas so rapidly the room feels like it's bursting with creativity. "Burstiness" is the opposite of an ineffective and sludgy brainstorm session: highly creative teams tend to be more "bursty," as members contribute ideas freely and quickly. But—and this is a crucial *but*—teams

PSYCHOLOGICAL SAFETY SIGNS

CAUTION
DON'T MAKE PEOPLE FEEL STUPID FOR ASKING QUESTIONS

Warning eye rolls are Corrosive

NO ZONE-OUT ZONE

STOP TALKING OVER OTHERS

need a base of psychological safety so members don't take the accidental interruptions that often come with rapid-fire-idea interruption personally. Uber's poisonous culture meant that the endorsement of "toe-stepping" was "too often used as an excuse for being an asshole," wrote one of the company's executives. "You want a whole bunch of different opinions in there and yet you don't want to get bogged down in conflict," explains Jill Soloway, creator of the TV show *Transparent*. "You want people who are shit-starters creatively, but not in real life." In the next section, we'll look at how to preserve all the good parts of burstiness without getting mired in conflict.

Unfortunately, you won't always be able to create psychological safety for your team. Cutthroat offices value bravado and bluster, traits that usually don't make for great team players. Or you may work with people who've spent years at institutions that prize individual effort in a competitive setting. After his first year in a prestigious graduate program, a friend of ours had learned to say, "You're of course familiar with the work of so-and-so?" His phrasing didn't make "no" feel like a safe answer. If you're on a psychologically unsafe team, take care of your mental well-being and focus on what you can control. Because "what you can control" differs depending on your role, we've broken out the bullet points below into what you can do as an individual and what you can do as a leader.

How to create an environment of
psychological safety as an individual:

- **Encourage open discussion.** Questions like "What does everyone think?" or "Does anyone disagree?" do not effectively invite opposing viewpoints. Especially if someone on the team is an introvert, ask each team member to write out their thoughts and then have everyone share out loud. And don't forget follow-up questions. "I've found that whenever you ask a question, the first response you get is usually not the answer," says Roshi Givechi, a former partner at IDEO. Roshi recommends asking team members to "say more about that" and advises suggestions be given only after a "scaffolding of thoughtfulness" has been established.

- **Suggest a bad ideas brainstorm.** Have team members throw out purposefully absurd ideas or ask them to come up with the worst suggestion they can think of. This exercise takes the pressure off and allows team members to be silly and adventurous.
- **Ask clarifying questions (to make it okay for others to do the same).** When team members use acronyms or jargon, ask them to explain (and avoid using them yourself). Although you may initially worry about how you'll be perceived for asking clarifying questions, remember you're modeling this behavior for others, and together you can all increase psychological safety.
- **Use generative language.** If someone has an interesting suggestion, respond with, "Let's try it!" If you like the gist of someone's idea, say, "Building on that idea . . ." or borrow from the world of improv and make "Yes and . . ." your catchphrase.

As a leader:

- **Create team agreements.** At the beginning of a meeting or project, create a list of ground rules for how you'll treat one another. Keep the list in a visible place (e.g., hang it on the wall). Example agreements: assume good; trust one another; be present.
- **Ask your team how you can help.** Don't put the onus on your team members to tell you they feel psychologically unsafe—they won't. As a leader, it's your job to start the conversation. Ask individual team members, "What's one thing I could do to help the team feel safer taking risks?"
- **Balance activities with communication.** B. Byrne, a product manager

at Coinbase, shared the following analogy: every relationship, professional or personal, is like building a tower of popsicle sticks. Experiences (e.g., eating together, working on a case together, or coauthoring an article) are the popsicle sticks, and communication is the glue. If you do things together but never take the time to discuss your feelings or needs, the tower will be constructed of only popsicle sticks and will eventually fall over. But if you overanalyze every interaction and never step back to simply enjoy each other's company, the tower will be weighed down by glue and melt in on itself.

- **Ask questions that get to a deeper level.** BlackRock uses a number of icebreakers when starting conversations. One has employees split into pairs (people are more trusting when they talk to a single person versus the whole room) and answer the prompt, "When you think of your childhood, what meal comes to mind and why?" This disarming question sets the stage for more disclosure later. "No one just says pizza," explains managing director Jonathan McBride. "Instead, they give you a story about their family, their culture and upbringing, and weekly traditions with their parents or grandparents. You get something like, 'My family baked pizzas together each Sunday and the whole family would prepare the meal together.' Even though you're discussing food, you get a story about someone's life and family that you wouldn't normally get in five minutes."

THERE WILL BE CONFLICT

"If two men on the same job agree all the time, then one is useless," wrote movie producer Darryl Zanuck. "If they disagree all the time, both are useless." At its best, conflict sparks breakthroughs. Early conflict between the creators of *Toy Story* led to two pivotal changes: the original mechanical drummer character was replaced with a karate-chop-style space toy that became the much loved Buzz Lightyear, and a ventriloquist's dummy character was changed to a pull-string cowboy doll named Woody.

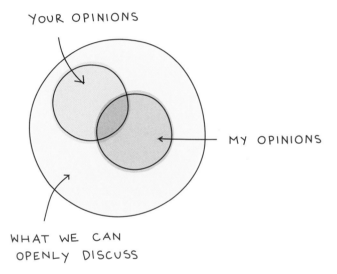

PSYCHOLOGICAL SAFETY

YOUR OPINIONS

MY OPINIONS

WHAT WE CAN
OPENLY DISCUSS

Of course, conflict can also upset us so much that we burn out or "rage quit" (a term our friend coined). Unmanaged debate leads to brainstorm breakdowns. When people get mired in disagreements or shut down, the group comes up with fewer and worse ideas than if everyone simply worked alone.

In this section, we'll talk about how to protect psychological safety even when you're butting heads. You need to learn to navigate two main types of conflict: *task conflict* (the clash of creative ideas) and *relationship conflict* (personality-driven arguments). Task and relationship conflict are often related: it's hard not to take disagreement over ideas personally.

	I LIKE YOU	I HATE YOU
I LIKE YOUR IDEA	NO CONFLICT	RELATIONSHIP CONFLICT
I HATE YOUR IDEA	TASK CONFLICT	FEUD

Task conflict

The two of us are not immune to creative clashes: we often dealt with task conflict while writing chapters of this book. Mollie likes to quickly write an initial draft and send it to our editor for immediate feedback whereas Liz prefers to mull over sections and send our editor a more polished version. Over time, we realized this difference is useful—Liz ensures we don't send out a half-baked chapter and Mollie prevents Liz from obsessing over syntax. We learned to find a healthy tension and talk through why we do or don't feel ready to hand over a chapter (but we still stepped on each other's toes sometimes!).

There's hope for you, too. Teams can create structures that encourage task conflict while making sure it stays productive. Every morning during Pixar dailies (daily reviews of draft films), animators look at one another's partially completed frames and propose edits to the motion, body, and facial expression of the characters. Participants are encouraged to make all comments about the shot, not the animator; comments on stills from the movie *Inside Out* included, "Vary shape of pupils" and "More on her toes." Another central rule at dailies: "You shouldn't change things just to make them 'yours'—you want to make them 'better,'" writes Pixar animator Victor Navone. When teams take the time to discuss the pros and cons of each member's suggestions, they make better decisions.

ROAD MAP OF TEAM OBSTACLES

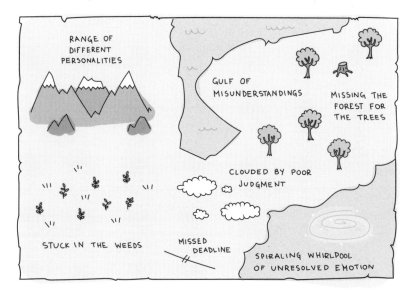

User Manuals

The best way to navigate potential conflict is to preemptively create structures that help communicate preferences and work styles. Many of the CEOs interviewed by *New York Times* columnist Adam Bryant create "user manuals" or "how to work with me" guides to make collaboration easier. To achieve the same with your team, Adam recommends blocking off an hour to answer the questions below. Ideally, invite a neutral facilitator to guide discussion.

WHAT EVERYONE SHOULD KNOW ABOUT YOU:

1. What are some honest, unfiltered things about you?
2. What drives you nuts?
3. What are your quirks?
4. What qualities do you particularly value in people who work with you?
5. What are some things that people might misunderstand about you that you should clarify?

HOW TO WORK WITH YOU:

1. What's the best way to communicate with you?
2. What hours do we want to work together? Where and how do we want to work? (Same room, what kinds of meetings, what kinds of file sharing?)
3. What are our goals for this team? What are our concerns about this team?
4. How will we make decisions? What types of decisions need consensus? How will we deal with conflict?
5. How do we want to give and receive feedback? (One-on-one, in a group, informally, or during a specified time each week—like at a retrospective?)

MOLLIE AND LIZ'S ANSWERS TO # 1:

- Mollie: I warm up to people slowly. Once you get to know me, I think you'll find that I'm warm, generous, and even silly. But I can come across as more reserved and serious at first. Be patient with me as you get to know me.

- Liz: I love to be left alone when I work. When I was an economic consultant I took a personality test called the DISC assessment, which stated that the best way to work with me is to "be brief, be bright, and be gone." So accurate. . . . For people who enjoy frequently emailing or messaging one another, my behavior can come across as antisocial, but I don't intend it to be. I can't concentrate if I'm constantly being pinged—cognitive switching is a productivity sinkhole.

Schedule time to check back in about your team's answers. It's always better to start with more structure and check-ins about everyone's work style at the beginning. You can always cancel planned meetings if you feel everything is going smoothly.

Relationship conflict

Let's go back to our conflict about whether or not to turn in a chapter draft. If Liz had at any point said to Mollie, "It's a dumb idea to send this chapter to our editor now," and Mollie responded with, "You never take my suggestions seriously," what started out as task conflict would have devolved into relationship conflict (and goodbye, psychological safety). No amount of time, talent, or money will save you if you let relationship conflict hijack a discussion. Pop culture is littered with examples of teams whose personal feuds led to public implosions. One member of the Eagles famously told another, "Only three more songs before I kick your ass"—the band didn't play together again for more than a decade. And the *Seinfeld* cast found it so difficult to work with Heidi Swedberg, the actress who played George's fiancée, Susan Ross, that they convinced show creator Larry David to kill her off.

It's easy to write relationship conflict off as a clear-cut case of irreconcilable differences, but it can often be resolved simply by hearing each other out. For example, you're probably either a Seeker (you like to argue) or an Avoider (you'd rather eat a slug than deal with confrontation). These two types run into problems when Seekers engage in ritual opposition, a form of verbal one-upmanship aimed at testing ideas (see: "How did you not think of . . . ," "That suggestion makes no sense," or simply "You're wrong"). To avoid hurt feelings between Seekers and Avoiders, discuss each person's conversational style and then decide how the team will handle conflict. Is it okay to immediately and aggressively poke holes in someone's idea, or should criticism be delivered more indirectly? In the moments when you're not able to sidestep clashes between these two types, Avoiders should remember that Seekers don't intend their comments as personal attacks or insults. And Seekers should remind themselves that confrontational debate might shut down input from others.

When you're having conflict within your team, validation preserves psychological safety (you could reconceptualize all conflict as a struggle for validation). Disagreement causes hurt feelings only when mutual respect hasn't been established. From now on, if you have something to say, let it (gently) rip! When sharing an honest point of view, "You fear people will become angry or vindictive,"

writes Kim Scott in the book *Radical Candor.* "Instead they are usually grateful for the chance to talk it through." On the flip side, one of the most disrespectful things you can do is to make someone else feel invisible—and validation helps people feel visible. We'll talk more about approaching these difficult conversations in chapter 6 on communication. Recognize that the people you disagree with are also human and have human needs. Paul Santagata, head of industry at Google, leads his teams through an activity called "Just Like Me," in which he asks team members who are arguing to remember the following:

- This person has beliefs, perspectives, and opinions, just like me.
- This person has hopes, anxieties, and vulnerabilities, just like me.
- This person wants to feel respected, appreciated, and competent, just like me.

THINGS TO SAY DURING AN ARGUMENT

I GET THAT

HOW CAN WE COMPROMISE

YOU'RE BECOMING HYSTERICAL

LET'S TAKE A BREAK*

WHAT'S WRONG WITH YOU

HOW DO YOU SEE THE SITUATION

#SORRY NOT SORRY

HELPFUL   UNHELPFUL

*HELPFUL UNLESS YOU'RE DATING

What if you've tried talking and you've offered validation but your co-worker still drives you nuts? The best thing to do might be nothing. Don't rehash the discussion. You'll risk going in circles and making interpersonal problems worse. You're better off taking a deep breath and realizing confrontation isn't going to get you what you want. Appreciate that some levels of chaos and conflict are part of the process, and try to focus less on your coworker and more on the thing you're doing.

A final comment on conflict: We hate the advice "Never go to bed angry." Go to bed angry! Emotions like jealousy, hatred, anger, or frustration skew your view on reality. Few disputes need to be resolved immediately. Take a break and revisit the discussion later.

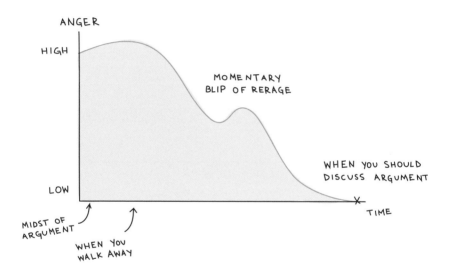

How to fight a good fight:

- **Get curious.** If others feel that you're blaming them, you become the enemy, and they become defensive. Instead, try to find out what they see as the root cause of disagreement. Ask something like, "Sounds like there are multiple factors at play, maybe we can uncover them together?" Then ask for solutions: "What do we think needs to happen here?"
- **Conduct premortems.** Set aside half an hour at the outset of a project

and have team members list everything they fear might go wrong. This allows the team to fully understand and address potential risks. "People are probably already saying these things in smaller groups, but they might not be saying it loudly, clearly, or often enough," writes Astro Teller, head of Google X. "Often because these are things that might get you branded as a downer or disloyal."

- **Conduct postmortems.** If you had conflict during a project (or within a phase of a project), schedule time after the work is done to figure out why there was conflict. Come together as a team to share what could have gone better and why—and brainstorm how you can avoid these issues in the future.

- **Understand your biases.** When you're working with a group of racially diverse colleagues, research shows that the biggest issue may be that group members *perceive* there will be more conflict. When a norm of fairness is encouraged, people are less likely to express prejudiced behavior or responses.

- **Invite structured criticism.** A great way to make critiques generative is to ask people to share ideas that are either quick fixes, small steps that make a meaningful impact, or a way to rethink the entire thing. These three buckets add helpful constraints and make conversation less likely to devolve into personal attacks.

- **Find a conflict role model.** We all know someone, personally or professionally, who tells it like it is, but in a way that is helpful. Next time you're around this person, observe how they act, and try to model your behavior after theirs.

Liz Lecture: Team Meetings

I know it's cliché to complain about unproductive team meetings, but they're still happening all the time, so whatever. Meetings are necessary for team discussion and decision making, but too many meetings are an expensive alternative to work. It's not just the time that the meeting itself takes up, but the fifteen minutes before and after the meeting when we think, "Oh I have/had a meeting, I might as well take a quick break."

Meetings happen so often because we are a species that loves to gather and loves to belong. Even I feel bad when I'm not invited to a meeting—and I hate meetings! It also *feels* productive to sit in a room with people and pontificate. Here are my rules for making meetings worth it.

1. **Pay attention.** Get off your phones and computers. If I'm talking and you're on your phone, you're telling me I'm less important and less informative than a Buzzfeed list. That is enraging! The point of a meeting is to solve problems and determine next steps. This is why we have so many meetings, because no one listened during the first meeting.

2. **Have an agenda.** If I don't know why we're meeting and you don't know why we're meeting, *why are we meeting?* A meeting without a point is excruciating, especially if I have a ton of other work to do. Research backs me up! When we don't find meetings effective, we are more dissatisfied with our jobs, regardless of how much we're getting paid or how much we like our managers.

3. **No longer than necessary.** If we end early, let me go. Just because our calendars default to thirty- or sixty-minute blocks doesn't mean the meeting needs to fill that entire time.

4. **Be smart about scheduling.** "A single meeting can blow a whole afternoon, by breaking it into two pieces each too small to do anything hard in," writes Paul Graham. Please make meetings happen at the beginning or end of the morning or afternoon. No more 10:30 A.M. meetings; they punch a hole in my productivity!

BINGO

FOR MEETINGS

SIDE CONVO	"GOING FORWARD"	LATE START	SWIPING	SOMEONE CHECKS SOCIAL MEDIA
"BANDWIDTH"	SOMEONE FORGETS MUTE	COMPLETE ZONE-OUT	RAMBLING BLAH BLAH	ENDS EARLY
"CIRCLE BACK"	UNADDRESSED TENSION	FREE	AWFUL HOLD MUSIC	COWORKER ARRIVES LATE
SURPRISE FOOD	COMMENT DISGUISED AS QUESTION	THE POP-IN	PLAYING GAME ON PHONE	FEMALE INTERRUPTED
CLEAR NEXT STEPS	"TO PLAY DEVIL'S ADVOCATE"	NO DECISION MAKER	MEETING SHOULD HAVE BEEN AN EMAIL	"LET'S TAKE THIS OFFLINE"

JERKS, DISSENTERS, AND SLACKERS

Unchecked, a bad apple spoils the bin. Researcher Will Felps paid actors to throw out insults, act annoyed, or openly slack off. These surly additions dropped group performance by almost forty percent. "When an employee demoralizes the entire team by undermining a project, or when a team member checks out and doesn't pull his weight, or when a bully causes future stars to quit the organization—too often, we shrug and point out that this person has tenure, or vocational skills or isn't so bad," writes Seth Godin. Managers, you *must* be intolerant of bad apples for the psychological safety of your team. If someone constantly makes others feel bad, the group will doubt your abilities as a leader. Of course, sometimes you can't get rid of a bad apple. What then?

DECK OF ANNOYING COWORKERS

JACKASS   QUEEN OF "THAT   WON'T STOP
                   WILL NEVER WORK"   SLACKING

JUST A JERK   ALWAYS DISSENTING   DOES NOTHING
                   WITH NO SUGGESTIONS

In this section, we'll look at how to handle three particularly rotten team members: jerks, dissenters, and slackers.

Jerks

Imagine you have two colleagues: one is a competent jerk and the other doesn't know much but is fun to be around. Who would you rather work with? Managers who were asked this hypothetical question overwhelmingly chose the competent jerk. One explained, "I can defuse antipathy toward the jerk if he's competent, but I can't train someone who's incompetent." But when the same managers had to put their money where their mouths were, no one hired the jerk (turns out competent jerks are like five-inch heels—we think we'll find a use for them, but then we decide they're too painful). And with good reason: working with jerks leaves us anxious, depressed, and unable to sleep.

Jerks undermine psychological safety by preying on vulnerability and leaving others feeling belittled and deenergized. And because a jerk usually isn't a jerk to just one person, they have the potential to kill a team's momentum and motivation. If you can't get rid of jerks, the best way to manage them is to constrain their negativity. Bob Sutton, author of *The No A$$hole Rule*, writes about a doctoral student whose adviser inundated her with nasty emails. The student decided to wait before replying and then send one message that addressed a batch of emails. This helped reduce the frequency of responses from the adviser.

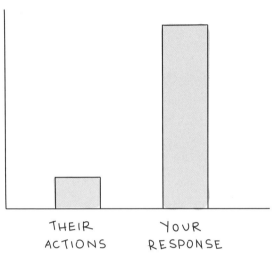

A word of caution: just because you don't get along with someone doesn't mean that person is a jerk. Studies show we tend to like people who are similar or familiar to us, who are good-looking, and who like us back. If you find someone irritating or unlikable, it might be because they are different from you. Or you don't know them well enough!

How to deal with jerks:

- **Reduce how often you rub elbows.** As a TV writer in Hollywood, Elizabeth Craft interacts with more than her share of jerks. "If someone handed you a literal glass of poison, you would not drink it—so don't drink the verbal poison," she says. "If someone's coming at you negatively at work, just don't ingest."
- **Have empathy . . .** Ask yourself what might have happened in a jerk's past to make them such a jerk?

- **. . . but do not open up.** A jerk may try to ruin your reputation or abuse your vulnerabilities by telling others about your limitations.
- **Keep physical distance.** MIT professor Thomas Allen found that people are four times more likely to communicate regularly with a coworker who sits six feet away than with one who sits sixty feet away.
- **Keep mental distance.** Try an imagination-based time-travel technique called temporal distancing. "Imagine it is a day, a week, or a year later," writes Bob Sutton. "And you are looking back on it, and it really didn't last that long or wasn't nearly as bad as it seemed at the time."
- **If you're a manager, get rid of them.** If nothing you've tried is working, it might be time to let the jerk go. Definitely don't promote them (unfortunately, this happens far more than it should). Dr. Jo Shapiro, founder of the Center for Professionalism and Peer Support at Brigham and Women's Hospital, told us powerful bullies used to be promoted in the medical field. "We overvalued certain competencies—'she's technically such a good surgeon,'" Jo told us. "But to be a good surgeon, you have to be respectful and a good leader, because that behavior has an effect on patient outcomes. We didn't understand personal issues negate technical competencies."

Dissenters

Work is a series of compromises. Impending deadlines, conflicting client demands, and limited resources mean your team's final output will never be perfect. (Ever found a glaring typo immediately after pressing Send?) A dissenter is a contrarian who points out every hole in the proposed plan but has no alternative suggestions. Dissenters "yell from the peanut gallery but never own results or the consequences of decisions," writes venture capitalist Mark Suster. "'That will never work' is their motto."

WILLINGNESS
TO RAISE
OBJECTIONS

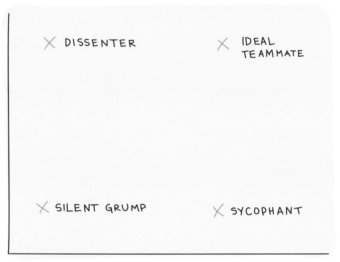

POSITIVE
INTENT

Of course, not everyone who raises questions is a dissenter. The goal in dealing with a dissenter is not to rid the team of healthy skepticism (pessimistic viewpoints are often based on sound logic) but to make sure Ebenezer Scrooge's suggestions are generative. Team members at Genius, the music-media company where Liz worked, are encouraged to add a "practical suggestion colon" to all criticism. If Mollie says to Liz, "I don't think the anecdote you included at the beginning of the chapter works," she has to add "(practical suggestion colon) what if we use the story about Dolly Parton's hairdresser instead?"

How to deal with dissenters:

- **Listen but set limits.** If the dissenter refuses to add anything productive, then excuse yourself or move on to the next person.
- **Seek more information.** Peter Senge, author of *The Fifth Discipline*,

asks dissenters: How did you arrive at your view? What data led to that viewpoint? What information might change your view? Could we design a better outcome?

- **Combat negativity.** Jon Katzenbach, author of *The Wisdom of Teams*, advises that teams should be at least as positive as they are negative. Researcher John Gottman believes a five-to-one ratio of positive to negative comments is necessary for sustaining happy relationships. We think groups should aim for at least a two-to-one ratio. Until you have hiring and firing capabilities, this might mean jumping in with a compliment after a dissenter throws out a criticism.

Slackers

"Doing more than the minimum amount of work is my definition of failing," shrugs Jeff Winger in the TV show *Community*. Nothing is as infuriating as having to do your job *and* someone else's. Ever heard of the sucker effect? If Liz begins to shrug off her responsibilities, Mollie will feel Liz is taking ad-

WHY DO YOU SOUND SO UPSET? YOU
TOLD ME I HAD UNLIMITED VACATION

vantage of her. Mollie might then refuse to pick up the slack (because she doesn't want to become a sucker) *and* reduce her own output because she is less motivated to work as part of an unequal group (again, because she doesn't want to be a sucker).

Those of us who aren't self-sacrificing saints will work on a group project only to the extent that we feel our individual efforts will contribute to a meaningful outcome. In the example above, if Mollie believes in the broader importance of her group's work, she will not shirk her responsibilities but will rather work *harder* in an attempt to compensate for Liz's laziness. But on bigger teams, it's easy to feel anonymous and irrelevant, making it more likely that people will slack off. To combat too-big teams, Amazon's Jeff Bezos uses a "two-pizza" rule: if two pizzas can't feed the whole group, it's too big. Depending on team members' appetites, this guideline usually keeps group size at five to seven people. Although we're always fans of ordering more pizza anyway.

How to deal with slackers:

- **Figure out why the team member is slacking.** The slacker may feel unnecessary, not fully understand their role, or be going through a difficult personal situation.
- **Divide into duos.** The culture transformation firm SYPartners pairs two employees together to form "the smallest atomic unit of trust." In a duo, group members have to figure out a way to work together because there is nowhere else to shovel the blame.
- **Evaluate team members on an individual basis**. When people know they'll be judged on team outcomes rather than on their own contribution, they are much more likely to slack off. By implementing social comparison standards like peer-evaluation forms, it becomes obvious who is completing their work on time and who isn't.
- **Talk to your manager about the slacker.** Remember that your job as

a team is to get the work done in the best possible way. "If you see a gap that needs to be filled, or part of the process that is breaking down, it is not being a tattletale to say this person isn't appropriately getting the work done," says Liz Dolan, former CMO at Nike, the Oprah Winfrey Network, and the National Geographic Channel. "As long as you're not going in and whining, it's okay."

- **Note to managers:** Slacker behavior needs to be addressed directly with the slacker(s). Although it may seem easier to address the problem with your entire team by saying, "Some people are slacking off," this approach will make the nonslackers worry unnecessarily about their performance while the slackers can remain oblivious. Don't punish the whole for the actions of a few.

TAKEAWAYS

1. Create psychological safety by encouraging open discussion, answering questions without condescension, and making it okay to take risks and admit mistakes.

2. Don't shy away from task conflict. Instead, create structures that prevent creative clashes from becoming personal.

3. For relationship conflict, listen to the other person and calmly share your perspective.

4. Get rid of (or if you can't, contain) bad apples to preserve psychological safety on your team.

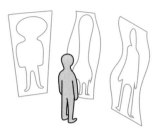

CHAPTER 6

Communication

Your feelings aren't facts:

Why you shouldn't get emotional about your emotions

om Lehman and Ilan Zechory are the cofounders of Genius, a music-media company where Liz used to work. The pair became fast friends at Yale, but the moment they stepped into a business relationship they began to drive each other crazy. "Tom has this manic energy that will drive us forward but will also create wreckage," Ilan explained to *The New York Times*. And Tom had to battle Ilan's tendency to get glum.

Their differences might have been complementary. Instead, Tom and Ilan found themselves unable to strike a balance between being overly cautious and blindly forging ahead. And as they kept bickering during business strategy discussions, their relationship became strained. "We had always related to each other as friends," Tom told us. "And that made it hard not to take disagreements about our company personally."

Their differences came to a head one day when they got mired in Manhattan traffic a few blocks from Penn Station. Their train was scheduled to depart in minutes to DC, where they had an important meeting. When Tom started anxiously poking Ilan about how late they were going to be, Ilan asked the cab driver to stop, paid the fare, and stalked up the sidewalk

YOU'RE NOT GETTING A SINGLE THING I'VE LEFT UNSAID!

toward the station. Tom was outraged that Ilan had so abruptly gone on without him.

Tom and Ilan managed to get on the train seconds before it pulled out of the station, but their relief quickly melted into fury. As they stood in the aisle snarling at each other, a new fear crept into Tom's mind. "Very frequently when I talked to people whose businesses failed, it boiled down to 'we couldn't get along,'" he told us. "It was always interpersonal issues." Something about his relationship with Ilan needed to change, or Genius might fail too. So Tom and Ilan decided to go to couples therapy.

• • • • •

"Every human will frustrate, anger, annoy, madden and disappoint us," writes philosopher Alain de Botton. "And we will (without any malice) do the same to them." Communication is one of the most powerful tools we have to effect change. That's where the fifth new rule of emotion at work comes in: *Your feelings aren't facts*. Effective communication depends on our ability to talk about emotions without *getting* emotional. We often react to one another based on assumptions we never bother to look at more carefully. But the words people say are not always what they mean. As the psychologist Steven Pinker points out, "Words themselves are not the ultimate point of communication. Words are a window into a world." In this chapter, we'll look at how to talk to your coworkers about hard things, highlight major differences between groups that can lead to bungled conversations, give advice on how to deliver useful feedback that doesn't sting, and walk through ways you can avoid digital miscommunication.

ADDRESSING THE ELEPHANT IN THE ROOM

Would you rather break up with someone or confront a coworker who took credit for your idea? In a survey, most people picked dumping a partner over sitting through a difficult work-related conversation. In this section, we'll make it a little less painful to navigate prickly situations. What should you say, for example, when your colleague Anita suddenly stops pulling her weight or when your teammate Amit CCs four people on what you thought was a private email thread?

TONIGHT'S MENU: AVOIDING DIFFICULT CONVERSATIONS

CAN'T LET
IT SLIDERS

CHIPS ON YOUR
SHOULDERS

STEAMED-UP BEEF
IN SEEING-RED SAUCE

NOODLE STEW
IN SILENCE

CLAMMED-UP
LINGUINE

BONE-TO-PICK
MARROW

Difficult conversations can feel so daunting that we're tempted to just avoid them. But if you avoid discussing an issue with a coworker, you deny him (and yourself) the opportunity to improve an uncomfortable situation.[5] We've all seen a miscommunication devolve into a long-held grudge, just because neither party addressed the initial issue. As Tom and Ilan's therapist taught them, "It is better to discuss a problem, because it will surface anyway." Flagging and calmly discussing issues as they arose, instead of letting them fester, repaired Tom and Ilan's relationship.

But it's also a mistake to rush into a difficult conversation: you're more likely to make incorrect assumptions about the other person or just start venting. At worst, confronting a problem without a plan makes the other person feel attacked or have a meltdown.

To prevent the discussion from devolving, wait until you can do the following:

1. Label your feelings. ("I'm hurt.")

2. Understand where those feelings are coming from. ("I'm hurt I wasn't included on the email about Evan's birthday celebration.")

3. Feel calm enough to hear the other person out. A good rule of thumb is, if you think you have all the facts ("You didn't CC me because you hate me"), you're not ready to have a difficult conversation.

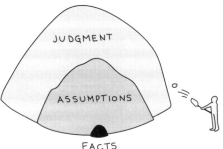

HOW TO MAKE A MOUNTAIN OUT OF A MOLEHILL

JUDGMENT

ASSUMPTIONS

FACTS

---

5 We recommend that you read the entire book *Difficult Conversations* by Douglas Stone, Bruce Patton, and Sheila Heen. We've referenced pieces of it here, but the book deserves a place on everyone's shelf.

This process takes time—don't decide to have a difficult conversation and then start the conversation five minutes later. As Ilan's grandfather told him, "Don't just do something, stand there!" When you're ready, calmly address your emotions, but *do* bring up how you feel. Most likely, you're sitting down with the other person because you feel frustrated, ignored, or upset. If you don't talk about those feelings, you guarantee a central piece of the problem will remain unresolved.

Getting visibly upset will only make the situation worse (often when we become extremely emotional we don't actually express much of anything). In studies of married couples, those who remain calm during arguments are the happiest and longest lasting. These couples frequently use humor and affection to defuse tension, which allows them to work through issues more quickly.

LIZ: I had a coworker who spoke very slowly every time he answered my questions. I found his measured replies condescending and infuriating. I eventually, very calmly, asked him about the change in his diction. Turns out he spoke so deliberately to make sure he didn't sound dumb in front of me!

HAVE YOU TRIED ASKING THEM?

To talk about feelings without letting them hijack the discussion, business school students at Stanford learn to use the phrase, "When you ____, I feel ____." "This avoids creating a victim and a perpetrator," Chris Gomes, an alum who now runs a start-up, told us. As Chris's company scrambled to launch its website and close a big partnership, his cofounder Scott became increasingly impatient. Finally Chris told him, "When you cut me off, I feel dumb and annoying. It makes me nervous to come to you with questions." Tom also used this structure when Ilan showed up five minutes late to a meeting carrying a shopping bag filled with just-purchased books. "Your whole . . . stroll-in-late vibe, that makes me feel bad," he said to Ilan.

Apologizing

Sometimes you'll be on the receiving end of a valid confrontation. There are three steps to constructing a great apology:

1. **Admit your mistake.** Suppress the impulse to explain your actions—this usually makes you look defensive or worse, like you're making excuses. If you do want to give context, make sure you're still taking responsibility for what you did. For example, say something like, "I fully admit that I snapped at you. I want you to know I slept really badly the night before, but that's no excuse for my behavior." And be specific! "Specific shows that you understand where someone is coming from," advises Tom. Finally, acknowledge the other person's feelings. You might say, "I didn't know you think my emails are curt. I'm glad you shared that with me."

2. **Say "I'm sorry."** Too many "apologies" don't contain an explicit apology. A good rule when saying "I'm sorry" is to stop after those two words. The fastest way to enter faux apology territory is to append "if [my rude behavior] made you feel that way." Don't imply the other person is being overly sensitive—take ownership of your mistake.

3. **Explain how it won't happen again.** Tell the other person what you're going to do differently in the future so you don't repeat your mistake.

Here's an example: "I didn't proofread the deck carefully enough before I sent it to the client, so there were several typos. I'm sorry, and it won't happen again. Next time, I'll slow down and have someone review my work."

What if you have a difficult conversation and nothing changes? If the other person seemed receptive during your conversation or you weren't able to communicate everything you wanted to, take another crack at it. Maybe you were nervous the first time and didn't quite get your point across. That said, some people won't care how you feel and won't change. In cases where the other person isn't ready to be self-reflective and meet you halfway, you are allowed to give up. Pursuing difficult conversations with these people is like trying to cook spaghetti with a straightening iron.

MISCOMMUNICATION PATTERNS

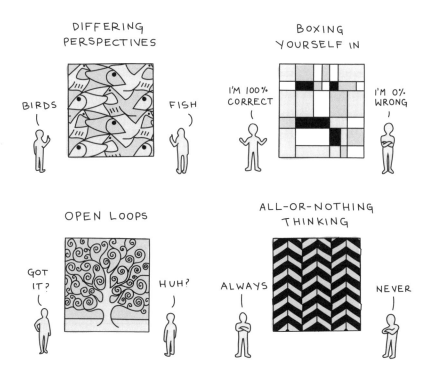

DIFFERING
PERSPECTIVES

BIRDS
(

FISH
)

BOXING
YOURSELF IN

I'M 100%
CORRECT
(

I'M 0%
WRONG
)

OPEN LOOPS

GOT
IT?
(

HUH?
)

ALL-OR-NOTHING
THINKING

ALWAYS
(

NEVER
)

THE TROUBLE WITH TALKING

Self-awareness is a powerful communication tool. Knowing you're an introvert, for example, might help you understand why you're constantly butting
heads with an extroverted coworker. When the People Operations team at
Google noticed female managers were much less likely to nominate themselves for a promotion than their male colleagues, an executive sent an email
to the managers explaining the issue. Just by receiving information, the

managers changed their behavior: the next promotion cycle, the gender gap was gone.

Awareness of others is equally important. Knowing someone's cultural background might help you understand they don't mean for their direct criticism to be personally offensive. In this section, we'll outline gender, race, age, cultural, and extraversion-level communication differences. The studies we reference are not meant to invalidate an individual experience or reduce someone to a single part of who they are. Each employee has a unique and complex identity and experience at work. Instead, we hope that learning about group trends may provide context that gives you better insight into the intention behind someone's words.

Gender

"I'm either a bitch or a bimbo," said Carly Fiorina, former CEO of Hewlett-Packard. As linguist Deborah Tannen observes, stereotypes about gender roles create a double bind for women: when women are kind and compassionate, they're well-liked but told they lack leadership potential. If they speak with confidence, they're chastised for being "aggressive." To avoid judgment, women often use qualifiers ("I'm not certain, but . . .") or hedging words ("might" and "I think"), frame requests as questions, and hesitate to speak up around men. In a study of school board meetings, women spoke as much as men only when the board was at least eighty percent female (men spoke the same amount whether or not they were in the minority).

VERMEER'S GIRL WITH THE PATRONIZING COWORKER

LET ME EXPLAIN YOUR JOB TO YOU

In contrast, men tend to dominate conversations by talking over others (especially their female colleagues) and are faster to deem themselves experts. Gerri Elliott, a former executive at Juniper Networks, told *The New York Times* about a presenter who asked a group of men and women if anyone had expertise in breastfeeding. "A man raised his hand," she recalled. "He had watched his wife for three months. The women in the crowd, mothers among them, didn't come forward as experts."

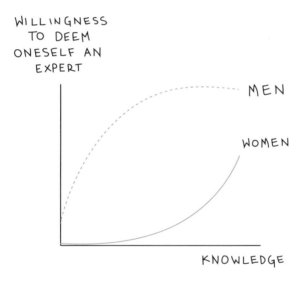

How to better communicate:

- **Use your voice to support women.** During President Obama's first term, his female staffers felt excluded from meetings and unheard in the meetings they did join. To make sure the men in the room recognized their contributions, the female staffers adopted a strategy called amplification. When one female staffer suggested an idea, another would repeat it and give the first credit. Obama took note, and began calling on women more frequently.

- **Be part of creating a workplace in which each person has an equal shot at success.** Men, speak up in the face of discrimination or harassment. Be mindful of the signals you send a female colleague—interrupting her, mansplaining, and calling her "sweetie" all make the workplace less hospitable. And always introduce your female colleagues as equals.

- **If you're being interrupted, try these two antidotes.** Plenty of interrupters don't know what they're doing—they're just excited and eager to chime in. Privately making these people aware of their habit, and how it makes you feel, might be enough. If nothing changes, workplace consultant Laura Rose suggests preempting interruptions by implementing a no-interruptions rule. Try saying, "There are a lot of different pieces to this explanation, so please bear with me. I want to tell you the entire story. Then I'd love to hear your thoughts on specific details."

Crying at Work

What should you do if you feel yourself tearing up at work? "The tendency is to stop the tears as quickly as possible. But it's important to understand the catalyst and then tease apart: What's going on? Are you not getting enough sleep? Are you undervalued or overworked? Do you hate this job? Are you scared to quit?" Anne Kreamer, author of *It's Always Personal*, advised us.

Of course, you shouldn't try to figure all this out while sobbing in a meeting. If you're around a lot of people, excuse yourself (go to the bathroom or get a drink of water) and calm down before returning. Research shows we feel better if we cry alone or around one other person who can provide emotional support. So if you have a confidant, it's okay to call in help!

Don't beat yourself up about crying on the job—it's often a signal you care about your work. In fact, reframing your distress as passion makes others view your tears more favorably. During the 2016 presidential campaign, Hillary Clinton's campaign staff cried so much that former communications director Jennifer Palmieri's office became an ad hoc "crying room." "No one I worked with—man or woman—thought anything of it other than that it was a human reaction to the inhumane crush a president and his or her staff endure," writes Palmieri. "No stigma was attached to anyone who had to use the crying room."

What if you see someone else crying? Understand that tears are not always a sign of sadness. Author Joanne Lipman found male managers often withhold feedback from female reports for fear of making them cry. Women do report crying more at work, but it's usually out of anger or frustration. "Men don't see it that way," Lipman explains. "A woman crying in the office is the same thing as a man screaming and yelling and getting angry."

DID YOU KNOW

YOU HAVE 3 TYPES OF TEARS

BASAL	REFLEX	EMOTIONAL
KEEP YOUR EYES LUBRICATED	PROTECT YOUR EYES; PRODUCED IN RESPONSE TO AN IRRITANT	CAUSED BY STRONG EMOTION

Race

We often avoid acknowledging race for fear of saying the wrong thing. But there are consequences to letting this fear dictate our behavior. At a previous job, Kisha, now a lead software engineer at Habit Inc., realized her coworkers' attempts to be inoffensive meant they were not giving her the advice she needed to improve. During code review, a type of peer review in which two people sit next to each other and go through code line by line to identify errors or areas for improvement, her white male colleagues would rip one another's work apart. "Your code is so bad I don't even want to sit here with you," one would say to the other. "I'm so embarrassed you missed the semicolon in line three."

But when it came time to give Kisha, who is African American, feedback, her colleagues' attitudes shifted completely. They would say, "Everything looks great. Maybe one thing I would change on line 79 is . . ." Kisha finally pointed out the clear difference in their behavior and how it was disadvantaging her ability to progress and learn. After the conversation, the other engineers began to treat her as simply another member of the team. At Habit, Kisha helped design the code-review process to make sure it was fair: engineers are asked to be specific, provide examples for how to fix issues, and note subjectivity.

Why do we shy away from directly addressing race or racial issues? "We are socialized to not talk about race," explains psychologist Kira Hudson Banks, "so if we wait until something blows up to have the conversation, we're not skilled and we're not as able to hear each other." Be willing to make mistakes—and, if you do, apologize and change your language or behavior. You might start by stating, "Please give me honest, constructive feedback if I say something that is hurtful or offensive to you, in the moment or later."

How to better communicate:

- **Watch for and call out racist coded language.** Coded language, which includes phrases like "inner city," "thug," and "illegal alien," allows people to insult members of certain groups without explicitly referencing those groups.
- **Don't ignore differences . . .** When we "don't see color," we tend to be more biased. Studies show organizations that openly discuss *cultural* diversity (e.g., a team whose members grew up in different countries) are falsely perceived as more fair—but conversations about diversity that don't explicitly address *race* may end up concealing racial discrimination. When giving feedback, keep potential biases in mind but don't withhold important critiques for fear of being seen as racist.
- **. . . but look for commonalities.** Avoid "us/them" language, which creates a divide and undermines any empathetic sentiment.
- **Practice makes progress.** "Don't wait for a/the black person at your company to say something. Don't wait for your HR . . . rep to send you an email," writes Mandela SH Dixon, CEO of Founder Gym. There may be misunderstanding and miscommunication when you discuss race, but humility and a willingness to learn can help smooth missteps.
- **Reflect on your behavior.** Not everyone will feel safe giving you feedback or correcting you when you've made a verbal misstep. An important part of getting more comfortable discussing race or racial issues is to inform and observe yourself. Be aware of how and why your communication patterns might change around certain coworkers.

Age

As Baby Boomers continue to delay retirement (the number of workers aged sixty-five and older has more than doubled since 2000), five generations are working together for the first time in history:

- Silent Generation, born 1925 to 1945
- Baby Boomers, born between 1946 and 1964
- Generation X, born between 1965 and 1976
- Millennials (aka Generation Y), born between 1977 and 1997
- Generation Z, born after 1997

Harping about intergenerational differences is a timeless tradition. "Youth were never more saucie, yea never more savagely saucie," lamented one grump in 1624. Four hundred years later, Boomers see Millennials as slovenly job-hoppers while Millennials think Boomers are digitally hopeless job-hoggers. Both see Gen X-ers as rebel slackers and Gen Z-ers as self-absorbed and Snapchat-obsessed.

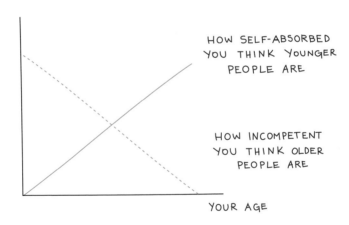

HOW SELF-ABSORBED YOU THINK YOUNGER PEOPLE ARE

HOW INCOMPETENT YOU THINK OLDER PEOPLE ARE

YOUR AGE

Despite these stereotypes, researchers find that differences between generations are partly attributable to life stage. "It's not that people born after 1980 are narcissists," writes *The Atlantic* columnist Elspeth Reeve. "It's that young people are narcissists, and they get over themselves as they get older." (Pablo Picasso painted a lot of self-portraits well before you could snap a selfie with an iPhone.) But generations do differ in how they prefer to communicate at work. Younger generations, for example, are more likely to text and email than pick up the phone (or, God forbid, leave a voice mail). These habits can come across as impersonal and even rude to older generations. Learn about other generations' preferences and find a communication balance between email, conference calls, and face-to-face conversations.

How to better communicate:

- **Start a cross-generational mentoring program.** These programs match younger employees with older employees, widening both parties' mental horizons and reducing discrimination. Chip Conley, founder of Joie de Vivre Hospitality, joined Airbnb as a strategic adviser at age fifty-two. "I heard an existential tech question in a meeting and didn't know how to answer it: 'If you shipped a feature and no one used it, did it really ship?,'" Conley recalls. "Bewildered, I realized I was in 'deep ship.'" His younger colleagues were far more digitally intelligent. But he also had something to contribute (and here's where the "talking about emotions" part comes in): Research shows our social skills peak in our forties and fifties. "Often I would leave a meeting and discreetly ask one of my fellow leaders, who might be two decades younger than I was, if they were open to some private feedback on how to read the emotions in the room, or the motivations of a particular engineer, a little more effectively," Conley explains. He began to act as their emotional intelligence mentor. That's some deep ship.

Multicultural diversity

"Even asking another's point of view can feel confrontational in our culture," an Indonesian interviewee explained to researcher Erin Meyer. "We had a meeting with a group of French managers from headquarters where they went around the table asking each of us: 'What do you think about this?' . . . We were just shocked that we would be put on the spot in a meeting with a lot of people."

A HANDY GUIDE TO
UNDERSTANDING AMERICANS

"I'M GREAT"	"I'M FINE"
"I'M FINE"	"THE WORLD IS CRUMBLING AROUND ME"
"JUST A SECOND"	"I NEED A MINUTE"
"JUST A MINUTE"	"I NEED 15 MINUTES"
"ANY WEEKEND PLANS?"	"WHY HASN'T ANYONE ELSE JOINED THE CONFERENCE CALL?"
"CORRECT ME IF I'M WRONG"	"I'M NOT WRONG, YOU ARE"
"LET'S TAKE THIS OFFLINE"	"PLEASE STOP TALKING"
"LET'S TALK ABOUT IT IN THE MEETING"	"PLEASE STOP EMAILING ME"
"LET'S GRAB COFFEE SOMETIME"	"LET'S PRETEND WE WANT TO GRAB COFFEE SOMETIME"

But the French managers saw the same situation differently. "We make our points passionately," an executive told Meyer. "We like to disagree openly . . . And afterwards we feel that was a great meeting and say, 'See you next time!'"

It's easy to step on someone's toes if you're unfamiliar with his or her cultural norms. Culture also affects which emotions we feel comfortable expressing. Americans often try to exude euphoria and excitement. "Americans have to say they're doing GREAT!" notes Stanford researcher Jeanne Tsai. "If you are only fine, people think you're depressed." The chart below, created by Meyer, plots cultural confrontation and emotional expression tendencies.

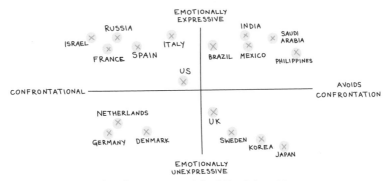

Chart from Erin Meyer's book The Culture Map

How to better communicate:

- **Do your research.** An awareness of cultural differences can prevent a lot of anguish and strife. If you're working with someone who is less comfortable with confrontation, try saying "I don't fully understand your point" or "Please explain a bit more" rather than "I disagree." And if an international colleague abruptly points out a mistake you've made, understanding their cultural background could help you better recognize their intention. The same dynamics apply to written messages. Although you might add "Thanks!" to the end of an email, your colleague may not be as outwardly appreciative (but still feel grateful for your work).

- **Talking might not always be the answer for multicultural groups.** Language barriers among coworkers can make it harder for them to feel connected. Music or physical activity can build empathy among all teams but are especially effective nonverbal ways to build empathy for multicultural groups.

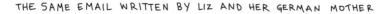

THE SAME EMAIL WRITTEN BY LIZ AND HER GERMAN MOTHER

Extroverts and introverts

"I'll go if I don't have to talk," says Elaine when Jerry asks her to join him for coffee on *Seinfeld*. Some of us need more quiet time than others. If you prefer one-on-one conversation to group discussion, want to think things through before acting, and feel drained after office happy hours, you're probably an introvert. If none of that makes sense to you, you're an extrovert.

Introverts and extroverts have different needs. Extroverts tend to react to social interactions more quickly. Introverts have a higher base rate of arousal: put an introvert in a crowded, noisy room and he'll quickly become overwhelmed. This might explain why introverts perform best in quiet environments whereas extroverts do better when it's noisy.

It's not immediately obvious whether someone is an introvert or an extrovert, especially when you're just getting to know each other. In the workplace, introverts often try to mask their introverted qualities to fit in. But if they don't talk openly about their differences, extroverts and introverts drive each other nuts. Introverts are more sensitive to external stimuli (an introvert will salivate more at the taste of lemon juice than an extrovert) and need quiet time to recharge. It can be hard for extroverts to understand why an introvert might turn down a lunch invitation or start to shut down after back-to-back meetings.

WHY WOULD I GO BIG WHEN
I COULD GO HOME?

How to better communicate:

Tips for introverts:

- Let people know when you need space. Start by saying something like, "I really like working and talking with you." Then explain you're better able to concentrate when you have quiet time by yourself. Expect to make some concessions; you do still have to work with others.
- Avoid sending extroverts excessively long emails. Extroverts, who often prefer to discuss issues or ideas in person, might skim through only the first paragraphs.
- Prepare for meetings in order to feel more comfortable speaking up and then try to chime in during the first ten minutes. Once you've broken the ice it will be easier to jump in again. And remember, a good question can contribute just as much as an opinion or statistic.

Tips for extroverts:

- Send out agendas before meetings to give introverts a chance to prepare their thoughts. This will help facilitate equitable discussion. For example, email a prompt to the group ahead of a meeting and then start by going around the table and having each person share their thoughts one by one.

- Don't rush to fill in pauses, and let introverts finish speaking before you chime in.
- Suggest breaking into duos or small groups to discuss ideas and then reporting back to the larger team.
- And our biggest pieces of advice: give an introvert time to come out of his shell, and don't stop extending invitations!

YOU'RE SO QUIET

FEEDBACK

Hearing what you're not doing well feels bad. Even people who say they want to learn from their mistakes report feeling unhappy and unmotivated after receiving critical feedback. A friend of ours got an overwhelmingly positive performance review but still obsessed over the few listed "areas for improvement." "Sure, it was helpful to understand what I could do better," she told us, "but that didn't stop me from spiraling into self-loathing and questioning my ability to do anything right." Studies show we tend to avoid colleagues who give us feedback that is more negative than our view of ourselves. But we

CRITICISM CRIME SCENE

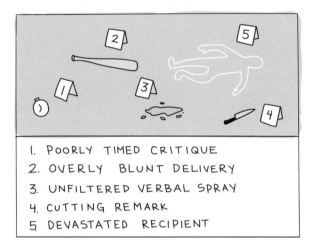

1. POORLY TIMED CRITIQUE
2. OVERLY BLUNT DELIVERY
3. UNFILTERED VERBAL SPRAY
4. CUTTING REMARK
5. DEVASTATED RECIPIENT

obviously need to know what we're doing wrong if we want to improve (and get promoted). How can you give feedback that doesn't pack such a painful punch?

Great feedback helps the receiver move past their knee-jerk, defensive reaction ("I've worked so hard, how could there be anything left to improve?") and on to determination and action ("I'm a work in progress, and I'm glad I know what I need to do to get better"). In this section, we'll walk through the three rules for giving feedback that makes the receiver feel good (or at least less bad): (1) focus on specific behavior, (2) make it about bridging the gap, and (3) remember: how you say it matters.

First, give feedback about specific behavior. Vague criticism is useless and makes it easy for the receiver to fall down the "I did a bad thing, therefore I am bad" rabbit hole. Consider these two statements:

- Your email could have been better.
- The second sentence in your email restated the first and should be deleted.

"NAUGHTY"? THAT'S NOT ACTIONABLE OR SPECIFIC

The first is ambiguous and demoralizing. The second points to a specific issue, which makes it harder to take personally and gives the recipient a clear directive on how to improve.

Be mindful of withholding specific feedback because you're afraid of hurting the other person's feelings. We're more likely to give the most valuable, actionable feedback to people we know—which means we might be keeping other colleagues from the information they need to get promoted. In predominantly male workplaces, men tend to receive specific, constructive advice whereas women receive generalized commentary. Where a man might hear, "You did not clearly communicate your results in the meeting about customer engagement. You could prevent that from happening again by adding a slide that outlines the main takeaways," a woman is told, "Your presentations are good though sometimes your comments miss the mark."

Second, don't simply criticize—suggest a different way of doing things *and* explain how it will benefit the person. Wharton professor Cade Massey recommends positioning feedback as bridging the gap: identify where you want the other person to be, give them clear advice on how to get there, and (most importantly) emphasize that you believe they have the ability to bridge that gap.

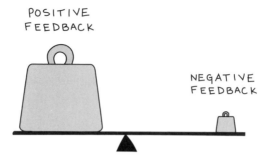

POSITIVE
FEEDBACK

NEGATIVE
FEEDBACK

"I've noticed you shut down people in discussion," former Netflix head of Talent Patty McCord once told an employee. "If your goal is to be a manager, people have to want to work for you. Here are some tips: Don't immediately tear apart an idea. Stop interrupting your colleagues. If someone hasn't said anything, invite them into the conversation by asking, 'What is your opinion on this?'" One more piece of advice: studies show people are much more receptive to negative feedback if you first say, "I'm giving you these comments because I have very high expectations of you and I'm confident you can reach them."

MOLLIE: At IDEO, the global innovation firm where I work, we use the C.O.I.N.S. (Context, Observation, Impact, Next, Stay) feedback model to keep feedback specific. Employees are encouraged to start on an emotional level and provide context for the conversation, share a factual observation of their behavior, explain the impact of their behavior on the team or organization, and then suggest ideas for how to handle a similar situation differently in the future. As an example, you could say, "Context: I know you want to move into a more senior position this year, and I want that for you too. Observation: You've been late to several key meetings. Impact: This makes your fellow colleagues feel like you don't respect their time. Next: Can you commit to being on time to meetings in the future? Stay: Does that make sense to you? I'm happy to continue to work with you on this."

HOW TO SOFTEN THE FEEDBACK BLOW

BE SPECIFIC

MAKE IT ABOUT
BRIDGING
THE GAP

ASK HOW IT
SHOULD BE GIVEN

PUT IT ON
A CAKE

Lastly, the best way to avoid hurting the other person's feelings is to ask how and when they prefer to receive feedback. Don't treat others how you want to be treated—treat them how *they* want to be treated. "Whether your advice comes from a place of caring is not measured at your mouth but at the other person's ear," Kim Scott, author of *Radical Candor*, told us. Liz loves in-the-moment feedback so she can immediately make improvements. Mollie prefers getting specific feedback in writing ahead of a longer conversation, so she can process it privately before discussing it. This advice is not limited to criticism—people also differ in how they like to receive positive feedback. "If someone praises me in front of my team, that counts ten times as much as if they tell me privately," our friend told us. But public praise makes Mollie (and many introverts) uncomfortable. If you're not aware of the other person's preferences, it's easy to think you're being kind and productive as you bull-doze over their feelings.

INTROVERT   EXTROVERT

PUBLIC PRAISE

How to Ask for Feedback

When a colleague sees you make a mistake, her first thought is usually, "Should I say something?" You want the answer to be a resounding yes. "Make it wonderful to tell you hard shit," writes Mark Rabkin, a vice president at Facebook.

TIPS TO HELP YOU HANDLE CRITICISM:

• **Remind yourself that you need critical feedback to improve.** The instant gratification of praise feels so good that we often willingly trade learning opportunities for easy successes that reinforce our positive self-image. But adopting a growth mind-set allows you to view criticism as a chance to get better—and makes it more likely you get promoted.

- **Ask someone who knows what they're talking about.** When we need help, we tend to prioritize trustworthiness and accessibility over expertise. But studies show feedback helps us improve only when it comes from an expert.

- **Use the word *what* instead of *any*.** If you ask, "Do you have any feedback on how my presentation went?" the person can easily default to saying no. If you instead ask, "What could I improve about my presentation?" you invite specific feedback.

- **Remind yourself the person is giving you advice to help you.** "A friend tells you that you have food on your face," writes Genius CEO Tom Lehman. "A non-friend doesn't give you the bad news because they don't want to feel uncomfortable!"

- **Keep a smile file (or folder).** Write down nice comments you receive. Save emails from colleagues thanking you for your hard work. Criticism will linger longer than praise, so being able to quickly remind yourself of what you do well will help you weather your inevitable gloomy moments.

- **Remember feedback is never objective.** Even well-intentioned advice might paint an inaccurate picture; women are twice as likely as men to be described as "aggressive." When evaluating feedback, ask yourself: How much does this person know about your work? How does their feedback map to your understanding of your strengths and weaknesses?

TYPES OF FEEDBACK

OREO

TWO POSITIVE
THOUGHTS AROUND
ONE NEGATIVE
THOUGHT

MACARON

ELEGANTLY WORDED
POSITIVE THOUGHTS
AROUND ONE VERY SMALL
NEGATIVE THOUGHT

BLACK AND WHITE

NO-NONSENSE
STRAIGHTFORWARD

OATMEAL RAISIN

POSITIVE, WITH BITS
OF NEGATIVE
SPRINKLED IN

SUGAR

OVERLY SWEET AND
ULTIMATELY
UNFULFILLING

UNCOOKED

COMPLETELY
UNFILTERED

DIGITAL MISCOMMUNICATION

We overestimate how easy it is for someone to figure out exactly what we're trying to communicate. To show this, psychologist Elizabeth Newton randomly assigned a group of people to be either a "tapper" or a "listener." Tappers had to pick a popular song and tap its rhythm on the table with their hand; listeners then had to guess the song. Before the experiment, tappers guessed listeners would be able to figure out half of the tapped songs. They were way off. The listeners correctly guessed only three out of more than a hundred tapped songs.

If you know something, it's really hard to imagine what it's like to not know that thing. When you tap "We Are the Champions," the accompanying melody seems obvious because you sing the music in your head. But the other person only hears *"Taaaap, tap, tap, taaap, tap,"* which sounds like . . . anything. A similar disconnect happens when we write to each other. "The single biggest problem in communication is the illusion that it has taken place," writes playwright George Bernard Shaw. How can you prevent texts and emails from accidentally torpedoing your relationships? Below are our DOs and DON'Ts for work-related digital communication.

DO add emoji (but proceed with caution). Emoji can help us express tone, meaning, and emotional cues. If Liz adds a ☺ to her "Don't be late!" text, she makes it easier for Mollie to see she's joking. But an outpouring of emoji, especially when you don't know the other person well, can undermine your professionalism. It's best to wait until you have an idea of how the other person will receive emoji before sending a slew of smileys.

DO realize typos send a message. A typo reveals we were in a rush or heightened emotional state when we hit Send (or that we're the boss and don't need to care about typos). Researcher Andrew Brodsky describes typos as emotional amplifiers: if Mollie sends Liz an angry email filled

with typos, Liz will imagine Mollie hammering out an email in a blind rage and perceive the message as *really* angry.

DO emotionally proofread your messages. Brian Fetherstonhaugh, the worldwide chief talent officer at the Ogilvy Group, frequently asks employees if they have ever successfully defused an emotional issue via email. The answer is almost always no. But when he asks the same group if they've ever *inflamed* an issue via email? "Everyone puts their hand up," he told us. Always reread what you've written before hitting Send to make sure your message is clear and conveys the intended tone. Sending "Let's talk" when

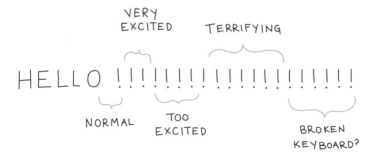

you mean "These are good suggestions; let's discuss how to work them into the draft" will make the recipient unnecessarily anxious.

DO use richer communication channels when you're first getting to know each other. We're most likely to interpret ambiguity as negative when we're texting or emailing with people we don't know well or with more

GOOGLE TRANSLATE FOR EMAILS FROM YOUR BOSS

"JUST WONDERING…"	"I'M ABOUT TO MAKE A RIDICULOUS REQUEST"
"WHERE ARE WE ON THIS?"	"YOU'RE STILL NOT DONE?"
"MAYBE I'M MISSING SOMETHING"	"WTF"
"I'M AWARE"	"I'M PISSED"
"I'M SURE YOU…"	"YOU BETTER HAVE"
"I'LL TAKE IT FROM HERE"	"YOU'RE DONE"

senior colleagues. Say Liz emails Mollie, "This draft is a good start, but I think a couple sections could be better." Mollie will take the email at face value. But if Mollie receives the same email from her boss or a new colleague, she'll feel anxious. Using videoconferences when you begin working together, especially if one of you is working remotely, helps build trust. In general, seeing each other's facial expressions allows you to better read between the lines, chitchat, and develop genuine relationships. After you know the person, you can use email more frequently.

DO default to video. At Trello, a project management software company, if even one person on a team works remotely, the group will jump on a video call; this ensures everyone feels included and makes it less likely for information to be lost.

MOLLIE: The first meeting Liz and I had with our editor, Leah, was a disaster. Leah and I are in New York, so we met in person at the Penguin offices and had Liz call in from Berkeley. I arrived early and started talking with Leah about her family, which meant that Liz dialed in halfway through our conversation. Later in the meeting, there was an issue with the phone line: Liz had been speaking, but we couldn't hear her at all. Liz tried to hang up and redial the conference line but couldn't rejoin. Then, she tried calling my cell, but I had no service. Meanwhile Leah and I were completely oblivious to Liz's struggles and kept chatting away about changes to our outline. Liz was extremely peeved (totally reasonable). We talked about it afterward and decided to all use Google Hangouts from then on.

LIZ: Yes, it felt awful!! But Leah and Mollie were very understanding afterward, and we began defaulting to videoconference. I have felt included ever since.

DANCE LIKE NOBODY IS WATCHING

EMAIL LIKE IT WILL ONE DAY
BE READ IN A DEPOSITION

DON'T panic. If an email makes you enraged, anxious, or euphoric, wait until the next day to write back. Even better, talk face-to-face when you've calmed down. When you do reply, reread your draft through the other person's eyes. It might be easier to imagine how your reader will interpret your email if you first send it to yourself. (Additional tip: always leave the "To:" field blank until you're ready to hit Send; a friend of ours lost a job offer because he accidentally sent out a half-baked salary negotiation email.)

DON'T use email when you need a yes. An in-person request is more than thirty times more successful than an emailed one. Research shows people see email asks as untrustworthy and nonurgent. If you do enter into an email negotiation, it helps to first schmooze in person, over video chat, or on the phone. In an experiment (titled "Schmooze or Lose") that pitted MBA students against one another, half were given only their counterpart's name and email. The other half were shown a photograph of the other person and told to talk about hobbies, job plans, and hometowns before negotiating. Seventy percent of the first group were able to reach a deal, compared to almost everyone in the second.

DON'T send emails during off-hours if it's not urgent. "I am away from the office and checking email intermittently. If your email is not urgent, I'll probably still reply. I have a problem," tweeted the parody account AcademicsSay. Even if you write "Don't read/respond to this until tomorrow/Monday," chances are the reader will still think about your email all weekend (and might even feel pressure to respond immediately). Try saving the email to your draft folder or schedule it to send later.

TAKEAWAYS

1. During a difficult conversation, calmly address your feelings without making assumptions.
2. Be aware of communication tendencies to better understand the intention behind someone's words.
3. Make criticism specific and actionable. Ask the recipient how they prefer to receive feedback.
4. Emotionally proofread what you write before hitting Send.

MICROACTIONS

CHAPTER 7

Culture

Emotional culture cascades from you:
Why small actions make a big difference

EMOTIONAL MAP OF THE OFFICE

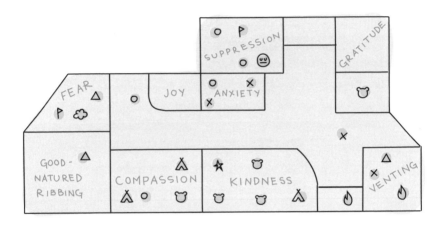

× CONSTANT COMPLAINER   ☆ A SHOULDER TO CRY ON
△ OVERSHARER   ⚑ HAPPY CAMPER
○ COOL CUCUMBER   ☈ NETWORKER
❀ GRUMP   ♜ TEDDY BEAR
♦ LOOSE CANNON   ☺ STOIC

O ne nod is good, two nods is very good. There's only one actual smile on record and that was Tom Ford in 2001. If she doesn't like it she shakes her head. Then of course there's the pursing of the lips . . . Catastrophe." This is how art director Nigel describes his boss, fashion magazine editor in chief Miranda Priestly, in the movie *The Devil Wears Prada*. Worshipped and feared, Miranda murmurs biting observations about her staff's incompetence and never reveals a chink in her hypercomposed workplace armor. All of Miranda's employees try to mirror her behavior. After a few weeks, Miranda's new assistant, Andy, also learns to hide her anxiety and frustration and stops warmly greeting her colleagues in the morning. In other words, Andy begins to act differently to better fit the office's implicit rules about how employees can and can't show emotion.

In this chapter, we'll walk you through the sixth new rule of emotion at work: ***Emotional culture cascades from you***. We'll look at how an emotional culture forms and spreads, how it affects every aspect of work (from productivity to willingness-to-live on Mondays), and finally how a sense of belonging is the best indicator of a healthy emotional environment. Whether you're a manager who can change policies or an employee trapped under a Miranda Priestly, you have the power to influence your office's emotional culture.

Emotional Contagion

Ever watched someone laugh and found yourself starting to giggle? We catch one another's feelings through an automatic process called emotional contagion. Whether you're chatting with a coworker in the elevator or reading an email she sent you from halfway across the world, you'll reflexively internalize her expressed emotion. That's right, feelings can spread digitally, through capitalization, spelling, message length, punctuation, GIFs, and emoji. "Passive-aggressive when we're texting, I feel the distance," rapper Drake laments in the song "From Time."

Emotions can also go viral. Researchers at Baylor University found that a nasty coworker not only makes you (and your family) grumpy but may have a ripple effect that extends as far as your partner's workplace. It happens like this: Mollie comes home irritated because of her crabby colleague and snaps at her husband. He catches Mollie's bad mood and goes to work the next day equally irritable. Mollie's colleague's sour attitude might then spread to her husband's coworkers.

Check-ins are a simple way to keep a grump from turning everyone into a grouch. At the beginning of meetings, leadership adviser Anese Cavanaugh has everyone rate their mood on a scale of zero to ten. Anese asks people who feel low (less than a five) if they can do anything in the next few minutes to raise their number. Say a team member feels stressed about an email he needs to answer. Anese will encourage him to leave the room, write and send his response, and then return. It's better to have someone leave a meeting for a bit than be present but so agitated they make everyone around them anxious too.

Gretchen Rubin, author of *The Happiness Project*, also recommends pinpointing the situations that stress you out and slowing down when you catch yourself projecting negative emotions. "Looming deadlines bring out the worst in me," she told us. "I become anxious and have the urge to rush everyone along. I now tell myself, 'This deadline is not as big of a deal as you're making it; stay calm.' I've realized when I speak in a less impatient, more cheerful way, everyone else remains cheerful, which is better for productivity than if we're all rattled."

AND THEN, DUE TO EMOTIONAL CONTAGION, THE GRINCH'S HEART GREW THREE SIZES THAT DAY

HOW CULTURE HAPPENS

Every company has its own emotional culture. To instantly learn about an organization's culture, Wharton professor Adam Grant says, "Tell me a story about something that would only happen here." When Liz left Genius, she

SPOT THE DIFFERENCES IN EMOTIONAL CULTURE

posted an emotional goodbye on the site that opened with, "I'll be forever grateful for the incredible + funny people that Genius has brought into my life." Genius site users responded with sad GIFs and rap memes; a troll commented, "Who r u again?" At Mollie's IDEO office in New York, Thursday lunches are dedicated to Make(believe) time. Creative activities like aromatic finger painting, writing group haiku poems, and blind contour drawing help employees get goofy.

There are other, subtle cues that indicate what emotions are acceptable in your office. Do people say hello to one another in the hallways? Are there tissues in meeting rooms (which might indicate it's okay to cry)? Do your coworkers seem more comfortable expressing frustration or joy? Is it okay to respond to emails with a funny cat GIF? Your answers may depend on which coworkers you're thinking about; several emotional cultures can exist within the same organization. (Ever walked into a section of your office and thought, "Weird vibes over here"?) Nurses at a hospital might vent to one another in the privacy of a breakroom but display only compassion around patients. Either way, whether you're dealing with one overarching culture or juggling different emotional cultures in the same day, understanding and relating to your company's culture(s) is key to feeling a sense of belonging (we'll cover this more in the next section).

Emotional culture is built on emotion norms, the unspoken rules that dictate what you're allowed to feel and express. Here are some examples of workplace emotion norms:

- On trading floors, no one bats an eye at obscenity-filled shouting.
- In hospitals, doctors delivering grim diagnoses suppress their grief to appear calm and professional in front of patients.
- In many offices, employees appear enthusiastic while sitting at their desks but head to the privacy of the bathroom when they need to cry.

- At any job, you'll likely receive scandalized looks if you sigh and bang your head on the table during a boring meeting.

Emotion norms are created and reinforced by small, repeated social signals that we often pick up on without realizing it. If your colleague Erica nods conspiratorially when you tell her how annoying John was during the meeting, you'll keep griping. If she crosses her arms and frowns (even ever so slightly), you'll find yourself changing the subject.

Few organizations talk about emotional cultures—or emotion norms—even though they affect how much we enjoy our jobs, how stressed we feel, and our ability to do work well and on time. And emotional culture *is* a tricky concept: a single "good" or "bad" emotional culture doesn't exist. It's also dangerous to be overly prescriptive, as any expression of emotion can be harmful when taken to an extreme. Putting too much of an emphasis on compassion might make people shy away from necessary conflict.

A few important trends do show up in the research. Organizations where compassion and gratitude are discouraged tend to have higher turnover rates. Ruthless and vindictive hedge fund managers bring in less money than their kinder colleagues. And people whose bosses are rude or punitive have a harder time remembering important information and are more likely to make bad decisions. In contrast, when we feel supported and motivated by our colleagues, we are happier, more productive, and stick around longer. We're also healthier and better able to cope with job stress. And when our bosses respond to our mistakes with patience instead of fury, we trust them more.

HOW TO HOLD AN EMOTIONAL ENVIRONMENT HOSTAGE

SULK   SCOFF   SLOUCH

SIGH   SNORE

A reasonable goal for organizations and individuals is to encourage some level of emotional expression. You can make this happen without a major organizational shift; norms are flexible. Compassion and generosity have a "cascade effect": they spread from person to person, meaning that you can influence your entire organization. Try the 10/5 rule that the Ritz-Carlton trains its staff to follow: when employees walk within ten feet of someone, they make eye contact and smile. If they walk within five feet, they say hello. This simple policy, which has also been implemented at hospitals, makes customers and employees happier. (As one hotel encourages its employees, "A smile today will keep guest complaints away!")

Or follow Giles Turnbull's example. While working as a writer at the UK Government Digital Service (GDS), Giles created an "It's OK to" poster for the organization (pictured below) and hung copies around his office. Giles told us that writing out which emotion norms the GDS valued helped new hires absorb the culture quickly and easily. The poster has since appeared on walls at Spotify, Salesforce, and even Goldman Sachs.

It's ok to...
say "I don't know"
ask for more clarity
stay at home when you feel ill
say you don't understand
ask what acronyms stand for
ask why, and why not
forget things
introduce yourself
depend on the team
ask for help
not know everything
have quiet days
have loud days, to talk, joke and laugh
put your headphones on
say "no" when you're too busy
make mistakes
sing
sigh
not check your email out of hours
not check your email constantly during hours
just Slack it
walk over and ask someone face-to-face
go somewhere else to concentrate
offer feedback on other people's work
challenge things you're not comfortable with
say yes when anyone does a coffee run
prefer tea
snack
have a messy desk
have a tidy desk
work how you like to work
ask the management to fix it
have off-days
have days off

The UK Government Digital Service's "It's OK to" list, designed by Sonia Turcotte

Normalizing some level of emotional expression can also give you valuable data. At Ubiquity Retirement and Savings, employees press one of five buttons representing their mood—they can choose between happy, neutral, or sad faces—every evening before they leave the office. Ubiquity uses the smiley face data to learn how it can increase workplace happiness and motivation.

But what if you work for a Miranda Priestly, who doesn't care about how you feel? Reframe discussions about emotion by using accepted language and tie your feelings to an organizational goal. "If saying 'I feel hurt and taken for granted,' will be poorly received," write the authors of the book *Difficult Conversations*, "consider something like this: 'I'd like to find a way to get this done earlier each quarter. I know I often leave these meetings frustrated, and I imagine you also periodically feel frustrated. Can we talk about

EMOTIONAL EXPRESSION IN A CULTURE OF SUPPRESSION

I'M UPSET   I'M EUPHORIC   I'M DYING   I'M EXPLODING!
                                     INSIDE

why that is and how we might design a better process?'" But when an emotional culture makes you *constantly* miserable, it's time to think about moving to a different group or company. "People don't take emotional culture seriously enough," advises Wharton professor Sigal Barsade. "They'll point to other parts of a job that are great on paper. But emotional culture affects you and your work a lot. If you're deeply unhappy, it may be better for you to leave."

How to encourage healthy emotional expression:

- **Acknowledge personal lives.** Even in the high-stress environment of a hospital, the late neurosurgeon Paul Kalanithi's colleague told him, "The chief is going through a divorce, so he's really throwing himself into his work right now. Don't make small talk with him." Understanding what the people around you might be enduring lets you better treat them with empathy and compassion.
- **Share coffee breaks and meals.** "Eating together has a long, primal tradition as a kind of social glue," explains Cornell professor Kevin Kniffin. When we eat together, we tend to like one another and our jobs more. Based on the advice of MIT researchers, a Bank of America call center switched everyone's schedules so team members could start taking coffee breaks together instead of individually.

Giving employees time for office chitchat made them happier and willing to work harder—which led to an estimated $15 million jump a year in productivity gains. At Starbucks, important meetings begin with a coffee tasting. This practice creates a collegial atmosphere that makes it easier for the group to agree on next steps or final decisions (no word on whether everyone writes their names on the coffee cups).

- **Celebrate the emotions you value.** Fashion retailer Tory Burch rewards its employees who most embody the company's collaborative values with a fully paid weeklong trip to anywhere in the world. A smaller way you can positively reinforce kindness is to model and

BEST FOOD + DRINK FOR BONDING

CHAIN COFFEE
INVITES DISCUSSION ABOUT THE SUPERIORITY OF ARTISANAL ROASTS

MICROWAVED FISH
SMELLS AWFUL, CREATES A COMMON ENEMY

SELTZER
DAIRY-FREE, GLUTEN-FREE, VEGAN-FRIENDLY

VOODOO COOKIES
FEAR BRINGS EVERYONE TOGETHER

explicitly acknowledge considerate gestures. ("Thanks for grabbing me a granola bar from the kitchen!")

- **Don't get pulled in by complainers.** If you have a coworker who gripes incessantly, try to push them toward action by asking, "What could you have done differently?" or "What can you do about it now?" These questions move the conversation in a positive direction—and make it less fun for them to vent to you. If that doesn't work, come up with an excuse to end the discussion ("I have a ton of emails waiting for a response").

BELONGING

What if you could bring yourself out of hiding and into the organization, even the parts of yourself that don't seem to belong on surface level? To do this, you'd have to feel like you truly belonged at the organization. But what is belonging, exactly? Diversity is having a seat at the table, inclusion is having a voice, and belonging is having that voice be heard. "We don't want to know we can survive in a space, we want to know we can thrive," Pat Wadors, the chief human resources officer at ServiceNow, told us. Pat explained that growing up as a girl with a learning disability, she often felt like an outsider. But in the moments when she did feel like she belonged? "I'd run up mountains for you," Pat said. "What unlocks me is when I can be my authentic self. When I am proud to be female, when I'm not embarrassed to tell you I'm dyslexic, when being odd is cool." *To assess your sense of belonging within your organization, see our flash assessment on page 247.*

Transition moments, like an employee's first day on the job, are particularly anxiety inducing—which makes them great opportunities to create a sense of belonging. Think back to how elated you felt the day you received

DIVERSITY

INCLUSION

BELONGING

a job offer. But as your start date drew closer, your excitement probably dissolved into self-doubt. To counteract first-day-on-the-job nerves, IDEO's San Francisco office gives new hires an "enterview" (a mash-up of *enter* and *interview*). Everyone who interviewed the new hire shares why they're excited for that individual to join and what necessary skills they bring to the team. These comments are written on a fold-out card that says, "Dear [new employee's name], we think you're kind of a big deal, and here's why."

THIS ONBOARDING PROCESS COULD
USE SOME MORE EMPATHY

MOLLIE: I was so excited to start working at IDEO. IDEO's culture is incredibly strong, which is wonderful, but it also means that new hires can feel like outsiders until they learn all the unique and nuanced norms. I felt nervous about whether or not I would fit in. It takes me months to loosen up around people.

The day I started, my desk was covered with Post-its from my colleagues telling me why they were excited to work with me. Someone had laid out my favorite office snacks; I filled out an IDEO onboarding survey the week before I started, including a question about my go-to snacks, but I assumed this information would just be used to help people get to know me. I was so relieved that my new team wanted to make me feel welcome. Another new hire tradition is to send around an email with fun facts and photos to introduce yourself. I shared that I love to watch comedy (my husband is a comedian), and that I once went on spring break with a Real Housewife of New York (for fans of the show: it was Sonja "Leopard Is My Neutral" Morgan). By 5:00 P.M., my first email had spawned an extensive thread.

As months passed, I gained a deeper understanding of the culture, so I started smiling, speaking up, and volunteering more (which included organizing and hosting an office-wide baking competition modeled after the *Great British Bake Off*). Once I felt a deeper sense of belonging, I wasn't constantly questioning if I fit in or not. I could share the sillier side of myself but also ask tough questions. A few months after I began to bring my full self to work, I was asked to lead my first project.

Microactions and Belonging

Microactions are small gestures that act as social signals. You might be more familiar with the term "microaggressions," indirect or unintentional moments of exclusion. "Microactions" (a term the culture transformation firm SYPartners coined, and uses in its own practice) are the antithesis—they are positive actions you can take to build meaningful belonging.

Here's an example: Karishma is a talented senior designer at SYPartners. In early 2015, she worked on a project with Keith Yamashita, the company's founder and chairman. After a few meetings, Karishma pulled Keith aside. "I am going to teach you how to say my name," she told him. "And then you can call on me by name like you call on everyone else by name." Keith thought he was being inclusive by asking Karishma questions and focusing his attention on her when she spoke. "But I didn't know how to pronounce Karishma's name, so I was shy about saying it," he recalled to us. "And if I refer to everyone else by name but never her, what does that tell her about how much I value her?" Keith now asks people how they pronounce their name when he first gets to know them (this gesture is a microaction).

To create a sense of belonging for others, try these micro-actions:

- Use a colleague's name in conversation. (This requires you to ask and remember how to correctly pronounce it!)
- Once a month, grab coffee or lunch with a coworker you don't know that well. Take the opportunity to learn more about who they are and what they do.
- When a new hire starts, help them get to know others. When you introduce them to someone, don't just say, "Hey, you two should talk!" Instead, find and mention an interest they share (ideally one that's not work related) to give them a conversational starting point.
- When someone joins a conversation, take a moment to bring them up to speed.
- If a colleague goes out of their way to help you, thank them!
- When someone is talking to you, don't multitask. Stop what you're doing and give them your full attention.
- If you notice someone get cut off midsentence, make a point to jump in and ask them to continue sharing their thoughts.

A sense of belonging is not the same as feeling similar to everyone else (our desire to fit in often compels us to hide who we really are). Belonging is when you feel safe and valued for embracing what makes you different. We feel a sense of belonging when we are confident the team passed on our idea simply

because it wasn't the best choice, not because something is innately wrong with us. *Not* belonging or a sense of isolation is among the strongest predictors of turnover. A study analyzing emails showed new employees who do not switch from "I" to "we" pronouns (which the researchers used as a sign of belonging) during the first six months at their jobs are more likely to leave.

Feeling like you belong doesn't mean work will be a walk in the park—it means the normal ups and downs of office life won't cause you quite so much stress. At Pinterest, managers are encouraged to share their experiences (good and bad) at the company to help their reports understand that some emotional swings are part of the job—and that you can go through difficult periods but still belong. In the next section, we'll discuss these types of conversations in more detail. They are called belonging interventions and often don't take more than an hour to implement.

How to create a culture of belonging:

- **Assume good intentions.** If a colleague you know and trust missteps, explain why their behavior made you feel excluded and propose an alternate action. "Intentions do matter," notes Pat Wadors. "Give people room to learn from their mistakes."
- **Belonging starts with onboarding.** At Warby Parker, employees call new hires before their start date to tell them what to expect at orientation and to answer any questions. New Google employees whose managers give them a warm welcome on their first day are more productive nine months down the line.
- **Assign "culture buddies."** Buffer, a social-media-management company, pairs new hires with employees who already understand the culture. At the end of the first week, this culture buddy sits down with the new hire to answer questions, give feedback (e.g., how the tone of their emails is coming across), and help them understand that feeling a bit out of place at first is normal.
- **Make sure belonging doesn't nosedive in meetings.** Appoint one person to be an objective observer during each meeting. That person's job is to record group dynamics, noting who speaks the most, who isn't given any time to speak, and who keeps talking over other people. At the end of the meeting, have the observer suggest ways to improve group dynamics.

Belonging and Remote Workers

What does culture mean to the growing number of people who work from home or as freelancers? Laura Savino is an iOS developer who lives in Seattle and works remotely for companies based around the world. When we spoke with her, Laura was up-front about the biggest drawback to her career: because she rarely gets to know her colleagues outside of work, she sometimes feels isolated and invisible. "One company, though," she recalled with a smile, "scheduled a weekly thirty-minute video teatime for all employees. It was explicitly social and really brought us closer."

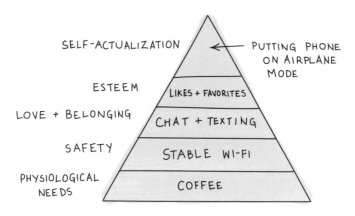

LIZ'S HIERARCHY OF REMOTE WORK NEEDS

SELF-ACTUALIZATION ← PUTTING PHONE ON AIRPLANE MODE

ESTEEM — LIKES + FAVORITES

LOVE + BELONGING — CHAT + TEXTING

SAFETY — STABLE WI-FI

PHYSIOLOGICAL NEEDS — COFFEE

Proverbial water coolers help remote workers connect with one another. Buffer's seventy-five employees, who are distributed across the world, share personal snippets of their lives on Instagram Stories. Buffer director of people Courtney Seiter told us, "Now I know what my colleague's day is like and what her work space looks like. I get to see my coworkers making cookies and walking their dogs. It's the things you would never share on a conference call, but seeing them helps you understand each other."

The "out of sight, out of mind" trap often means remote

workers rarely receive praise. When we work with our colleagues in person, we compliment one another after meetings, in the hall, or over drinks. Remote workers have fewer chances to receive this kind of informal feedback. "Many remote workers receive assignments, deliver them on time, and hear back only when their managers need more work done on these assignments," explains Kristen Chirco of E Group. Publicly pointing out when a remote team member has done a good job goes a long way.

iSPY : VIDEOCONFERENCE

HAS A CAT

DRAWS?

READS A LOT OF KAFKA

LOVES CALVIN + HOBBES

MAKES BED

BOYFRIEND WEARS POLKA-DOT BOXERS

PLAYS CELLO

UNEXPECTEDLY HIGH STILETTOS

Liz's Tips on Helping Remote Workers
Feel Belonging

LIZ: Because I am a freelancer, I can work anywhere with wi-fi. My dad's a retired pathologist; he had to commute forty minutes by train to get to his laboratory. I have to constantly remind him that when I'm wearing sweatpants and using my laptop at the dining table, I'm doing work. One morning when I was visiting my parents, I was lying in bed working. My dad poked his head into the room and asked with real concern, "When are you going to work in a building?"

The best advice for making remote workers feel like they belong: do as close to the same things you would do if you were together in person.

- **Once we've earned it, trust us.** Because you don't see us working, it's easy to assume any lull in communication means we're twiddling our thumbs. The nicest part of working remotely is that you can easily build blocks of uninterrupted concentration time into your day. Set clear expectations for remote workers but don't worry if you don't get a ping from them every five minutes.

- **Be mindful of time zones.** To help people in all time zones feel included, delay decision making until you've heard from everyone who should be involved. And if you ask a colleague to join a meeting at 6:00 A.M. or 10:00 P.M. their time, this is when I recommend skipping video. It's much easier to jump on a call if you don't have to put on mascara or button a shirt first.

- **Send us stuff!** One of my clients had a little cake delivered to me on my birthday. I was thrilled! Another sent my paychecks in illustrated thank-you cards. When everything is digital, a physical package (think company swag, books, snacks, or hand-written notes) is delightful.

- **Help us meet one another.** This can be done by setting up virtual lunches, teatimes, or what Buffer calls "Pair calls." For Pair calls, Buffer employees opt in to be randomly paired with someone else at the company once a week. Calls have no set agenda; coworkers get to know one another by talking about their families, their hobbies, and their favorite shows.

MAKING SURE WE GET BELONGING RIGHT

"No matter how liberal and open-minded some of my white professors and classmates try to be toward me, I sometimes feel like a visitor on campus; as if I really don't belong," wrote Michelle Obama while studying at Princeton. "It often seems as if, to them, I will always be black first and a student second."

Although everyone experiences periods of self-doubt, members of under-represented groups are much more likely to feel alienated at work. Individuals from marginalized communities not only ask themselves "Do I belong?" but contend with the additional question, "Does my group belong?" Many minority professionals admit feeling pressure to display a workplace identity that both conforms to dominant standards and counters stereotypes about their own group. "Black men often say managing their emotions so others don't view them as the stereotypical 'angry black man' is just part of their job," sociologist Adia Harvey Wingfield told us. And black and Latina women frequently report taking pains to speak without an accent or avoid slang.

Feeling like you have to continually and carefully cultivate a work identity is taxing. And if you're *not* a minority, research shows you probably underestimate how isolating this can be. Minorities who cannot bring up the biases they encounter in their professional and personal lives are more than twice as likely as non-minorities to feel alone—and to leave their companies within a year. Research also shows black employees from disadvantaged backgrounds who work hard to succeed tend to have lower life expectancies—this may be because they undergo so much stress acclimating to uninclusive work environments.

These dynamics mean many people silently bear heavy emotional burdens at work. After the police shootings in the summer of 2016, tech executive Leah McGowen-Hare didn't feel comfortable showing how upset she was. "I had to go into a bathroom stall because I couldn't keep it together and everyone else acted like nothing was happening," she recalled. "The level of empathy for the black community wasn't there."

Diversity-training sessions, especially ones in which "diversity" is defined broadly (as, for example, "diversity of thought"), are not a cure-all. In fact, these sessions often become another source of emotional distress for members of underrepresented groups. In interviews, black professionals told Adia they found little to no equality in terms of who was able to express emotion. "While white workers felt free to articulate racial biases," she told us, "their black colleagues were not comfortable expressing their emotional responses. The training session became another place where minorities had to hide their feelings." This inequality in emotional expression often occurs when diversity training sessions are used as one-off attempts to correct for an unhealthy emotional culture. "Organizations can't simply demand trust," writes Erica Baker, a senior engineering manager at Patreon. "Trust needs to be earned."

Emotional Labor

How often have you chosen your words carefully to make sure you come across as nonthreatening? What about smiling and nodding when your boss hasn't said anything particularly insightful? We lost count a long time ago. These are both forms of emotional labor, the often invisible and unpaid work we do to fulfill the emotional expectations of a job. Emotional labor usually involves surface acting, or expressing emotions we don't feel. Author Seth Godin describes this as "listening when we'd rather yell." Surface acting is draining; people who do it frequently are more likely to feel stressed and eventually burn out.

Although everyone performs some degree of emotional labor at work, women and minorities feel more pressure than their colleagues to appear nonthreatening or empathetic. At universities, students often use female professors' office hours as "confessional time" and are more likely to lean on them for emotional support. Writing in *The Toast*, Jess Zimmerman argues women should start pricing and charging for "soothing a man's ego" ($100) and "pretending to find him fascinating" ($150). Nadia, a copywriter in the tech industry, told *The Outline* she spent a significant amount of mental energy at a recent job carefully choosing her words. "I was one of the youngest people on the team, I'm a woman, and I'm black," she explained. "I'd watch other people say things, and I would think, 'Oh my God, if those words came out of my mouth, people would cringe.'"

So how do we create a workplace where each employee feels a true sense of belonging? First, commit to creating a diverse workforce at all levels. When members of all groups are visibly represented among and supported by senior management, there is less of a need for individuals to check their real selves at the door. In the spring of 2018, Utah-based software company Domo unveiled six new billboards near its headquarters that stated, "DOMO ♥ LGBTQ+ (and everyone else too)." Domo executives decided to launch the campaign after hearing stories about LGBTQ+ individuals who were ostracized by the local conservative community. "We need to make sure our workplaces are welcoming and inclusive for everyone," wrote CEO Josh James.

Second, look into belonging interventions. In a study, Stanford professor Greg Walton had a group of African American college freshmen read essays

WHO YOU FEEL
YOU CAN BE
AT WORK

EVERYTHING
THAT MAKES
YOU SPECIAL

WHERE THE
MAGIC HAPPENS

INITIAL PERCEPTION

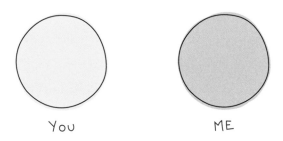

YOU

ME

AFTER SHARING STORIES

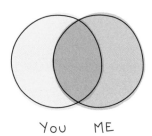

YOU   ME

written by upperclassmen about the difficult emotions they had experienced when they arrived at college. "When I got here, I thought I was the only one who felt left out," wrote one upperclassman. "But then I found out that everyone feels that way at first, and everyone gets over it. I got over it, too." Over the next three years, the intervention halved the GPA gap between white students and the African Americans who were part of the intervention group. A similar intervention eliminated the gender GPA gap in a highly selective engineering program.

Finally, create emotion norms that encourage minorities to talk about how they feel. After the police shootings in the summer of 2016, Pricewaterhouse-Coopers (PwC) brought its employees together in small groups to openly discuss racial issues. One African American executive described his suit as his cape: when he wears it, he's a good guy, but when he takes it off, he's suddenly more likely to be seen as threatening. PwC chairman Tim Ryan and minority initiatives and talent management leader Elena Richards discussed what they learned from the conversations on video, and then used social media to encourage employees to continue sharing their stories with one another. "Discussing these types of difficult topics is usually assumed to be the responsibility of community leaders, politicians, and activists," wrote Ryan. "But our people spend a good portion of their lives within the walls of this firm and more than anything, I want them to be able to bring their whole selves to work."

How to help make sure everyone feels belonging:

- **Acknowledge that members of different groups face different challenges.** "Let's start with gender" is a flawed approach to creating a culture of belonging for all employees. Conversations about women in the workplace often focus on white women and ignore the experiences of members of other underrepresented groups.
- **Remember that it's never "not your problem."** "No one marginalized group has ever successfully advocated on behalf of themselves— alone—to enact change," writes CNN content strategist Cameron

Hough. Many people who are progressive in their personal lives give themselves a pass in their professional lives. If someone on your team says something that raises a few eyebrows but is not directly prejudiced toward you, speak up or pull them aside later. People are more likely to feel guilty and apologize if their prejudiced comment is pointed out by someone outside of the targeted group.

- **Identify missing voices.** In every meeting, Pat Wadors asks participants which voices they wish were part of the conversation and how to involve them. "It's about taking care of individuals even when they're not in the room," she told us.
- **Ask questions instead of immediately trying to problem solve.** You won't understand another person's perspective unless you listen and show compassion. "You want to hold your ideas very lightly so you can change your mind, so you can be moved by what someone says," advises Mellody Hobson, president of Ariel Investments. "When you ask questions . . . it takes the edge off." Your instinct might be to quickly patch things over, as if the issue is just a matter of momentary emotional conflict. But the reality is that these are often structural issues, not interpersonal ones.
- **Play in your lane.** Hobson encourages people to work with the power they have. If you're a manager, start conversations and set a team norm of asking questions. If you're a member of a team, reach out to people who are different from you.

For further resources on gender and leadership: *We recommend Mellody Hobson's TED talk "Be Color Brave, Not Color Blind"; research and writing by Professors Adia Harvey Wingfield and Kira Hudson Banks; "The Belonging Guide" by Professor Greg Walton; diversity and inclusion consulting firm Paradigm's research white papers; and the resources on the CODE2040, Kapor Center, and Catalyst websites.*

TAKEAWAYS

1. Be kind; emotions are contagious, which means your actions can have a positive influence on your entire organization's emotional culture.
2. Create a culture of belonging through microactions: say "hello," invite people into conversations, or help a new hire meet others.
3. Share stories about who you are, not what you do, and invite others to do the same.
4. Don't ignore the emotional burdens your colleagues may carry.

IT'S A WILD WORLD BUT I'M HERE FOR YOU

CHAPTER 8

Leadership

Be selectively vulnerable:

Why how you share matters

THE LIFE OF A LEADER

ANOTHER POTENTIALLY DISASTROUS
SITUATION IS HERE TO SEE YOU

L aszlo Bock sat on a couch in the sparsely furnished conference room and listened to the last of his employees update the assembled group about her work. Then it was Laszlo's turn. "Last week, my brother died unexpectedly."

Laszlo Bock, who led HR at Google for ten years, is the founder and CEO of Humu, a machine learning company that aims to make work better. One August morning in 2017, he got a call with news about his brother. Citing a personal emergency, Laszlo immediately dropped everything and flew to Florida to be with his family.

When he returned to California a week later, Laszlo decided to tell his employees about his brother's death. "I had to acknowledge why I might be in and out for the next few months," Laszlo told us. "I knew if I didn't, I would feel guilty for seeming less focused. These people quit amazing jobs to work with me and three months in, I felt I was breaking an unspoken contract with them."

After Laszlo spoke, his employees rallied around him. Though each member of his team responded differently—some didn't bring it up again while others asked Laszlo every so often how he and his family were doing—everyone showed up in ways that made him feel supported. "That made it easier for me to come to work," Laszlo recalled. "It was a relief to just be there and work hard and sometimes suppress my feelings and know that people understood why I was doing that and be okay with it." His vulnerability also created an environment where employees could share and support one another. A few months later, Laszlo saw one employee hesitate to confide something to another. "I don't want to burden you with this," she said. Her colleague responded, "It doesn't feel like a burden when you share."

SELECTIVE VULNERABILITY

Laszlo isn't the first powerful figure to use his platform to destigmatize vulnerability, nor is he the first CEO to realize the value of letting your guard down. Apple CEO Tim Cook likes to have lunch with random employees. Simon Sinek's viral TED talk "Why Good Leaders Make You Feel Safe" indicated that command and control management—which uses dominance to get results—is on its way out. A relational leadership style has emotional *and* financial benefits. Research shows that our brains respond more positively to empathetic bosses; when we feel a personal connection with a leader, we try harder, perform better, and are kinder to our colleagues.

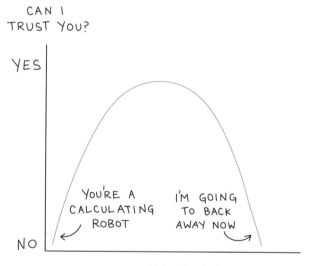

Vulnerability matters because we're really good at picking up on fakeness, especially in our leaders. Workers are already predisposed to question the sincerity of leaders when they show emotion, but trust between leaders and workers breaks down completely if leaders never show any emotion at all, especially after a round of layoffs or when the company is doing poorly. We have an uncanny ability to pick up on one another's moods. Research by Stanford's James Gross shows that when someone is upset but keeps their feelings bottled up, our own blood pressure goes up when we're around them—even if we don't consciously realize they're angry.

MY BODY LANGUAGE? I'M TELLING YOU, EVERYTHING IS FINE

The unique problem leaders face is that they have to think longer and harder than the rest of us about when to be transparent. Too much disclosure (or "Workplace TMI") might diminish how much people respect you and make them question your ability to do your job. Researchers found sharing personal stories that expose a weakness can undermine a leader's authority (sharing with a peer did not trigger the same negative response in the listener).

So what's the line between sharing, which builds trust, and oversharing, which destroys it? Our seventh new rule of emotion at work is: *Be selectively vulnerable*. This chapter is a guide for how to open up while still prioritizing emotional stability and psychological safety for yourself and your colleagues. Our goal is to end any agonizing about what to say and when.

If you're about to flip to another chapter because you think you're not a leader, think again. Leadership is a skill, not a role. Do you influence the people around you? Do they look to you for help in making decisions? Julie Zhuo, VP of Design at Facebook, writes that "anyone can exhibit leadership regardless of their specific role. Think of a store clerk calmly directing shoppers to safety when the screeching tornado bell goes off in a mall." Or think of "an individual contributor who surfaces important customer complaints and then coordinates solutions across multiple teams." No matter your official job title, you're almost certainly a leader in some way.

Managing Other People's Emotions

Successfully making the transition from individual contributor to leader requires a major mind-set shift. In addition to managing your emotions, you have to start helping other people manage and effectively express their emotions.

If you're an individual contributor and someone comes to you in tears, you can provide a shoulder to cry on and then get back to work. But if you're a leader, you need to think about the best next step for this person, both personally and professionally. You have to be empathetic but still able to objectively assess the situation.

Avoid telling people what to feel. Try not to say, "Don't be mad," "It's not personal," or "You'll be fine" (and never, ever use "we," as in "We think you should be coming in earlier..."). If an employee gets emotional, try to understand where his feelings are coming from. You might ask, "What would be helpful to you right now?" "You already know how to react to an emotion with compassion," *Radical Candor* author Kim Scott points out. "You do it all the time in your personal life. Somehow, at work, we are primed to forget these basics." Don't make your employees immediately feel bad for feeling bad.

Don't waffle. Being an empathetic manager is not the same as being a pushover. Own your decisions and discuss and set expectations with your reports as soon as you know there's a problem. This can be as simple as saying, "I'm not happy with the work you're doing. What's going on?" If you let someone underperform for months or even years without saying anything, you've failed as a manager.

Listen. It sounds basic, but it bears repeating. The question Wharton professor Adam Grant most frequently fields is how to have your suggestions heard when you're not in charge. "These are not questions asked by leaders," Grant notes. "They're fundamental questions of followership." Listening helps leaders understand the source of problems or strong emotions. Harvard Business School professor Bill George told us, "Ninety to ninety-five percent of what we teach at HBS is intellectual [as opposed to emotional]. Our faculty isn't comfortable asking students to probe about emotional motivations in case studies, like, 'Why did this person do what they did? Why did this happen?' I actually think we can take people the wrong way in their two years [in business school]."

Manage individually. After surveying almost eighty thousand people, researcher Marcus Buckingham's biggest insight was, "Average managers play checkers, while great managers play chess." In checkers, every piece is the same. But winning a game of chess requires you to understand each piece's strengths and weaknesses. Your reports will not all enjoy the same tasks or perceive situations in the same way, so it's important to treat them as individuals.

PROVIDE A PATH TO FOLLOW

The best leaders show vulnerability when assessing a situation but then present a clear path forward. Jerry Colonna is a former venture capitalist who's become a beloved coach to entrepreneurs (he's known as the "CEO Whisperer") through Reboot, the coaching firm he cofounded. Jerry gave us the following example: "Let's imagine that you're the CEO of a start-up and you're about to run out of money but close to raising another round. You're probably terrified. Now picture yourself walking into a meeting with all twelve of your employees and saying, 'I'm terrified.' That's an unhelpful strategy. A better strategy is to say, 'I'm scared, but I still believe—in you, our product, our mission.' Both approaches involve you being authentic," Jerry told us. But saying, "I believe in our product" is a way of presenting a clear path forward. It's a promise to work toward a solution *in spite of* emotions. "The call of leadership isn't just to be real. It's also to be able to manage and soothe your own anxieties, so that you don't infect others."

Cynthia Danaher knows firsthand the perils of putting emotion above a call to action. After she was promoted to general manager of Hewlett-Packard's Medical Products Group, she told her fifty-three hundred employees, "I want to do this job, but it's scary and I need your help." At the time, in 1999, revealing her true feelings made sense; now, the memory makes her cringe. Cynthia told *The Wall Street Journal* she wishes she had instead outlined her growth goals for the business. "People say they want a leader to be vulnerable just like them, but deep down they want to believe you have the

— HOW LEADERS FEEL

-- WHAT GREAT LEADERS EXPRESS

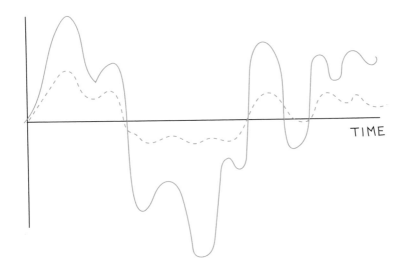

TIME

skill to move and fix things they can't." (Of course, gender might have factored heavily into the negative reaction she received—we'll discuss this more in the next section.)

"An important part of being a leader is understanding how much weight the people around you can bear," Laszlo told us. "You can't burden your employees with more than they can carry or expect them to hold you up all the time." As our friend put it, "The best managers are good shit umbrellas. When the shit hits the fan, they do what they can to protect their team from the emotional fallout."

Another way to use the "vulnerability + path forward" formula is to ask yourself, "How can I be realistic *and* optimistic?" Tony Schwartz, CEO of The Energy Project, describes realistic optimism as confronting and dealing with difficult facts while still having the self-confidence and faith in your team's ability to tell the most uplifting and empowering story possible.

THIS IS NOTHING. AT MY OLD JOB I HAD
TO SHOULDER MY BOSS'S EMOTIONAL BURDENS

In the following, you'll find additional tips on how to practice selective vulnerability and provide a clear path forward. Of course, great managers need to do more than these two things (they should also define strategic goals, communicate clearly, and master the necessary technical skills), but we'll focus on emotional action items.

How to be selectively vulnerable and provide a clear path forward:

- **Figure yourself out.** The best leaders are able to hit a pause button when they become emotional. Instead of immediately acting, they ask themselves, "What exactly am I feeling? Why? What is the need behind this emotion?" An average manager might quickly answer these questions with, "I'm so annoyed by this project," but a great manager will realize that the root cause of her irritability is anxiety about meeting an impending deadline. With this understanding, she can go back to her team and put structures into place that ensure work is done on time.

YOUR REPORTS' EMOTIONAL ROLLER COASTER

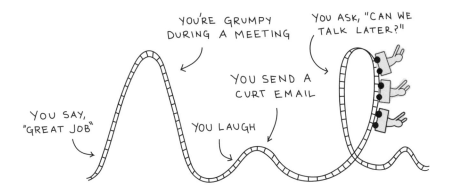

YOU'RE GRUMPY DURING A MEETING

YOU ASK, "CAN WE TALK LATER?"

YOU SEND A CURT EMAIL

YOU SAY, "GREAT JOB"

YOU LAUGH

- **Regulate your emotions.** In *Radical Candor,* author Kim Scott recalls a morning when a report told her, "I know what kind of day I'm going to have by the kind of mood you're in when you walk in the door." Managing your feelings is as important as managing your reports; what you consider a throwaway comment or a momentary bad mood can ruin someone's day. Reactive, hot-tempered managers are hurtful, demoralizing, and the top reason people quit their jobs. In a lab experiment, employees confronted by an angry manager were less willing to work hard—especially if they didn't know why the manager was mad. In contrast, after a group of managers were taught to control their words and body language during tense situations, their reports' stress levels dropped by more than 30 percent.

- **Address your feelings without becoming emotionally leaky.** "The idea that you're never going to have a bad day as a boss is bullshit," Kim Scott told us. "The best thing to do is to cop to it. Say to your team, 'I'm having a bad day, and I'm trying my best not to take it out on you. But if it seems like I'm having a bad day, I am. But it's not because of you that I'm having a bad day. The last thing I want is for my bad day to make your day bad.'"

- **Find time to prioritize yourself.** Managing means cooking something on every burner without burning anything. Your job is to simultaneously bring the fusilli to a boil (al dente, please), keep the risotto at a simmer, sauté a mix of veggies, and add just the right amount of salt to the sauce. You also have to time every step perfectly to make sure the meal comes together. That's exhausting! Try taking a "Shultz hour" for yourself. When he was in office, former secretary of state George Shultz protected one hour each week for solitary reflection with paper and pen. No one was allowed to interrupt him except the president or his wife.

- **If you feel isolated, seek support.** Maintaining selective vulnerability can be a draining exercise; half of leaders report feeling alone in their roles. Seek support from peers with whom you feel safe talking openly about personal and professional issues. As Liz Koenig, who managed Teach for America teachers, told us, "You can't pour out of an empty cup."

- **Don't be upset when your employees move on.** They might become valuable contacts in another company or even come back. Anthropologist Ilana Gershon says the best managers communicate this to new hires. One leader Gershon talked to said she takes every new member of her team out to lunch in the week they start and says things like, "You don't work for me, I work for you . . . my job is to make sure you can do your job well. And one day, you're going to leave this job. . . . When you want to leave this job, I hope to be here to help you move on to the next job." McKinsey and Ernst & Young cultivate alumni communities as a great source of new business and referrals.

When Your Manager Can't Manage

What if you work for someone whose mean flashes and knee-jerk reactions make work miserable? Because you can't fire up, your best bet is to manage up.

- **Call it out ... carefully.** If you think your boss will be receptive to feedback, have a conversation about how their mood affects you. Calmly describe a specific behavior you've noticed and ask how you can improve the situation. For example, say your manager snaps at you anytime you need help. You might say, "I've noticed when I stop by to ask you a question, you seem irritated. How can I better approach you?" Often managers don't know how their reactions come across, and because their days are so packed, they don't have time to reflect on or apologize for their negative reactions. Our friend and licensed social worker Julia Byers explains, "If you have a disagreement with your partner in the morning as you're heading out the door, your partner can text you later in the day and say, 'Sorry, I love you.' But in a professional setting, your boss isn't going to text you."

- **Don't get sucked in.** Researchers Shawn Achor and Michelle Gielan recommend trying to neutralize the negative effects of a frazzled boss. "Instead of returning a harried coworker's stressed nonverbals with an equally stressed grimace of your own," they write, "return it with a smile or a nod of understanding." If you have a meeting with your boss, set the tone on a positive note. If you say, "It's so great to get to meet with you today" (of course, you need to say this sincerely, not sarcastically), it will be hard for your boss to follow that positive comment by saying, "I'm so aggravated."

- **Schedule smart.** Watch for patterns in your manager's mood. Is he always stressed on Thursdays before his weekly call with a fussy client? Does she seem unapproachable until she's had her second cup of coffee? If you know when your boss will be anxious or preoccupied, schedule meetings at other times. One of Mollie's past bosses was always brusque in the morning, so Mollie tried to avoid meeting with him before 10:00 A.M.

- **Protect your self-esteem.** Unless you can easily identify something you did that could be causing your boss's bad mood, don't assume it's about you. That said, it's still easy to take a stormy encounter personally. Make sure to protect yourself. Self-confidence or work friends can enable you to better weather your boss's negative emotions—think of them as providing you with an emotional flak jacket. Self-esteem also helps you remind yourself that you're still capable, even if your boss is bringing you down. Keeping a smile file (the folder of positive feedback we mentioned in chapter 6, "Communication") can give you a mood boost when you need it.

- **If nothing else works, move on.** If your manager makes you completely miserable and you can't switch teams, it might be time to look for a new job. As the saying goes, "People don't quit jobs, they quit managers."

DIFFERENT LEADERSHIP STYLES

When Harvard Business School professor Bill George analyzed more than a thousand leadership studies, he found that a single best profile of a leader doesn't exist. That's because the key to being a great leader doesn't have much to do with specific personality traits. It has to do with emotional intelligence.

"Anyone can improve their emotional intelligence," Bill George told us. "The key is self-awareness. You need to develop a keen understanding of who you are in the world." In this section, we'll go through challenges different types of leaders face and how to address them. Again, our intent is not to box in individuals—gender, race, age, culture, and extraversion level (not to mention ethnicity, religion, sexual preference, and class) can intersect to shape identities and perceptions in complex ways—but to contextualize some experiences.

Gender

Female leaders often feel pressure to avoid appearing either too emotional or too emotionless to lead. We've heard stories of senior female employees whose managers coached them to be more "measured" during meetings. But studies also show that as women move up in an organization, their colleagues may begin to see them as less friendly or approachable and as more competitive.

THANKS JULIA, BUT TO BE FULLY
CONVINCED I'LL NEED TO HEAR
JOHN RESTATE YOUR IDEA

How can female leaders strike the right balance? First, they shouldn't shy away from being decisive and straightforward when delegating. Phrase requests confidently and clearly. Instead of asking, "Would it be possible for you to finish a one-page memo by tomorrow?" try, "The client needs the memo by tomorrow end of day. Can you complete it by then?" Your team will appreciate clarity and be happy their manager is working to ensure no balls are dropped.

But female leaders also shouldn't shy away from opportunities to show some emotion. One of Mollie's former bosses openly expressed her delight at team members' accomplishments, which motivated them. Emotion can be an extremely effective tool to help bond and inspire reports. "Don't stifle your emotions or your ambitions," writes author Jennifer Palmieri. "Men spent centuries building the professional world, devising rules to make sure it was a comfortable place for them and that it was geared toward their particular qualities and skills. Like any good guest, women have looked for clues on how we are to behave in this foreign land. We have intuited that in this world we are to be obliging, calm under pressure, diligent, and to always keep our emotions in check." But we are now living in a different world, one that needs leaders who are in tune with their emotions—and their team's emotions.

"Let's embrace a new way of working that is equally geared toward our own qualities and skills," urges Palmieri.

"CONFIDENT"   "AGGRESSIVE"

Male leaders also benefit from investing in empathy. Research by Daniel Goleman, author of *Emotional Intelligence*, shows that men's brains are more likely to tune out emotion and start problem solving when presented with an issue. The ability to block out others' distress works in their favor during a crisis but can leave those around them feeling lost or unsupported in an emotionally trying situation. Studies show that high emotional intelligence makes for a top-performing leader, no matter their gender.

Sadly, it still needs to be said: treat your colleagues equally. Don't ask your male colleagues only about their work and your female colleagues only about their families. Make sure to reward competent female reports, even if they don't ask for promotions or raises as frequently as male reports. And address everyone by the same honorifics; when men introduce speakers at medical conferences, they tend to introduce male doctors as "Doctor [Last Name]" but introduce females by their first names.

For further resources on gender and leadership: *We recommend the* *books* Dear Madam President *by Jennifer Palmieri,* Playing Big *by Tara Mohr, and* That's *What She Said by Joanne Lipman. The Catalyst and LeanIn.Org websites and the annual Women in the Workplace report by McKinsey also contain valuable information.*

When Women Cut Each Other Down

Would you rather work for a male or female boss? In surveys, more than half of female respondents pick a male boss. Even women who are managers themselves are more likely to want to work for a man (men also prefer male bosses, but by a smaller margin). When asked why, some women explained they didn't want to work for another woman for fear she would be too "emotional," "catty," or "bitchy."

Writing for *The Atlantic*, journalist Olga Khazan describes her interviews with women who have been undermined by both genders, but "it somehow felt different—worse—when it happened at the hands of a woman, a supposed ally." One of Khazan's own mentors told Khazan that she "divides her past female managers into 'Dragon Ladies' and 'Softies Who Nice Their Way Upward.' She'd rather work for men because, she says, they're more forthright. 'With women, I'm partly being judged on my abilities and partly being judged on whether or not I'm 'a friend' or 'nice' or 'fun.'"

A lack of leadership opportunities can make women feel like they have to compete with one another—and makes younger ambitious female employees seem threatening. Research shows that women who are optimistic about their career paths are less likely to tear one another down. "We need to change our society so that it becomes normative for women to see other women succeeding in all kinds of roles," writes psychologist Laurie Rudman.

Race

Studies show we are more likely to see white people as management material, which introduces bias into the promotion process. Take the "bamboo ceiling," a phrase coined by executive coach Jane Hyun: while Asian Americans are more likely to have a college degree than the average person, and account for roughly one in five students at elite business schools, they're notably absent from the list of Fortune 500 CEOs. Racial minorities often feel they must act, look, and sound like the prevailing white male leadership model if they want to be taken seriously. "For many black professionals, remaining in leadership positions can be an emotional challenge," sociologist Adia Harvey Wingfield told us. Especially if you are an organization's first minority leader, you might limit how open you are with white colleagues to avoid jeopardizing your perceived credibility.

Gender and race intersect to create unique disadvantages for female

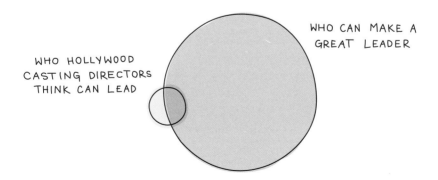

WHO HOLLYWOOD CASTING DIRECTORS THINK CAN LEAD

WHO CAN MAKE A GREAT LEADER

minorities. Black women can be disproportionately punished for making mistakes in a leadership role. And Latina leaders tend to be seen as overly emotional: "[We're] always told, 'Calm down. You've got to be more cool. Be careful with your voice, be careful with your hands,'" describes a Latina executive.

Mentors help minority leaders maintain a positive sense of self and get honest feedback. Talking to someone who has faced similar challenges and can offer emotional support might reduce doubts about your ability to succeed. But, of course, it's hard to find a mentor who can relate to your experience when there aren't many people like you in leadership positions. Women of color are least likely to find mentors in large corporations. Which brings us to our next point.

If you are in a leadership position, make diversity a priority. From 2005 to 2011, eight black, twelve Latino, and thirteen Asian executives were promoted to CEOs at Fortune 500 companies. But in more recent years, those numbers have fallen again as white men replaced minority CEOs who retired or were forced out. One theory is that these pushes for diversity have stalled; when it appeared as if some success had been made, companies felt less pressure to push for equal representation at all levels. Leaders must continually evaluate what they can do to increase diversity at their organizations.

For further resources on race and leadership: *We recommend work by Professor Adia Harvey Wingfield, Professor Tina Opie, and Candice Morgan, head of Inclusion and Diversity at Pinterest. Also check out Project Include and the* Inclusion Insights *blog from Paradigm, a diversity and inclusion consulting firm.*

Age

It's historically unusual for a boss to be younger than her reports—and this can make young leaders uncomfortable. As Wharton professor Peter Cappelli explains, young leaders might worry, "I can't manage somebody who's older than I am."

Stepping out of traditional roles is valuable for employees and managers at all ages. For leaders who are younger than your reports: be open but stay confident and demonstrate maturity. Don't go overboard on proving why you deserve to be in a leadership role; racing through conversations or shutting down feedback will only make you look arrogant and deepen a divide between you and your team. "Admit honestly to your senior reports what you do and do not know, and work together on a plan for how you can help support them," advises Julie Zhuo, who was just a few years out of college when she became a manager at Facebook.

For leaders who are older than your reports: realize that younger employees can keep you up-to-date. Forty-one-year-old SoulCycle CEO Melanie Whelan meets monthly with a younger mentor who helps her get "hip with what the kids are doing these days" by suggesting what

I HEARD HE'S WORKING WITH A MILLENNIAL NOW

Whelan should be reading and what apps she should be using. This isn't a new phenomenon. In the 1990s, former GE CEO Jack Welch paired five hundred of his top managers with younger employees so the managers could learn from them.

Introverts and extroverts

Though we're quick to assume the best leaders must be larger-than-life spotlight hogs, the meek are just as likely to inherit the world. Some of the most powerful leaders, including Bill Gates, Warren Buffett, and Larry Page, are described as "quiet," "soft-spoken," and "unassuming." In offices where employees tend to offer ideas, introverted leaders are tied to higher profits. And when economists analyzed the linguistic patterns of CEOs, they found reserved leaders were connected to a better bottom line.

But introverted leaders do face challenges. Leadership roles are highly visible and require a lot of time spent managing and building connections. It's easy for introverts to feel exhausted if they don't schedule alone time to recharge. But this tendency toward solitude (and away from networking events) can make introverts appear withdrawn or even rude. It also puts them at risk for career derailment. And a bias against promoting introverts into leadership positions may still exist: more than half of executives view introversion as a barrier to leadership (though this survey was conducted in 2006, six years before Susan Cain's book *Quiet: The Power of Introverts in a World That Can't Stop Talking* was published, which we hope has changed this view).

Introverted leaders succeed by being open about their preferences and by pushing themselves to override their tendency to want to be alone. That doesn't mean you can *never* be alone again—your creativity and the quiet time you spend thinking are probably why you got promoted in the first place—but it does mean that you need to be strategically social. Don't shy away from public-speaking opportunities. "Just the sheer act of being in front of a group can change people's perceptions of you and have them start thinking of you as a leader," advises Susan Cain. Former Campbell Soup CEO Doug Conant would give people he worked with a "DRC (Doug R. Conant) orientation": he would explain that he was an introvert and how that affected his work style. This helped him "quickly get beyond all the little superficial dances people do when they first start working with each other."

The harder introverts prepare and push themselves to be slightly more extroverted, the easier it will become. When introverts manage extroverts primarily by email from the silence and safety of their office, the extroverts don't get the in-person contact they need. They feel the ball is always in their court to have to go and interrupt their introverted boss to discuss their work or ask questions. Introverts, if you manage extroverts, set standing meetings with them daily or weekly so they know they'll have time to talk things through.

AN INTROVERTED LEADER'S REWARD CARD

DO 9 SUPER SOCIAL THINGS AND EARN 1 DAY OFF

Extroverted leaders: please be aware of your tendency toward MBWA, or "management by wandering around." Though you thrive on impromptu Q&As, we guarantee your introverted colleagues would be grateful for a bit more time to think about their responses to your questions. Even drive-by chitchat is draining for introverts. Studies show that extroverts are most productive when there is a lot of noise, whereas introverts work best in quiet spaces. A few tips: if you do ask a difficult question, give an introvert until the next day to get back to you with an answer. Be conscious of when you drop by. If you've spent all morning in meetings with an introvert, he is probably ready for some space. And finally, err toward one-on-one meetings in private or on walks.

Great leaders bring out the best in those around them—and that means accommodating both introverts and extroverts. "Your personality is a tendency that is in part biological, part learned," explains Wharton professor Adam Grant. "But we can choose to override that tendency when the time is right, and I think that is something we all need to get comfortable doing . . . I think the best leaders end up operating like ambiverts."

SHARING TOO MUCH

SHARING TOO LITTLE

TAKEAWAYS

1. Show vulnerability when assessing a difficult situation, but present a clear path forward.
2. Become a student of the people you manage: avoid telling people what to feel, listen carefully, and manage individually.
3. Prioritize yourself and seek support from other leaders to avoid emotional leaks that negatively affect your reports.
4. Understand the challenges you and others may face in leadership positions and take steps to reduce them.

Conclusion

Most of us grew up with the idea that mixing feelings and work is a recipe for disaster. We wrote this book to dispel that myth. You *can* bring emotion into the workplace without causing chaos, but timing, context, and delivery all matter. Try not to schedule meetings with your boss on days when you know she'll be stressed or frustrated. During a difficult conversation, calmly address how you feel; don't raise your voice or roll your eyes. Save kind or funny notes in a folder you can revisit when work gets tough. These are all ways to make your work life better—and they all center around feelings. Success (*real* success, the kind measured not only in dollars and perks) happens when you open yourself to emotion.

Our hope is that you go in to work tomorrow and start to listen to, learn from, and express your emotions in a more effective and fulfilling way (you can use the seven New Rules of Emotion at Work as your cheat sheet). It's not always easy to accept and discuss emotion at work. But when you do, you'll find that feelings stop getting in the way and instead become signposts to guide you on your career path. After all, anticipation and regret let us narrow down our set of choices and make better decisions. Envy can be an internal compass that reveals what we value. Gratitude and a sense of purpose give us the willpower to come into the office on dreary Monday mornings.

WHAT PEOPLE THINK
BEING EMOTIONAL MEANS

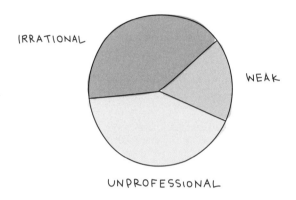

IRRATIONAL

WEAK

UNPROFESSIONAL

WHAT IT REALLY MEANS

YOU ARE
HUMAN

If you're looking for more ways to better understand and harness your feelings, here are three resources we've put together for you:

- For handy reference, we've collected all the chapter takeaways for you in the next section.
- A guide to useful emotional skills (including emotional intelligence,

emotional regulation, and emotional agility) and a detailed look at how scientists define emotion on page 239.

- An emotional tendencies assessment on our website: lizandmollie .com/assessment. You can find a flash version of the assessment on page 247.

Feel feelings!

Liz AND Mollie

New Rules of Emotion at Work

Phew—this book has many pages. Here are two handy summaries:

Twitter summary: *No Hard Feelings* is a visual guide for how to embrace emotion at work and become more authentic and fulfilled—while still staying professional.

Slightly longer summary: *No Hard Feelings* is a wickedly funny illustrated guide to unrepressing your emotions at work, finding constructive channels even for jealousy and anxiety, demystifying digital interactions and coworker communication styles, and ultimately allowing you to bring your best self to work.

TAKEAWAYS FROM ALL CHAPTERS

Health

1. Take the break you can, whether it's a vacation, a day off, or a mini-break.
2. Make time to be rigorously unproductive, see friends and family, and step away from your email and phone.

3. Stop feeling bad about feeling bad. Reframe your stress as motivation or excitement.

4. Prevent rumination by viewing your thoughts as simply thoughts, not as inevitable truths. Stay in the present and take care of the things within your control.

Motivation

1. To increase your autonomy, make small changes to your schedule.

2. Job craft: shift your responsibilities toward the things you enjoy to make your work more meaningful.

3. Push yourself to acquire new skills. The more you know, the more you'll enjoy your work.

4. Invest in workplace friendships to give yourself another reason to look forward to work.

Decision Making

1. Recognize that listening to your feelings is not the same as acting on your feelings.

2. Keep relevant emotions (those related to the decision you're facing), toss irrelevant emotions (those unrelated to the decision you're facing).

3. Do not rely on emotion when deciding whether or not to hire a candidate. Use structured interviews to reduce biased hiring decisions.

4. Before an external negotiation, come to an inner consensus.

Teams

1. Create psychological safety by encouraging open discussion, answering questions without condescension, and making it okay to take risks and admit mistakes.

2. Don't shy away from task conflict. Instead, create structures that prevent creative clashes from becoming personal.

3. For relationship conflict, listen to the other person and calmly share your perspective.

4. Get rid of (or if you can't, contain) bad apples to preserve psychological safety on your team.

Communication

1. During a difficult conversation, calmly address your feelings without making assumptions.

2. Be aware of communication tendencies to better understand the intention behind someone's words.

3. Make criticism specific and actionable. Ask the recipient how they prefer to receive to feedback.

4. Emotionally proofread what you write before hitting Send.

Culture

1. Be kind; emotions are contagious, which means your actions can have a positive influence on your entire organization's emotional culture.

2. Create a culture of belonging through microactions: say hello, invite people into conversations, or help a new hire meet others.

3. Share stories about who you are, not what you do, and invite others to do the same.

4. Don't ignore the emotional burdens your colleagues may carry.

Leadership

1. Show vulnerability when assessing a difficult situation, but present a clear path forward.

2. Become a student of the people you manage: avoid telling people what to feel, listen carefully, and manage individually.

3. Prioritize yourself and seek support from other leaders to avoid emotional leaks that negatively affect your reports.

4. Understand the challenges you and others may face in leadership positions and take steps to reduce them.

Further Resources on Emotions

Still curious? We've put together a guide to the most common emotional skills needed for the workplace: emotional intelligence, emotion regulation, and emotional agility. But first . . .

WHAT EVEN IS AN EMOTION?

The psychologists Beverley Fehr and James Russell said it best: "Everyone knows what an emotion is, until asked to give a definition." The most visible aspect of an emotion is a facial expression. If we asked you to show us "fear," you would probably widen your eyes and open your mouth. But would any person, regardless of how or where they were raised, be able to interpret your expression as "fear"?

Scientists fall into two camps. The first argues that humans share an innate set of emotions, which they express in the same way. This camp tends to view emotions as hardwired products of evolutionary instincts that motivate us to act in ways that promote survival. The plot of the Pixar movie *Inside Out* is based on this theory. The movie's five main characters, Joy, Sadness, Fear, Anger, and Disgust, represent the emotions that live inside our brains as separate entities and press buttons to control our behavior.

The second camp points to scientific evidence that emotions are not universal but rather learned and shaped by culture. Psychologist and neuroscientist Lisa Feldman Barrett, a leading proponent of this view, explained to us, "Emotions are not your reactions to the world; they are your brain's way of making meaning."

Say your heart starts beating wildly. Are you afraid or are you excited? If your boss just emailed you, "We need to talk about your performance lately," you might attribute your racing heart to fear. But if instead your crush just confessed how much they like you, you might interpret the thump in your chest as excitement (although Liz says for her this is another "fear" situation).

CAMP 1: EMOTIONS ARE UNIVERSAL

CAMP 2: EMOTIONS ARE SHAPED
BY CULTURE

Barrett explains, "Utku Eskimos have no concept of 'anger.' The Tahitians have no concept of 'sadness.' This last item is very difficult for Westerners to accept . . . life without sadness? Really? When Tahitians are in a situation that a Westerner would describe as sad, they feel ill, troubled, fatigued, or unenthusiastic, all of which are covered by their broader term *pe'ape'a*." Westerners, in comparison, are taught the concepts of "anger" and "sadness" as children. Why does this matter? When you're judging someone's emotion based on their facial expression, that perception is coming from you, not from the other person. According to Barrett, we're able to perceive a "happy" face as happy because we are socialized to do so, not because of evolution.

Barrett's research also shows there is nothing inherently "bitchy" about resting bitch face, or RBF (here's a handy definition from *Urban Dictionary*: "a person, girl especially, whose regular facial expression makes them look like a bitch"). In 2015 *The New York Times* reported that women were resorting to plastic surgery to escape the tyranny of RBF. "When you look at someone's face, it feels like you read emotion," Barrett told us. "But you're reading it based on past experience. These faces are structurally neutral. When you see a bitchy face, that perception is coming from you." So the next time someone mentions RBF, you can correct them: "Actually it's resting neutral face."

Dealing with Emotion, Day-to-Day: Three Core Emotional Skills

Here are three core skills that will help you understand and effectively express emotion.

Emotional Intelligence

Emotional intelligence (EQ) is the ability to acknowledge, understand, and express your emotions and to handle relationships with empathy. Workers high in EQ are better able to cooperate, manage conflict, and make thoughtful decisions. Without emotional intelligence, warns psychologist Daniel Goleman, "no amount of attention to the bottom line will protect your career."

EQ does *not* involve sharing every feeling you have with every person you encounter. People with high EQ channel and filter emotions in ways that help them become more effective. This requires:

JOB CHECKLIST

☑ REVIEW DECK
☑ RESEARCH
☑ WRITE MEMO
☐ EMAIL CLIENT
☐ SCHEDULE MEETINGS
☐ ACKNOWLEDGE EMOTION
☐ UNDERSTAND EMOTION
☐ EXPRESS EMOTION EFFECTIVELY

• **Acknowledgment.** Mollie wakes up and feels anxious. She doesn't suppress (or express) this emotion, she simply gives herself permission to feel and observe it.

• **Understanding.** Mollie realizes she is nervous because of an upcoming book deadline. Liz is working on a chapter draft but hasn't emailed Mollie in a few days.

• **Expression.** That morning, Mollie sends Liz a friendly text. "Hi!" she writes. "I'm confident you're going to get this done, but you know me—I get anxious about deadlines. I want to respect your process, but do you think we could review the chapter together this afternoon?" After a few minutes, Liz writes back, "Of course! Didn't mean to make you anxious," and Mollie feels the tension drain from her shoulders.

Emotion Regulation

Surveys about fear reveal that we are more afraid of public speaking than we are of dying. Say you have to give a presentation in front of fifty of your colleagues. Your anxiety might make you stumble over your words, sweat profusely, or freeze.

The ability to regulate your emotions can be a life- (and job) saver. You can manage which emotions you experience, when you experience them, and how you react to them. Even though emotions can be useful signals, they can also hurt, come at the wrong time, or be too intense. Three common ways to regulate your emotions are reappraisal (when you reframe how you see a situation), suppression (when you actively avoid an emotion by shifting your focus), and response control (when you stifle your laughter or take deep breaths to calm your body).

Say you're the anxious public speaker we described above. If you practice extensively, you will build confidence and decrease the anxiety you feel during the presentation (and the amount of emotion you need to regulate). If you memorize the first few sentences of your presentation, you will be able to launch into the talk without any initial anxieties.

Emotional Agility

LIZ: My partner and I have a rule where we tell the other when one of us is stuck in an emotion. For example, if I feel irritable, I say, "I'm grumpy right now, but it has nothing to do with you—I think it might have to do with an upcoming deadline or the humidity." This prevents us from getting into a grump spiral where he feels like I'm upset with him so he becomes confused and grumpy, which makes me confused and more grumpy.

At work, we tap into a constant stream of emotions. Some of these emotions are positive and some are downright difficult. Psychologist Susan David advises that instead of trying to distract yourself from your difficult emotions through affirmations and to-do lists, you can unhook yourself from them. This does not mean you should ignore them, but rather, work through them so their existence doesn't define your entire mood. There are four steps to unhooking yourself from difficult emotions:

1. Notice difficult emotions

Let's say you're on a project team and one of your team members suggests big changes right before the deadline. You start to get annoyed. Instead of snapping at your coworker, pause and observe the feeling.

2. Label each emotion

EMOTIONAL GRANULARITY BIRD

I'M NOT ANGRY, I'M JUST DISAPPOINTED

The ability to describe complex feelings, to distinguish awesome from happy, content, or thrilled, is called emotional granularity. Emotional granularity is linked with better emotion regulation and a lower likelihood to become vindictive when stressed. People who have this skill "have a texture to the way they are able to talk about emotions: not only what they are feeling but the intensity with which they are feeling," says LeeAnn Renninger, neuroscientist and founder of workplace training firm LifeLabs Learning.

In the project team example, without emotional granularity you might say something lacking specifics. "I have a bad feeling and I'm not liking the way this project is going." But with emotional granularity, you'll be able to realize that by "I'm feeling annoyed," you really mean, "I'm worried that we won't have time to make these changes."

Emotional vocabulary words: To help you get started on expanding your emotional vocabulary, here are three of our favorite lesser-known emotion words. *Ilinx* (French): the elated disorientation caused by random acts of destruction, like kicking the office copy machine. *Malu* (Dusun Baguk people of Indonesia): the awkward feeling around people of higher status, like riding an elevator with the CEO of your company. *Pronoia* (English): the creeping feeling that everyone is involved in a conspiracy to help you.

3. Understand the need behind each emotion

Once you've labeled each emotion, flip your perspective and explicitly state what you'd like to be feeling instead. Dwelling on a difficult feeling will only enhance that feeling. Instead, ask yourself, "What do I *want* to feel?" If you'd like to feel calm instead of anxious, figure out what you need to do to successfully relax. In the project team example, that might be ensuring stability: you want the project plan to stay on track.

4. Express your needs

Once you've identified your need, articulate it. Don't say, "I'm annoyed by this request for last-minute changes." Try, "Your edits are good, but because we are down to the wire, stability and predictability are important. What edits do we have time for? How can we make this work?"

THE EMOTIONAL EMPLOYEE'S JOURNEY

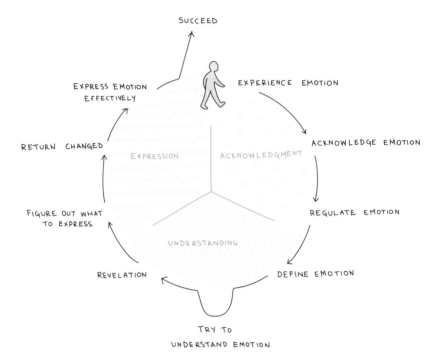

SUCCEED

EXPRESS EMOTION
EFFECTIVELY

EXPERIENCE EMOTION

ACKNOWLEDGE EMOTION

RETURN CHANGED

EXPRESSION

ACKNOWLEDGMENT

REGULATE EMOTION

FIGURE OUT WHAT
TO EXPRESS

UNDERSTANDING

REVELATION

DEFINE EMOTION

TRY TO
UNDERSTAND EMOTION

Emotional Tendencies Assessment

How do I apply everything I've learned?

To help you make the skills in this book actionable, we've created a three-part assessment. The assessment will help you learn about:

1. Your own emotional tendencies
2. Your team's emotional culture
3. Your organization's emotion norms

An awareness of these three areas means you will know where to focus your energy as you apply what you read in this book.

To take the full free assessments, go to lizandmollie.com/assessment.

We recommend taking the full version, but we've included a short flash-assessment version on three topic areas here in the book.

Flash assessment

Assess: Your emotional expression tendency

1. You've just lost some of your work due to a Save error right before a deadline. You're upset. Which of the following best describes you?
   a. I'm fuming on the inside but not showing or verbalizing it at all

      b. My facial expression is pained, I'm taking deep breaths, and I tell my immediate neighbor I'm annoyed

      c. I'm visibly upset and venting to anyone around me

2. Your team just finished an important milestone. Which of the following best describes you?

      a. Proudly but subtly smiling

      b. Excitedly texting my partner

      c. On top of the world. I'm hugging my team and gushing to everyone we see in the hallway

3. How would your colleagues most likely describe you?

      a. Mysterious

      b. Even-keeled

      c. An open book

Mostly As: You're an **under-emoter**, meaning you are less expressive about your emotions. People feel they can come to you if they are upset or have a problem, because you'll be able to calmly figure out a way forward. However, they sometimes misinterpret your silence as a lack of urgency or excitement. It may take time for people to trust you, because it's hard for them to read you.

Your main opportunity: Try to find moments when you can be more vulnerable (**especially if you're a leader—see the section on selective vulnerability in chapter 8: "Leadership"**). Be careful to not bottle up your negative feelings so much that they begin to negatively affect you or come out in unhealthy ways. **See the section on the positivity paradox in chapter 2: "Health."**

Mostly Bs: You're an **even-emoter**. You are somewhat emotionally expressive. You can get visibly excited but you usually rein in your excitement or frustration.

Your main opportunity: Focus on understanding what types of situations make you feel comfortable expressing your emotions and what situations don't. **See the section on selective vulnerability in chapter 8: "Leadership."**

Mostly Cs: You're an **over-emoter,** meaning you are highly emotionally expressive. People always know how you're feeling, and others come to you when they have exciting news or just need an energy boost. Your open emotional expression signals trustworthiness, but it might also make people perceive you as unstable.

Your main opportunity: Focus on understanding when it's productive to express your unfiltered emotions and when you might be unconsciously affecting those around you. Instead of getting swept up by your feelings, take a moment to calm down before acting on them. **See the section on emotional contagion in chapter 7: "Culture," and the section on emotional regulation in chapter 8: "Leadership."**

(Source: LeeAnn Renninger, LifeLabs Learning)

Assess: Your team's psychological safety

Respond to each statement by selecting a number to indicate how much you agree or disagree with the statement.

1. If I make a mistake on my team, it is often held against me
   Strongly disagree 1 — 2 — 3 — 4 — 5 — 6 — 7 Strongly agree

2. Members of my team are able to bring up problems and tough issues
   Strongly disagree 1 — 2 — 3 — 4 — 5 — 6 — 7 Strongly agree

3. It is safe to take a risk on this team
   Strongly disagree 1 — 2 — 3 — 4 — 5 — 6 — 7 Strongly agree

4. It is difficult to ask other members of this team for help
   Strongly disagree 1 — 2 — 3 — 4 — 5 — 6 — 7 Strongly agree

5. Working with members of this team, my unique skills and talents are valued and utilized
   Strongly disagree 1 — 2 — 3 — 4 — 5 — 6 — 7 Strongly agree

Scoring: Step 1: Add up your score from 2, 3, and 5 to find a subtotal. Step 2: 1 and 4 are reverse scored, so subtract each of your answer choices from 8 (8 minus your answer choice number) and then add them together with the subtotal.

Score of 0–15: Your team is psychologically unsafe! Team members do not feel comfortable throwing out new ideas or pointing out potential problems.

You and your team's main opportunity: Start small and model the behavior you wish to see. Invite someone on your team to weigh in with a point of view or contribute a new idea, even when it might challenge the group. Then acknowledge and thank the person on the team for taking a risk. **See the section on psychological safety in chapter 5: "Teams."**

Score of 16–30: Your team has some psychological safety, but could increase it. You and/or other team members sometimes, but not always, feel you can suggest ideas, admit mistakes, and take risks without being embarrassed by the group.

Your team's main opportunity: Identify the behaviors that are contributing to a sense of psychological safety and try to increase them. Try asking each team member to write their thoughts and then have everyone share out loud. Additionally, ask follow-up questions such as "Can you say more about that?" **See the section on psychological safety in chapter 5: "Teams."**

Score of more than 30: Your team has a good amount of psychological safety. You and your team members feel that you can usually share your thoughts and ideas and know you'll be respected.

Your team's main opportunity: You can always increase psychological safety by trying new methods. Try doing unusual team-building activities together to build trust. Or try asking questions such as "When you think of your childhood, what meal comes to mind and why?" to get a deeper story about someone's life and family. **See the section on psychological safety in chapter 5: "Teams."**

(Source: Modified from Amy Edmondson's Team Psychological Safety Assessment)

Assess: Your sense of belonging within your organization

Respond to each statement by selecting a number to indicate how much you agree or disagree with the statement.

1. I generally feel that people accept me in my organization
   Strongly disagree 1 — 2 — 3 — 4 — 5 — 6 — 7 Strongly agree

2. I feel like a misplaced piece that doesn't fit into the larger puzzle of the organization
   Strongly disagree 1 — 2 — 3 — 4 — 5 — 6 — 7 Strongly agree

3. I would like to make a difference to people around me at work, but I don't feel that what I have to offer is valued
   Strongly disagree 1 — 2 — 3 — 4 — 5 — 6 — 7 Strongly agree

4. I feel like an outsider in most situations in my organization
   Strongly disagree 1 — 2 — 3 — 4 — 5 — 6 — 7 Strongly agree

5. I am uncomfortable that my background and experiences are so different from those who are usually around me in the organization
   Strongly disagree 1 — 2 — 3 — 4 — 5 — 6 — 7 Strongly agree

Scoring: Step 1: 2, 3, 4, and 5 are reverse scored, so subtract each of your answer choices from 8 (8 minus your answer choice number) and then add them up to get a subtotal. Step 2: Add your answer choice number from 1 to your subtotal.

Score of 0–15: You don't feel a sense of belonging. You do not feel safe and valued for expressing your true self.

Your main opportunity: Understand that it's normal to lack a sense of belonging in the first year of a new job. Try to identify the situations in which you don't feel a sense of belonging: Is it in certain settings (like video calls) or with certain groups of people? Then try to find a culture buddy or mentor who can help you decode these situations. This is someone who understands the culture and can answer your questions and give feedback on items small (e.g., how the tone of your emails is coming across) to large (e.g., helping you understand that feeling out of place is normal). **Note:** When you still frequently lack a sense of belonging after two years, it's time to think about moving to a different group or organization. **See the section on belonging in chapter 7: "Culture."**

Score of 16–30: You feel some sense of belonging. You mainly feel safe and valued for expressing your true self, but there is still room for improvement.

Your main opportunity: Remember that feeling like you belong doesn't mean work will suddenly be a walk in the park—it means the normal ups and downs of office life won't cause you quite so much stress. Look for ways to model creating a sense of belonging in your own team. For example, assume good intentions. If a colleague you know and trust makes a misstep, explain why their behavior made you feel excluded and propose an alternate action. **See the section on belonging in chapter 7: "Culture."**

Score of more than 30: You feel a good sense of belonging. You feel that you can usually share your thoughts and know you'll be respected and heard.

Your main opportunity: You can always increase the sense of belonging for others on the team. Offer to be a culture buddy or mentor for someone else. Help them understand the culture by answering questions and giving feedback on small items like email tone. Remind them that it's normal to not feel a sense of belonging during the first few months of a new job. **See the section on belonging in chapter 7: "Culture."**

(Source: Modified from the Sense of Belonging Inventory)

Acknowledgments

Writing a book takes a village. Mollie and Liz would like to thank the following:

Leah Trouwborst, true believer and editor extraordinaire, was generous with time, ideas, and enthusiasm. Lisa DiMona, phenomenal agent and friend, was our earliest champion and thought partner. Julie Mosow, our wise editing partner, helped us shape our narrative and brought out the best of our voices.

Team at Writers House: Nora Long was a patient and sage editor who helped us clarify our message. Alessandra Birch, Natalie Medina, Maja Nikolic, Katie Stuart, Peggy Boulos Smith, and everyone else at the agency were a joy to work with.

Team at Penguin: Adrian Zackheim, whose elegant articulation of the need for our book inspired us, Niki Papadopoulos, Will Weisser, Helen Healey, Tara Gilbride, Chris Sergio, Karl Spurzem, Alyssa Adler, Cassie Pappas, Madeline Montgomery, Margot Stamas, and Lillian Ball were helpful from start to finish.

All of the experts who gave us valuable time and ideas: Angela Antony, Erica Baker, Lisa Feldman Barrett, Sigal Barsade, Matt Breitfelder, Laszlo Bock, Julia Byers, B. Byrne, Jerry Colonna, Susan David, Brian Fetherstonaugh, Bill George, Chris Gomes, Paul Green, James Gross, Frans Johansson, Sarah Kalloch, Rem Konig, Anne Kreamer, Tom Lehman, Niki Lustig,

Cade Massey, Jonathan McBride, Patty McCord, Julianna Pillemer, Daniel Pink, LeeAnn Renninger, Kisha Richardson, Jonathan Roiser, Carissa Romero, Julia Rozovsky, Gretchen Rubin, Laura Savino, Jill Schwartzman, Kim Scott, Courtney Seiter, Jo Shapiro, Ashleigh Showler, Deborah Stamm, Deborah Tannen, Emily Stecker Truelove, Giles Turnbull, Pat Wadors, Greg Walton, Hannah Weisman, Brian Welle, Megan Wheeler, Cameron White, Adia Harvey Wingfield, Keith Yamashita, and Ilan Zechory.

For early conversations with us that helped shape the direction of our book: Dana Asher, Mette Norgaard, Wendy Palmer, Duncan Coombe, Art Markman, Karl Pillemer, and Kate Earle.

To Susan Cain, for helping us embrace being introverts and for giving us the opportunity to share with your Quiet Revolution community.

To Gabe Novais, for introducing us and for many years of friendship.

FROM LIZ:

To Mollie, for the perfect balance of patience and push and for making this one of the most fun and rewarding things I've done in my life.

Mom and Dad, for always picking up the phone, for telling me my punch lines are funny and (when you don't understand the punch lines) my drawings are cute, for supporting me in all my creative pursuits, and for making me happy when life becomes sad. I am grateful to be your daughter and proud you are my parents.

Maxim, for the illustration brainstorms, syntax improvements, and research audits. Your edits, advice, patience, and humor made this book better. You make my life better. I'm very lucky.

All of my past colleagues and bosses, especially Andy Wong for being my guiding light, the Rap Genius #beehive for all the LOLs, and Peter Sims for all your support and generosity.

To everyone who helped make this book happen. Some of you read drafts of this book, some of you shared your most personal work highs and lows, and some of you made me smile when I was in the creative dumps. Thank you to Marina Agapakis, Carmen Aiken, Vivek Ashok, Mat Brown, B. Byrne,

Meghan Casserly, Amit Chatwani, Misha Chellam, Mathew Chow, Nick DeWilde, Ryan Dick, Elicia Epstein, Tomi Fischer, Kevin Frick, Brenna Hull, Becca Jacobs, Iris Jong, Hee-Sun Kang, Clare Lambert, Maya Lopuch, Nathalie Miller, Lila Murphy, Jason Nemirow, The Red Wine Society, Jess Seok, Natalie Sun, Erik Torenberg, Christine Tsang, Charley Wang, and Hannah Yung.

Finally, no thank you to Reddit for distracting me so much throughout this process.

FROM MOLLIE:

To Liz, for friendship, commitment to working through ups and downs to build a dream partnership, and for all the smiles your illustrations bring me.

To all the Seattle public school teachers who encouraged my writing: Molly Peterson, Norm Hollingshead, Tara McBennett, Mark Lovre, Laura Strentz, and Steve Miranda. Three professors at Brown inspired my interest in studying organizations: Barrett Hazeltine, Danny Warshay, and Alan Harlam. I still remember what I learned from each of you, and I wouldn't be here today without you.

To my 444 sisterhood, for being a constant source of ideas, laughs, and positivity. To my Seattle ladies, for both inspiring me and grounding me. Sophie Egan, thank you for encouragement and always being a phone call away.

To my Culture Lab friends: Liza Conrad, Kelly Ceynowa, Allie Mahler, Aimee Styler, Josh Levine, and Emily Tsiang.

To all my current and former IDEO colleagues, who helped inform my thinking on emotions at work. In particular, Duane Bray, Roshi Givechi, Ingrid Fetell Lee, Diana Rhoten, Heather Currier Hunt, Anna Silverstein, and Mat Chow were excellent sounding boards. Loren Flaherty Blackman provided invaluable design guidance for the cover. Debbe Stern, Whitney Mortimer, and Hailey Brewer, thanks for the writing guidance and support during my time at IDEO.

To all of my past colleagues and managers for expertise and guidance over the years.

Lifelong thanks to my family for believing in me and teaching me what's important. Particularly Laura, for knowing and loving the realest version of me, and for our shared sense of humor that only sisters can understand; Kate, for unconditional support, teaching me the value of curiosity, and encouragement to do what I love; David, for a strong set of values, an interest in the world of work, and for reminding me not to take life too seriously; Jackie, for emotional wisdom and warmth; and the Duffys, for generosity, positivity, and laughter.

Most of all: Chris, my better half, for bringing out the best in me and for leaning in extra through this writing process. You are a constant source of wonder, kindness, and humor to everyone who's lucky enough to be around you. You make me the happiest.

Notes

CHAPTER 1: THE FUTURE IS EMOTIONAL

10 **EQ is a better predictor of success in the workplace than IQ:** Harvey Deutchendorf, "Why Emotionally Intelligent People Are More Successful," *Fast Company*, June 22, 2015, www.fastcompany.com/3047455/why-emotionally-intelligent-people-are-more-successful.

10 **capacity to productively sense emotion:** Chip Conley, *Emotional Equations* (New York: Atria, 2013).

10–11 **capacity to communicate verbally with others:** Susan Adams, "The 10 Skills Employers Most Want in 2015 Graduates," *Forbes*, November 12, 2014, www.forbes.com/sites/susanadams/2014/11/12/the-10-skills-employers-most-want-in-2015-graduates/#6920eae42511.

11 **"collaboration is next to godliness":** "The Collaboration Curse," *The Economist*, January 23, 2016, www.economist.com/news/business/21688872-fashion-making-employees-collaborate-has-gone-too-far-collaboration-curse.

CHAPTER 2: HEALTH

19 **time to take Drake's advice:** The rapper, not Sir Francis.

22 **lobby of its Manhattan headquarters:** Joseph Heath, *The Efficient Society* (Toronto: Penguin Canada, 2002), 153.

22 **"You work, and then you die":** Andrea Peterson, "Metaphor of Corporate Display: 'You Work, and Then You Die,'" *Wall Street Journal*, November 8, 1996.

23 **after working about fifty hours per week:** Gretchen Rubin, "The Data Revealed a Big Surprise: Top Performers Do Less," GretchenRubin.com, accessed April 8, 2018, https://gretchenrubin.com/2018/02/morten-hansen.

23 **"unplugging, recharging, and renewing yourself":** Grace Nasri, "Advice from 7 Women Leaders Who Navigated the Male-Dominated Tech Scene," *Fast Company*, June 12, 2014, www.fastcompany.com/3031772/advice-from-7-women-leaders-who-navigated-the-male-dominated-tech-scene.

24 **Extended time off keeps us healthy and productive:** "A 20-Year Retrospective on the Durfee Foundation Sabbatical Program from Creative Disruption to Systems Change," September 2017, https://durfee.org/durfee-content/uploads/2017/10/Durfee-Sabbatical-Report-FINAL.pdf.

24 **half of Americans don't take all of their paid vacation:** Quentin Fottrell, "The Sad Reason Half of Americans Don't Take All Their Paid Vacation," *MarketWatch*, May 28, 2017, www.marketwatch.com/story/55-of-american-workers-dont-take-all-their-paid-vacation-2016-06-15.

25 **everyone would use more vacation time:** "The High Price of Silence: Analyzing the Business Implications of an Under-Vacationed Workforce," *Project: Time Off*, accessed April 8, 2018, www.projecttimeoff.com/research/high-price-silence.

25 **"make sure that people were not getting burned out":** "Remaking the Workplace, One Night Off at a Time," *Knowledge@Wharton*, July 3, 2012, http://knowledge.wharton.upenn.edu/article/remaking-the-workplace-one-night-off-at-a-time.

26 **friendly-looking faces as menacing:** Matthew Walker, *Why We Sleep: Unlocking the Power of Sleep and Dreams* (New York: Scribner, 2017), Kindle.

26 **helps you relax—and stay focused:** "Brief Diversions Vastly Improve Focus, Researchers Find," *Science Daily*, February 8, 2011, www.sciencedaily.com/releases/2011/02/110208131529.htm.

26 **Danish students who were given a short break:** Hans Henrik Sievertsen, Francesca Gino, and Marco Piovesan, "Cognitive Fatigue Influences Students' Performance on Standardized Tests," *Proceedings of the National Academy of Sciences*, February 16, 2016, www.pnas.org/content/early/2016/02/09/1516947113.

26 **help you de-stress faster than a solo break:** Dan Pink, *When: The Scientific Secrets of Perfect Timing* (New York: Riverhead, 2018), Kindle.

27 **weight training boosts your mood more than cardio:** Bertheussen GF et al., "Associations between Physical Activity and Physical and Mental Health—a HUNT 3 Study," *Med Sci Sports Exercise* 43, no. 7 (July 2011): 1220–28, www.ncbi.nlm.nih.gov/pubmed/21131869.

27 **"I said the termination phrase":** Cal Newport, "Drastically Reduce Stress with a Work Shutdown Ritual," CalNewport.com, June 8, 2009, http://calnewport.com/blog/2009/06/08/drastically-reduce-stress-with-a-work-shutdown-ritual.

28 **tracking our steps or measuring miles hiked:** Jordan Etkin, "The Hidden Cost of Personal Quantification," *Journal of Consumer Research* 42, no. 6 (April 1, 2016): 967–84, https://academic.oup.com/jcr/article-abstract/42/6/967/2358309.

28 **Beyoncé told *GQ* in an interview:** Amy Wallace, "Miss Millennium: Beyoncé," *GQ*, January 10, 2013, www.gq.com/story/beyonce-cover-story-interview-gq-february-2013.

29 **"having enough time for yourself":** Rebecca J. Rosen, "Why Do Americans Work So Much?" *The Atlantic*, January 7, 2016, www.theatlantic.com/business/archive/2016/01/inequality-work-hours/422775.

29 **people we care about makes us happy:** Cristobal Young and Chaeyoon Lim, "Time as a Network Good: Evidence from Unemployment and the Standard Workweek," *Sociological Science* 1, no. 2 (February 18, 2014), www.sociologicalscience.com/time-network-good.

29 **a leading researcher of burnout:** Kenneth R. Rosen, "How to Recognize Burnout before You're Burned Out," *New York Times*, September 5, 2017, www.nytimes.com/2017/09/05 /smarter-living/workplace-burnout-symptoms.html.

31 **"can do the work while I'm away":** Sarah Green Carmichael, "Millennials Are Actually Workaholics, According to Research," *Harvard Business Review*, August 17, 2016, https://hbr .org/2016/08/millennials-are-actually-workaholics-according-to-research.

32 **pleasure networks in our brains:** Annie McKee and Kandi Wiens, "Prevent Burnout by Making Compassion a Habit," *Harvard Business Review*, May 11, 2017, https://hbr.org /2017/05/prevent-burnout-by-making-compassion-a-habit.

32 **author of** *Where the Wild Things Are***:** Emma Brockes, interview with Maurice Sendak, *The Believer*, November 2012, www.believermag.com/issues/201211/?read=interview_sendak.

33 **twice as much as she thinks she does:** Sally Andrews et al., "Beyond Self-report: Tools to Compare Estimated and Real-World Smartphone Use," *PLoS ONE* 10, no. 10 (October 2015), https://doi.org/10.1371/journal.pone.0139004.

33 **only to realize it's not even there:** Michelle Drouin, "Phantom Vibrations among Under-graduates: Prevalence and Associated Psychological Characteristics," *Computers in Human Behavior* 28, no. 4 (July 2012): 1490–96, www.sciencedirect.com/science/article/pii/S07475 63212000799.

33 **you feel tired and unfocused:** Daniel J. Levitin, "Hit the Reset Button in Your Brain," *New York Times*, August 9, 2014, www.nytimes.com/2014/08/10/opinion/sunday/hit-the-reset -button-in-your-brain.html.

34 **"SUGGEST: PUT DOWN YOUR PHONE":** Shonda Rhimes, *Year of Yes* (New York: Simon & Schuster, 2016), Kindle.

34 **Employees cannot send one another emails on weeknights:** "Zzzmail," Vynamic.com, ac-cessed April 8, 2018, https://vynamic.com/zzzmail.

35 **writes psychologist Donald Campbell:** Steven Pinker, *How the Mind Works* (New York: W. W. Norton, 1997), Kindle.

35 **something bad happened, but something good resulted:** Brad Stulberg, "Become More Resilient by Learning to Take Joy Seriously," *New York*, April 28, 2017, http://nymag.com /scienceofus/2017/04/become-morresilient-by-learning-to-take-joy-seriously.html.

36 **a lot of employees sulked in satisfaction:** T-Mobile USA, Inc. v. NLRB, No. 16–60284 (5th Cir. 2017), https://law.justia.com/cases/federal/appellate-courts/ca5/16–60284/16–60284 –2017–07–25.html.

37 **lower well-being than their more self-accepting peers:** Brett Q. Ford et al., "The Psychological Health Benefits of Accepting Negative Emotions and Thoughts: Laboratory, Diary, and Lon-gitudinal Evidence," *Journal of Personality Social Psychology*, July 2017, www.ncbi.nlm.nih .gov/pubmed/28703602.

37 **"cope with their stress more successfully":** Yasmin Anwar, "Feeling bad about feeling bad can make you feel worse," *Berkeley News*, August 10, 2017, http://news.berkeley.edu/2017/08 /10/emotionalacceptance.

38 **work hard to avoid those situations:** Julie K. Norem and Nancy Cantor, "Defensive Pessi-mism: Harnessing Anxiety as Motivation," *Journal of Personality and Social Psychology* 51, no. 6 (1986): 120817, http://psycnet.apa.org/record/1987–13154–001.

38 **defensive pessimists are forced to cheer up:** Julie K. Norem and Edward C. Chang, "The Positive Psychology of Negative Thinking," *Journal of Clinical Psychology* 50, no. 9 (2002): 993–1001, http://homepages.se.edu/cvonbergen/files/2012/12/The-Positive-Psychology-of-Negative-Thinking.pdf.

38 **identical to our body's response to excitement:** Olga Khazan, "Can Three Words Turn Anxiety into Success?" *The Atlantic*, March 23, 2016, www.theatlantic.com/health/archive/2016/03/can-three-words-turn-anxiety-into-success/474909.

38 **reframing their stress as excitement:** Alison Wood Brooks, "Get Excited: Reappraising Pre-Performance Anxiety as Excitement," *Journal of Experimental Psychology* 143, no. 3 (2014): 114458, www.apa.org/pubs/journals/releases/xge-a0035325.pdf.

38–39 **better able to handle stress:** Emma Janette Rowland, "Emotional Geographies of Care Work in the NHS," *Royal Holloway University of London*, https://pure.royalholloway.ac.uk/portal/files/23742468/final_submission_1st_december_2014.pdf.

39 **people listening to you feel worse:** Margot Bastin et al., "Brooding and Reflecting in an Interpersonal Context," *Personality and Individual Differences* 63 (2014): 100–105, https://lirias.kuleuven.be/bitstream/123456789/439101/2/post+print+Brooding+and+Reflecting+in+an+Interpersonal+Context_Bastin+(2014).pdf.

39 **women feeling more anxious and depressed:** Amanda J. Rose, "Co-rumination in the Friendships of Girls and Boys," *Child Development* 73, no. 6 (November–December 2002): 1830–43, www.ncbi.nlm.nih.gov/pubmed/12487497.

40 **push you to resolve the issue:** Adam Grant, "*The Daily Show*'s Secret to Creativity," *WorkLife Podcast*, March 7, 2018, www.linkedin.com/pulse/daily-shows-secret-creativity-adam-grant.

40 **Uncertainty feels bad:** Achim Peters et al., "Uncertainty and Stress: Why It Causes Diseases and How It Is Mastered by the Brain," *Progress in Neurobiology* 156 (September 2017): 164–88, www.sciencedirect.com/science/article/pii/S0301008217300369.

40 **lack of direction from our bosses:** Morten Hansen, *Great at Work* (New York: Simon & Schuster, 2018).

40 **twice as much vacation as their colleagues:** Amanda Eisenberg, "Vacation Time Can Boost Employee Performance," *Employee Benefit Advisor,* July 31, 2017, www.employeebenefitadviser.com/news/vacation-time-can-boost-employee-performance.

40 **notes Flickr cofounder Caterina Fake:** Caterina Fake, "Working Hard Is Overrated," *Business Insider*, September 28, 2009, www.businessinsider.com/working-hard-is-overrated-2009-9.

41 **half our time focused on the present:** Matthew A. Killingsworth and Daniel T. Gilbert, "A Wandering Mind Is an Unhappy Mind," *Science* 330, no. 6006 (Nov 2010): 932, www.ncbi.nlm.nih.gov/pubmed/21071660.

41 **wandering mind is usually an unhappy mind:** Ibid.

41 **elements of a problem to better understand it:** Nicholas Petrie, "Pressure Doesn't Have to Turn into Stress," *Harvard Business Review*, March 16, 2017, https://hbr.org/2017/03/pressure-doesnt-have-to-turn-into-stress.

43 **If you find yourself pessimistically obsessing:** Stulberg, "Become More Resilient."

43 **step outside negative thinking patterns:** LeeAnn Renninger, phone interview with the authors, April 19, 2018.

44 **it must be done in the next day or two:** Nick Wignall, "How to Fall Asleep Amazingly Fast by Worrying on Purpose," *Medium*, February 12, 2018, https://medium.com/swlh/how-to -fall-asleep-amazingly-fast-by-worrying-on-purpose-db0078acc6b6.

CHAPTER 3: MOTIVATION

49 **"happier employee to boot":** Cali Ressler and Jody Thompson, *Why Work Sucks and How to Fix It: The Results-only Revolution* (New York: Penguin Press, 2010), Kindle.

49 **rolled out to the entire company:** Seth Stevenson, "Don't Go to Work," *Slate*, May 11, 2014, www.slate.com/articles/business/psychology_of_management/2014/05/best_buy_s_rowe _experiment_can_results_only_work_environments_actually_be.html.

49 **thirteen guideposts for ROWE:** Ressler, *Why Work Sucks and How to Fix It.*

50 **workers feel engaged at work:** "Employee Engagement," Gallup, accessed February 17, 2018, http://news.gallup.com/topic/employee_engagement.aspx.

51 **jobs that gave them a lot of freedom:** Joris Lammers, "To Have Control over or to Be Free from Others? The Desire for Power Reflects a Need for Autonomy," *Personality and Social Psychology Bulletin* 42, no. 4 (March 2016): 498–512, http://journals.sagepub.com/doi/abs /10.1177/0146167216634064?rss=1&

52 **absenteeism and turnover both dropped:** Lydia DePillis, "Walmart Is Rolling Out Big Changes to Worker Schedules This Year," *Washington Post,* February 17, 2016, www .washingtonpost.com/news/wonk/wp/2016/02/17/walmart-is-rolling-out-big-changes-to -worker-schedules-this-year.

53 **attend after-school activities:** Stevenson, "Don't Go to Work."

53 **Voluntary turnover dropped:** Ibid.

53 **supervisor who had expressed reservations:** Ressler, *Why Work Sucks and How to Fix It.*

53 **"The answer is almost always yes":** Daniel Pink, phone interview with authors, February 27, 2018.

54 **"afternoon is doable for most people":** Ibid.

54 **Bezos once said this to an engineer:** Brad Stone, *The Everything Store: Jeff Bezos and the Age of Amazon* (New York: Back Bay Books, 2014), Kindle.

54 **released when we seek a reward:** "Dopamine Regulates the Motivation to Act, Study Shows," *Science Daily*, January 10, 2013, www.sciencedaily.com/releases/2013/01/13011009 4415.htm.

54 **near-miss as when they won:** Henry W. Chase and Luke Clark, "Gambling Severity Predicts Midbrain Response to Near-miss Outcomes," *Journal of Neuroscience* 30, no. 18 (May 2010): 6180–87, www.jneurosci.org/content/30/18/6180.full.

56 **to-do list energizes us:** Karl E. Weick, "Small Wins Redefining the Scale of Social Problems," *American Psychologist* 39, no. 1 (January 1984): 40–49, http://homepages.se.edu /cvonbergen/files/2013/01/Small-Wins_Redefining-the-Scale-of-Social-Problems.pdf.

56 **happier and more engaged with our work:** Teresa Amabile and Steven Kramer, *The Progress Principle* (Boston: Harvard Business Press, 2011), Kindle.

56 **losing sight of the bigger picture saps motivation:** Dr. Pranav Parijat and Jaipur Shilpi Bagga, "Victor Vroom's Expectancy Theory of Motivation—An Evaluation," *International*

Research Journal of Business Management 7, no. 9 (September 2014), http://irjbm.org /irjbm2013/Sep2014/Paper1.pdf.

56 **signals inclusivity and teamwork:** Leah Fessler, "Three Words Make Brainstorming Sessions at Google, Facebook, and IDEO More Productive," *Quartz*, July 10, 2017, https://qz .com/1022054/the-secret-to-better-brainstorming-sessions-lies-in-the-phrase-how -might-we.

56 **to come to you with questions:** Pink, *Drive*, 166.

57 **"sense that work itself has an impact":** Dan Ariely, Emir Kamenica, and Dražen Prelec, "Man's Search for Meaning: The Case of Legos," *Journal of Economic Behavior & Organization* (September 2008): 671–77, www.sciencedirect.com/science/article/pii/S0167268108000127.

57 **"than work on hard problems":** Paul Graham, "How to Do What You Love," *Paul Graham's Top Business Tips* (blog), accessed February 18, 2018, www.paulgraham.com/love.html.

57 **lighthearted and happy moments:** "The Most and Least Meaningful Jobs," PayScale, accessed February 18, 2018, www.payscale.com/data-packages/most-and-least-meaningful -jobs.

57 **through particularly dreary days:** Shelley A. Fahlman, "Does a Lack of Meaning Cause Boredom? Results from Psychometric, Longitudinal, and Experimental Analyses," *Journal of Social and Clinical Psychology* 28, no. 3 (2009): 307–40, https://psyc525final.wikispaces .com/file/view/Does+a+lack+of+meaning+cause+boredom+-+Results+from+psychometric, +longitudinal,+and+experimental+analyses.pdf.

57 **brief interactions with the people who benefit:** Bock *Work Rules!*

58 **scholarship recipients had raised almost twice as much:** Adam Grant, "How Customers Can Rally Your Troops," *Harvard Business Review*, June 2011, https://hbr.org/2011/06/how -customers-can-rally-your-troops.

58 **"highest compliments I've ever received":** Alexandra Petri, "Maurice Sendak and Childhood—We Ate It Up, We Loved It," *Washington Post*, May 8, 2012, www.washingtonpost.com /blogs/compost/post/maurice-sendak-and-childhood—we-ate-it-up-we-loved-it /2012/05/08/gIQAhfcwAU_blog.html.

59 **there are no absolutes, our mind-set matters:** Catherine Bailey and Adrian Madden, "What Makes Work Meaningful—or Meaningless," *MIT Sloan Management Review*, Summer 2016, https://sloanreview.mit.edu/article/what-makes-work-meaningful-or-meaningless.

59 **cracking jokes to make passengers feel better:** Dave Isay, *Callings: The Purpose and Passion of Work* (New York: Penguin, 2017), Kindle.

59 **"environment to be maximally fun":** "I Am Joi Ito of MIT Media Lab, Ask Me Anything," Reddit, May 29, 2015, www.reddit.com/r/IAmA/comments/37qf9h/i_am_joi_ito_director _of_mit_media_lab_ask_me.

60 **"platform in the Atlantic after launch":** Ali Rowghani, "What's the Second Job of a Startup CEO?" *Y Combinator*, November 29, 2016, https://blog.ycombinator.com/the-second-job -of-a-startup-ceo.

62 **language that has not yet been written:** "Human Capital Outlook," World Economic Forum, June 2016, http://www3.weforum.org/docs/WEF_ASEAN_HumanCapitalOutlook.pdf.

62 **"who you choose to learn from":** Seth Godin, "17 ideas for the modern world of work," altMBA, accessed February 18, 2018, https://altmba.com/ideas.

62 **until they could leave the office:** Kim Willsher, "Frenchman Takes Former Employer to Tribunal over Tedious Job," *Guardian*, May 2, 2016, www.theguardian.com/world/2016/may/02/frenchman-takes-former-employer-to-tribunal-over-tedious-job.

62 **nearly two hundred shocks:** *HBR Ideacast*, "Episode 592: Why Everyone Should See Themselves as a Leader," released August 31, 2017, hbr.org/ideacast/2017/08/why-everyone-should-see-themselves-as-a-leader.

63 **memories and begin connecting ideas:** Elle Metz, "Why Idle Moments Are Crucial for Creativity," *BBC*, April 14, 2017, www.bbc.com/capital/story/20170414-why-idle-moments-are-crucial-for-creativity.

63 **associated with memory and imagination:** Jennifer Schuessler, "Our Boredom, Ourselves," *New York Times*, January 21, 2010, www.nytimes.com/2010/01/24/books/review/Schuessler-t.html.

63 **schedule time to simply sit and think:** Ibid.

63 **"finds the hole in your roof":** Graham, "How to Do What You Love."

63 **counteracting stress than simply relaxing:** Chen Zhang et al., "More Is Less: Learning but Not Relaxing Buffers Deviance under Job Stressors," *Journal of Applied Psychology* 103, no. 2 (September 21, 2017): 123–36, www.ncbi.nlm.nih.gov/labs/articles/28933912.

63 **"Using what I learned from the course":** Niki Lustig, phone and email interview with authors, January 10, 2017.

64 **order to be on a winning team:** Thomas Zimmerfaust, "Are Workers Willing to Pay to Join a Better Team?" *Economic Inquiry*, December 26, 2017, http://onlinelibrary.wiley.com/doi/10.1111/ecin.12543/abstract.

64 **They value their self-constructed furniture more:** Michael Norton et al., "The 'IKEA Effect': When Labor Leads to Love," Harvard Business School Working Paper, 2011, www.hbs.edu/faculty/Publication%20Files/11-091.pdf.

64 **performed better than their peers:** Paul P. Baard et al., "Intrinsic Need Satisfaction: A Motivational Basis of Performance and Well-Being in Two Work Settings," *Journal of Applied Social Psychology* 34, no. 10 (2004): 2045–68, https://selfdeterminationtheory.org/SDT/documents/2004_BaardDeciRyan.pdf.

64 **cookbook until she was fifty-one:** Ruth Reichl, "Julia Child's Recipe for a Thoroughly Modern Marriage," *Smithsonian*, June 2012, www.smithsonianmag.com/history/julia-childs-recipe-for-a-thoroughly-modern-marriage-86160745.

65 **which both lead to higher achievement:** Carol Dweck, *Mindset: The New Psychology of Success* (New York: Random House, 2006), Kindle.

66 **anxious or depressed don't learn:** Bruce D. Perry, "Fear and Learning: Trauma Related Factors in Adult Learning," *New Directions for Adult and Continuing Education*, no. 110 (2006): 21–27.

67–68 **People with friends at work:** Christine M. Riordan and Rodger W. Griffeth, "The Opportunity for Friendship in the Workplace: An Underexplored Construct," *Journal of Business and Psychology* 10, no. 2 (December 1995): 141–54, https://link.springer.com/article/10.1007/BF02249575.

68 **satisfying and are less affected by stress:** Faith Ozbay et al., "Social Support and Resilience to Stress: From Neurobiology to Clinical Practice," *Psychiatry (Edgmont)* (2007): 35–40, www.ncbi.nlm.nih.gov/pmc/articles/PMC2921311.

68 **presentation and finally ask for that raise:** "The Positive Business Impact of Having a Best Friend at Work," *HR in Asia*, June 23, 2016, www.hrinasia.com/hr-news/the-positive-business -impact-of-having-a-best-friend-at-work.

69 **more successful than those who went alone:** Erica Field et al., "Friendship at Work: Can Peer Effects Catalyze Female Entrepreneurship?" National Bureau of Economic Research Working Paper No. 21093, April 2015, www.nber.org/papers/w21093.

69 **number had dropped to a third:** Adam Grant, "Friends at Work? Not So Much," *New York Times*, September 4, 2015, www.nytimes.com/2015/09/06/opinion/sunday/adam-grant-friends -at-work-not-so-much.html.

69 **"camaraderie for outside work":** Ibid.

69 **people who keep to themselves:** Shawn Achor, *Before Happiness* (New York: Crown Business, 2013), 178.

69 **steer us toward the right career moves:** Edith M. Hamilton et al., "Effects of Mentoring on Job Satisfaction, Leadership Behaviors, and Job Retention of New Graduate Nurses," *Journal for Nurses in Professional Development*, July–August 1989, http://journals.lww.com /jnsdonline/Abstract/1989/07000/Effects_of_Mentoring_on_Job_Satisfaction,.3.aspx.

69 **advises economist and author Tyler Cowen:** Ezra Klein, Interview with Tyler Cowen, Longform Podcast, Episode 270, November 2017, https://longform.org/posts/longform -podcast-270-tyler-cowen.

70 **important members of our networks:** Bert N. Uchino et al., "Heterogeneity in the Social Networks of Young and Older Adults," *Journal of Behavioral Medicine* 24, no. 4 (August 2001): 361–82, https://link.springer.com/article/10.1023/A:1010634902498.

71 **effort to succeed and network:** Jessica R. Methot et al., "The Space Between Us: A Social-functional Emotions View of Ambivalent and Indifferent Workplace Relationships," *Journal of Management* 43, no. 6 (July 2017): 1789–1819, http://journals.sagepub.com/doi/abs /10.1177/0149206316685853?journalCode=joma.

71 **rushing to meet deadlines takes effort:** David Burkus, "Work Friends Make Us More Productive (Except When They Stress Us Out)," *Harvard Business Review*, May 26, 2017, https://hbr.org/2017/05/work-friends-make-us-more-productive-except-when-they-stress -us-out.

71 **PhD candidate at the Wharton School:** Julianna Pillemer, phone interview with authors, January 8, 2017.

72 **Integrators don't create boundaries:** Christena Nippert-Eng, "Calendars and Keys: The Classification of 'Home' and 'Work,'" *Sociological Forum* 11, no. 3 (September 1996): 563–82, https://link.springer.com/article/10.1007/BF02408393.

72 **Unfortunately for segmentors, it's becoming harder:** Robert Half, "Many Employees Think It's OK to Connect with Colleagues on Social Media, but Not All Managers Agree," Robert Half, accessed February 18, 2018, http://rh-us.mediaroom.com/2017-09-12-Should -You-Friend-Your-Coworkers.

72 **friend request from a coworker:** Adam Grant, "Why Some People Have No Boundaries Online," *Huffington Post*, November 11, 2013, www.huffingtonpost.com/adam-grant/why -some-people-have-no-b_b_3909799.html.

72 **negatively by their colleagues:** Leslie K. John, "Hiding Personal Information Reveals the

Worst," Harvard Business School, January 26, 2016, www.hbs.edu/faculty/Pages/item
.aspx?num=50432.

72 **"coworkers outside of a work context"**: Pillemer, interview.

74 **beginning of a meaningful relationship:** Grant, "Friends at Work?"

74 **"mostly bond with similar colleagues":** Ibid.

CHAPTER 4: DECISION MAKING

80 **instead of the other way around:** Myeong-Gu Seo and Lisa Feldman Barrett, "Being Emotional During Decision Making—Good or Bad? An Empirical Investigation," *Academy of Management Journal* 50, no. 4. (August 2007): 923–40, www.ncbi.nlm.nih.gov/pmc/articles/PMC2361392.

81 **William James described gut feelings:** Beryl W. Holtam, *Let's Call It What It Is: A Matter of Conscience: A New Vocabulary for Moral Education* (Berlin: Springer Science & Business Media, 2012).

81 **narrow down and prioritize your options:** Marcel Zeelenberg et al., "On Emotion Specificity in Decision Making: Why Feeling Is for Doing," *Judgment and Decision Making* 3, no. 1 (January 2008): 18–27, http://journal.sjdm.org/bb2/bb2.html.

82 **suddenly decide her colleagues' ideas are all bad:** Scott S. Wiltermuth and Larissa Z. Tiedens, "Incidental Anger and the Desire to Evaluate," *Organizational Behavior and Human Decision Processes* 116 (2011): 55–65, https://pdfs.semanticscholar.org/53d4/6c8475881cf891 1e235418f9a13acf56d4cd.pdf.

84 **compare apples and oranges:** Michel Cabanac, "Pleasure: The Common Currency," *Journal of Theoretical Biology* 155, no. 2 (April 1992): 173–200, www.ncbi.nlm.nih.gov/pubmed /12240693.

84 **good indication it's a relevant emotion:** Scott S. Wiltermuth and Larissa Z. Tiedens, "Incidental anger and the desire to evaluate," *Organizational Behavior and Human Decision Processes* 116, no. 1 (September 2011): 55–65, https://pdfs.semanticscholar.org/53d4/6c8475 881cf8911e235418f9a13acf56d4cd.pdf.

84 **pick between good choices:** Amitai Shenhav and Randy L. Buckner, "Neural Correlates of Dueling Affective Reactions to Win-win Choices," *Proceedings of the National Academy of Science* 111, no. 3 (July 29, 2014): 10978–83, www.ncbi.nlm.nih.gov/pubmed/25024178.

84 **"neural correlates of First World problems":** Maria Konnikova, "When It's Bad to Have Good Choices," *New Yorker*, August 1, 2014, www.newyorker.com/science/maria-konnikova /bad-good-choices.

85 **anxiety often lasts for days or months:** "When Fear Is a Competitive Advantage—4 Steps to Make It Work for You," *First Round Review*, accessed on April 21, 2018, http://firstround .com/review/when-fear-is-a-competitive-advantage-4-steps-to-make-it-work-for-you.

85 **"design a new path based on reality":** Ibid.

86 **option you think will minimize regret:** Michael Lewis, *The Undoing Project* (New York: W. W. Norton, 2016), Kindle.

86 **"change led to some disaster":** Ibid.

87 **"facing life-changing choices":** Steven D. Levitt, "Heads or Tails: The Impact of a Coin Toss

on Major Life Decisions and Subsequent Happiness," *NBER Working Paper* No. 22487 (August 2016), www.nber.org/papers/w22487.

87 **"I became sick with envy":** Gretchen Rubin, Phone interview with authors, February 23, 2018.

87 **"relative to her at this job":** "Envy at the Office: A Q&A with Tanya Menon, PhD," accessed April 21, 2018, http://goop.com/envy-at-the-office.

87 **copying machine can affect our mood:** Daniel Västfjäll et al., "The Arithmetic of Emotion: Integration of Incidental and Integral Affect in Judgments and Decisions," *Frontiers in Psychology* 7 (March 2016): 325, www.ncbi.nlm.nih.gov/pmc/articles/PMC4782160.

88 **quickly able to discount them:** Ibid.

88 **remember more happy memories with her:** Seo and Barrett, "Being Emotional," 923–40.

89 **regulate emotion or go for a quick walk or run:** Christina Zelano et al., "Nasal Respiration Entrains Human Limbic Oscillations and Modulates Cognitive Function," *Journal of Neuroscience* 36, no. 49 (December 7, 2016): 12448–67.

89 **set lower expectations for ourselves:** Jennifer S. Lerner et al., "The Financial Costs of Sadness," *Psychological Science* 24, no. 1 (November 13, 2012): 72–79, http://journals.sagepub .com/doi/abs/10.1177/0956797612450302?journalCode=pssa.

89 **opposite effect of sadness:** Jennifer S. Lerner et al., "Emotion and Decision Making," *Annual Review of Psychology* 66 (January 2015): 799–823, http://scholar.harvard.edu/files /jenniferlerner/files/emotion_and_decision_making.pdf.

89 **benefits lasting more than a month:** Martin Seligman et al., "Positive Psychology Progress: Empirical Validation of Interventions," *American Psychology* 60, no. 5 (July 2005): 410–21, www.ncbi.nlm.nih.gov/pubmed/16045394.

90 **had the right to fire Stanton:** Alex Crippen, "Warren Buffett: Buying Berkshire Hathaway Was $200 Billion Blunder," *CNBC*, October 18, 2010, www.cnbc.com/id/39710609.

90 **$100 billion more than it is today:** Modesto A. Maidique, "Intuition Isn't Just about Trusting your Gut," *Harvard Business Review*, April 13, 2011, https://hbr.org/2011/04/intuition -good-bad-or-indiffer.

90 **shrug off advice:** Daphna Motro et al., "Investigating the Effects of Anger and Guilt on Unethical Behavior: A Dual-Process Approach," *Journal of Business Ethics* (2016), https:// link.springer.com/article/10.1007/s10551–016–3337-x.

91 **then made worse guesses:** Francesca Gino, *Sidetracked: Why Our Decisions Get Derailed, and How We Can Stick to the Plan* (Cambridge, MA: Harvard Business Review Press, 2013), 45–47.

91 **decision-making behavior differently:** Eddie North-Hager, "When Stressed, Men Charge Ahead, Women More Cautious," *USC News*, June 2, 2011, http://news.usc.edu/30333/When -Stressed-Men-Charge-Ahead-Women-More-Cautious.

91 **women tend to choose the low-risk option:** Ruud van den Bos et al., "Stress and Decision-making in Humans: Performance Is Related to Cortisol Reactivity, Albeit Differently in Men and Women," *Psychoneuroendocrinology* 34, no. 10 (November 2009): 1449–58, www .ncbi.nlm.nih.gov/pubmed/19497677.

92 **writes psychologist Therese Huston:** Miranda Green, "Make Better Decisions by Using Stress to Your Advantage," *Financial Times*, August 28, 2016, www.ft.com/content/9e751970 -6a0b-11e6-a0b1-d87a9fea034f.

92 **"decision will often be the right choice":** North-Hager, "When Stressed, Men Charge Ahead, Women More Cautious."

92 **as if dating is never a hot mess:** Rivera, "Go with Your Gut."

92 **effectively over after the first ten seconds:** Frank J. Bernieri, "The Importance of First Impressions in a Job Interview," Midwestern Psychological Association Conference, May 2000, www.researchgate.net/publication/313878823_The_importance_of_first_impressions _in_a_job_interview.

92 **hire people who make us feel good:** Rivera, "Go with Your Gut."

92 **person for (or even able to do) the job:** Ibid.

92 **led HR at Netflix for fourteen years:** Patty McCord, phone interview with the authors, February 5, 2018.

92 **perceived is how similar they are to the interviewer:** Angela Antony, phone interview with authors, March 13, 2018.

93 **Women have a harder time:** "Recruiting Men, Constructing Manhood: How Health Care Organizations Mobilize Masculinities as Nursing Recruitment Strategy," *Gender & Society* (blog), February 4, 2014, https://gendersociety.wordpress.com/2014/02/04/recruiting-men -constructing-manhood-how-health-care-organizations-mobilize-masculinities-as-nursing -recruitment-strategy.

93 **"Are you man enough to be a nurse":** Claire Cain Miller, "Why Men Don't Want the Jobs Done Mostly by Women," *New York Times*, January 4, 2017, www.nytimes.com/2017/01/04 /upshot/why-men-dont-want-the-jobs-done-mostly-by-women.html.

93 **women who act assertively:** Joan C. Williams et al., "Double Jeopardy? Gender Bias against Women in Science," *Tools for Change in STEM*, January 21, 2015, www.toolsforchangeinstem .org/double-jeopardy-gender-bias-women-color-science.

93 **working for unbiased managers:** Dylan Glover et al., "Discrimination as a Self-Fulfilling Prophecy: Evidence from French Grocery Stores, *Quarterly Journal of Economics* 132, no. 3 (August 1, 2017): 1219–60, https://doi.org/10.1093/qje/qjx006.

94 **have a poor work ethic:** Adia Harvey Wingfield, "Being Black—but Not Too Black—in the Workplace," *The Atlantic*, October 14, 2015, www.theatlantic.com/business/archive/2015 /10/being-black-work/409990.

94 **"start by defining the problem":** McCord, interview.

94 **audition behind a curtain:** Claudia Goldin and Cecilia Rouse, "Orchestrating Impartiality: The Impact of 'Blind' Auditions on Female Musicians," National Bureau of Economic Research, January 1997, www.nber.org/papers/w5903.

94 **hired more women and minorities:** Adam Grant, "*The Daily Show*'s Secret to Creativity."

94 **"What did your approach look like":** Bock, *Work Rules*.

95 **focusing on a single candidate for too long:** Iris Bohnet et al., "When Performance Trumps Gender Bias: Joint vs. Separate Evaluation," *Management Science* 62, no. 5 (2016): 1225–34, https://ofew.berkeley.edu/sites/default/files/when_performance_trumps_gender_bias _bohnet_et_al.pdf.

96 **random and sometimes nonsensical responses:** Jason Dana, "Belief in the Unstructured Interview: The Persistence of an Illusion," *Judgment and Decision Making* 8, no. 5 (September 2013): 512–20, http://journal.sjdm.org/12/121130a/jdm121130a.pdf.

96 **study was done in 1989:** Marianne Bertrand and Sendhil Mullainathan, "Are Emily and Greg More Employable than Lakisha and Jamal? A Field Experiment on Labor Market Discrimination," National Bureau of Economic Research, July 2003, www.nber.org/papers /w9873.

96 **judge candidates based on skills:** John E. Hunter and Ronda F. Hunter, "Validity and Utility of Alternative Predictors of Job Performance," *Psychological Bulletin* 96, no. 1 (1984): 72–98, www.uam.es/personal_pdi/psicologia/pei/diferencias/Hunter1984JobPerformance.pdf.

97 **sixth candidate is less likely to be good:** Uri Simonsohn and Francesca Gino, "Daily Horizons: Evidence of Narrow Bracketing in Judgment from 10 Years of MBA-Admission Interviews," *Psychological Science* 24, no. 2 (2013), https://papers.ssrn.com/sol3/papers.cfm?abstract _id=2070623.

98 **less than your confident colleagues:** Alison Wood Brooks and Maurice E. Schweitzer, "Can Nervous Nelly Negotiate? How Anxiety Causes Negotiators to Make Low First Offers, Exit Early, and Earn Less Profit," *Organizational Behavior and Human Decision Processes* 115, no. 1 (May 2011): 43–54, www.sciencedirect.com/science/article/pii/S0749597811000227.

98 **projects than their male colleagues:** Kathy Caprino, "Intimidated to Negotiate for Yourself? 5 Critical Strategies to Help You Nail It," *Forbes*, October 29, 2014, www.forbes.com /sites/kathycaprino/2014/10/29/intimidated-to-negotiate-for-yourself-5-critical-strategies -to-help-you-nail-it/#1584039173f6.

98 **just as much money as the men did:** Emily T. Amanatullah and Michael W. Morris, "Negotiating Gender Roles: Gender Differences in Assertive Negotiating Are Mediated by Women's Fear of Backlash and Attenuated When Negotiating on Behalf of Others," *Journal of Personality and Social Psychology* 98, no. 2 (February 2010): 256–67, www.ncbi.nlm.nih.gov /pubmed/20085399.

98 **"non-salary-based benefits":** Andreas Jäger et al., "Using Self-regulation to Successfully Overcome the Negotiation Disadvantage of Low Power," *Frontiers in Psychology* 8 (2017): 271, www.ncbi.nlm.nih.gov/pubmed/28382005.

99 **deaths all declined:** Atul Gawande, "The Checklist," *New Yorker*, December 10, 2007, www. newyorker.com/magazine/2007/12/10/the-checklist.

100 **"current job and ask for a promotion":** Therese Huston, *How Women Decide: What's True, What's Not, and What Strategies Spark the Best Choices* (New York: Houghton Mifflin Harcourt, 2016).

101 **writes psychologist Tasha Eurich:** Tasha Eurich, "To Make Better Decisions, Ask Yourself 'What,' Not 'Why,'" *New York*, May 2, 2017, www.thecut.com/2017/05/to-make-better -decisions-ask-yourself-what-not-why.html.

101 **end up with objectively better options:** Sheena S. Iyengar et al., "Doing Better but Feeling Worse: Looking for the 'Best' Job Undermines Satisfaction," *Psychological Science* 17, no. 2 (February 2006): 143–50, http://journals.sagepub.com/doi/abs/10.1111/j.1467–9280.2006 .01677.x.

102 **best option from the pile of winners:** Tibor Besedeš et al., "Reducing Choice Overload without Reducing Choices," *Review of Economics and Statistics* 97, no. 4 (October 2015): 793–802, www.mitpressjournals.org/doi/abs/10.1162/REST_a_00506?journalCOde=rest# .VNI34mTF8rM.

102 **evidence for or against each option:** Stephen M. Fleming, "Hesitate! Quick decision-making might seem bold, but the agony of indecision is your brain's way of making a better choice," *Aeon*, January 8, 2014, https://aeon.co/essays/forget-being-boldly-decisive-let-your-brain-take-its-time.

CHAPTER 5: TEAMS

108 **"spelling mistakes annoy you":** Stu Woo, "In Search of a Perfect Team at Work," *Wall Street Journal*, April 4, 2017, www.wsj.com/articles/in-search-of-a-perfect-team-at-work-148937 2003.

109 **"equation didn't seem to matter":** Charles Duhigg, "What Google Learned from Its Quest to Build the Perfect Team," *New York Times*, February 25, 2016, www.nytimes.com/2016/02/28/magazine/what-google-learned-from-its-quest-to-build-the-perfect-team.html.

109 **embarrassed by the group:** Julia Rozovsky, "The Five Keys to a Successful Google Team," Google re: Work, November 17, 2015, rework.withgoogle.com/blog/five-keys-to-a-successful-google-team.

109 **twice as often by executives:** Ibid.

109 **doesn't guarantee a smart team:** David Engel et al., "Reading the Mind in the Eyes or Reading between the Lines? Theory of Mind Predicts Collective Intelligence Equally Well Online and Face-to-Face," *PLOS One*, December 16, 2014, http://journals.plos.org/plosone/article?id=10.1371/journal.pone.0115212.

109 **sensitive to one another's feelings:** Ibid.

110 **prescribed the wrong medications:** Jennifer Breheny Wallace, "The Costs of Workplace Rudeness," *Wall Street Journal*, August 18, 2017, www.wsj.com/articles/the-costs-of-workplace-rudeness-1503061187.

110 **comes to building diverse teams:** Duhigg, "What Google Learned."

111 **bursting with creativity:** Christoph Riedl and Anita Williams Woolley, "Teams vs. Crowds: A Field Test of the Relative Contribution of Incentives, Member Ability, and Emergent Collaboration to Crowd-Based Problem Solving Performance," *Academy of Management Discoveries* 3, no. 4 (December 2016), https://pdfs.semanticscholar.org/6687/637acceb6a73a803d0be60eed2f94aebe631.pdf.

112 **one of the company's executives:** Dara Khosrowshahi, "Uber's New Cultural Norms," LinkedIn, November 7, 2017, www.linkedin.com/pulse/ubers-new-cultural-norms-dara-khosrowshahi.

112 **"shit-starters creatively, but not in real life":** Tim Adams, "Secrets of the TV Writers' Room: Inside Narcos, Transparent and Silicon Valley," *Guardian*, September 23, 2017, www.theguardian.com/tv-and-radio/2017/sep/23/secrets-of-the-tv-writers-rooms-tv-narcos-silicon-valley-transparent.

112 **a former partner at IDEO:** Daniel Coyle, *The Culture Code: The Secrets of Highly Successful Groups* (New York: Bantam, 2018).

113 **"scaffolding of thoughtfulness":** Ibid.

113 **B. Byrne, a product manager:** B. Byrne, interview with the authors, January 14, 2018.

114 **"normally get in five minutes":** Jonathan McBride, phone interview with authors, November 29, 2017.

115 **cowboy doll named Woody:** Bryan Bishop, "Toy Story, 20 Years Later: How Pixar Made Its First Blockbuster," *The Verge*, March 17, 2015, www.theverge.com/2015/3/17/8229891/sxsw -2015-toy-story-pixar-making-of-20th-anniversary.

115 **a term our friend coined:** Debra Gilin Oore, "Individual and Organizational Factors Promoting Successful Responses to Workplace Conflict," *Canadian Psychology* 56, no. 3 (2015): 301–10, www.researchgate.net/profile/Michael_Leiter/publication/282295599_Individual _and_Organizational_Factors_Promoting_Successful_Responses_to_Workplace _Conflict/links/5645f7a008ae451880aa2295.pdf.

115 **if everyone simply worked alone:** Ibid.

116 **stills from the movie *Inside Out*:** "*Inside Out* Animation Dailies at Pixar," *Arts & Craft Family*, May 26, 2015, www.artcraftsandfamily.com/inside-out-animation-dailies-at-pixar -animation-studios.

117 **writes Pixar animator Victor Navone:** Victor Navone, "Inside Dailies at Pixar: Expressing Your Opinion about Changes in Animation," *Animation Mentor*, September 20, 2017, http://blog.animationmentor.com/inside-dailies-at-pixar-expressing-your-opinion-about -changes-in-animation.

117 **When teams take the time:** Kristin J. Behfar et al., "The Critical Role of Conflict Resolution in Teams: A Close Look at the Links Between Conflict Type, Conflict Management Strategies, and Team Outcomes," *Journal of Applied Psychology* 93, no. 1 (2008): 170–88, www .socialresearchmethods.net/research/JAP%20Conflict%20Resolution%202008.pdf.

117 **to discuss the pros and cons:** Tony L. Simons and Randall S. Peterson, "Task Conflict and Relationship Conflict in Top Management Teams: The Pivotal Role of Intragroup Trust," *Journal of Applied Psychology* 85, no. 1 (2000): 102–111, http://scholarship.sha.cornell.edu /cgi/viewcontent.cgi?article=1723&context=articles.

117 **guides to make collaboration easier:** David Politis, "This Is How You Revolutionize the Way Your Team Works Together: And All It Takes Is 15 Minutes," LinkedIn, March 29, 2016, www.linkedin.com/pulse/how-you-revolutionize-way-your-team-works-together-all -david-politis.

117 **blocking off an hour to answer the questions:** Ibid.

119 **Larry David to kill her off:** Joe Tacopino, "'Seinfeld' cast hated Susan so Larry David killed her off," *New York Post*, June 4, 2015, https://nypost.com/2015/06/04/seinfeld-cast-didnt-like -susan-so-larry-david-killed-her-off.

120 **one-upmanship aimed at testing ideas:** Amy Gallo, "Dealing with Conflict Avoiders and Seekers," *Harvard Business Review*, April 6, 2017, https://hbr.org/ideacast/2017/04/dealing -with-conflict-avoiders-and-seekers.

120 **conflict as a struggle for validation:** Joseph Grenny, "How to Save a Meeting That's Gotten Tense," *Harvard Business Review*, December 29, 2017, https://hbr.org/2017/12/how-to-save -a-meeting-thats-gotten-tense.

121 **"chance to talk it through":** Kim Scott, *Radical Candor* (New York: St. Martin's, 2017).

121 **team members who are arguing to remember:** Laura Delizonna, "High-performing Teams Need Psychological Safety. Here's How to Create It," *Harvard Business Review*, August 24,

2017, https://hbr.org/2017/08/high-performing-teams-need-psychological-safety-heres-how-to-create-it.

121 **coworker still drives you nuts:** Amy Gallo, "4 Types of Conflict and How to Manage Them," *Harvard Business Review,* November 25, 2015, https://hbr.org/ideacast/2015/11/4-types-of-conflict-and-how-to-manage-them.

122 **skew your view on reality:** Barbara L. Fredrickson and Christine Branigan, "Positive Emotions Broaden the Scope of Attention and Thought-action Repertoires," *Cognition and Emotion* 19, no. 3 (May 1, 2005): 313–32, www.ncbi.nlm.nih.gov/pmc/articles/PMC3156609.

122 **"we can uncover them together":** Delizonna, "High-performing Teams Need Psychological Safety."

123 **"branded as a downer or disloyal":** Astro Teller, "The Head of 'X' Explains How to Make Audacity the Path of Least Resistance," *Wired,* April 15, 2016, www.wired.com/2016/04/the-head-of-x-explains-how-to-make-audacity-the-path-of-least-resistance.

123 **prejudiced behavior or responses:** Alexander M. Czopp et al., "Standing Up for a Change: Reducing Bias through Interpersonal Confrontation," *Journal of Personality and Social Psychology* 90, no. 5 (2006): 784–803, https://pdfs.semanticscholar.org/f3c7/4aa95cb2d4ce04cfccbf7298290ce3cbb370.pdf.

123 **model your behavior after theirs:** Amy Gallo, "Why We Should Be Disagreeing More at Work," *Harvard Business Review,* January 3, 2018, https://hbr.org/2018/01/why-we-should-be-disagreeing-more-at-work.

124 **much we like our managers:** Steven G. Robelberg et al., "Employee Satisfaction with Meetings: A Contemporary Facet of Job Satisfaction," *Human Resource Management,* 49, no. 2 (March–April 2010): 149–72, https://orgscience.uncc.edu/sites/orgscience.uncc.edu/files/media/syllabi/9fcfd510ec7a528af7.pdf.

124 **"two pieces each too small to do anything":** Paul Graham, "Maker's Schedule, Manager's Schedule," PaulGraham.com, July 2009, www.paulgraham.com/makersschedule.html.

126 **dropped group performance by almost forty percent:** "Ruining It for the Rest of Us," *This American Life,* Episode 370, December 19, 2008, www.thisamericanlife.org/radio-archives/episode/370/ruining-it-for-the-rest-of-us.

126 **"vocational skills or isn't so bad":** Seth Godin, "Let's Stop Calling Them 'Soft Skills,'" *Medium,* January 31, 2017, https://itsyourturnblog.com/lets-stop-calling-them-soft-skills-9cc27ec09ecb.

127 **"train someone who's incompetent":** Tiziana Casciaro and Miguel Sousa Lobo, "Competent Jerks, Lovable Fools, and the Formation of Social Networks," *Harvard Business Review,* June 2005, https://hbr.org/2005/06/competent-jerks-lovable-fools-and-the-formation-of-social-networks.

127 **belittled and deenergized:** Ellen Simon, "He Wrote the Book on Work Jerks," *Washington Post,* March 15, 2007, www.washingtonpost.com/wp-dyn/content/article/2007/03/15/AR2007031501044_pf.html.

127 **team's momentum and motivation:** Amy Gallo, "How to Handle the Pessimist on Your Team," *Harvard Business Review,* September 17, 2009, https://hbr.org/2009/09/how-to-handle-the-pessimist-on.

128 **like people who are similar or familiar to us:** Casciaro and Lobo, "Competent Jerks."

128 **"If someone handed you a literal glass of poison"**: Liz Dolan and Larry Seal, "Sexism: from Annoyance to Conspiracy," *I Hate My Boss* podcast, Season 1, Episode 13, June 19, 2017, https://itunes.apple.com/us/podcast/i-hate-my-boss/id1148704291?mt=2.

129 **telling others about your limitations**: Casciaro and Lobo, "Competent Jerks."

129 **who sits sixty feet away**: Thomas J. Allen, *Managing the Flow of Technology* (Cambridge, MA: MIT Press, 1984).

129 **"Imagine it is a day, a week, or a year later"**: Bob Sutton, "The Asshole Survival Guide: The Backstory," *Quiet Rev*, accessed April 22, 2018, www.quietrev.com/asshole-survival-guide -backstory.

129 **"negate technical competencies"**: Jo Shapiro, phone interview with author, January 16, 2018.

129 **"'That will never work' is their motto"**: Mark Suster, "Lead, Follow or Get the Fuck Out of the Way," *Medium*, April 28, 2016, https://bothsidesofthetable.com/lead-follow-or-get-the -fuck-out-of-the-way-668000be6e47.

131 **Could we design a better outcome**: Peter M. Senge, *The Fifth Discipline: The Art and Practice of the Learning Organization* (New York: Doubleday, 2006).

131 **five-to-one ratio of positive to negative comments**: Amy Gallo, "How to Handle the Pessimist."

131 **Ever heard of the sucker effect**: Min Zhu, "Perception of Social Loafing, Conflict, and Emotion in the Process of Group Development," University of Minnesota PhD dissertation, August 2013, https://conservancy.umn.edu/handle/11299/160008.

132 **contribute to a meaningful outcome**: Steven J. Karau and Kipling D. Williams, "Social Loafing: A Meta-analytic Review and Theoretical Integration," *Journal of Personality and Social Psychology* 65, no. 4 (October 1993), https://pdfs.semanticscholar.org/dbfb/3c9153d3 aa75d98460e83fa180bc9650d6fd.pdf.

132 **anonymous and irrelevant**: James A. Shepperd and Kevin M. Taylor, "Social Loafing and Expectancy-Value Theory," *Personality and Social Psychology Bulletin* 25, no. 9 (September 1, 1999): 114758, http://journals.sagepub.com/doi/abs/10.1177/01461672992512008?journalCode=pspc.

132 **pizzas can't feed the whole group**: Alan Deutschman, "Inside the Mind of Jeff Bezos," *Fast Company*, August 1, 2004, www.fastcompany.com/50106/inside-mind-jeff-bezos.

132 **"atomic unit of trust"**: Keith Yamashita, "Keith Yamashita on the 9 Habits of Great Creative Teams," *Rethinked*, June 10, 2013, http://rethinked.org/?tag=duos.

132 **rather than on their own contribution**: Karau and Williams, "Social Loafing: A Meta-analytic Review."

132 **completing their work on time**: Christel G. Rutte, "Social Loafing in Teams," *International Handbook of Organizational Teamwork and Cooperative Working* (Chichester, UK: Wiley, 2008), 1372–75, https://onlinelibrary.wiley.com/doi/10.1002/9780470696712.ch17.

133 **"you're not going in and whining"**: Liz Dolan and Larry Seal, "After Hours 8: The Slacker and the Over-sharer," *I Hate My Boss* podcast, June 15, 2017, www.stitcher.com/podcast /wondery/i-hate-my-boss/e/50486806.

CHAPTER 6: COMMUNICATION

137 **Ilan explained to *The New York Times***: Laura M. Holson, "Anger Management: Why the Genius Founders Turned to Couples Therapy," *New York Times*, April 17, 2015, www

.nytimes.com/2015/04/19/fashion/anger-management-why-the-genius-founders-turned
-to-couples-therapy.html.

137 **"disagreements about our company personally"**: Tom Lehman, interview with the authors, July 2017.

138 **Ilan had so abruptly gone on without him:** Holson, "Anger Management."

138 **"always interpersonal issues"**: Lehman, interview.

138 **writes philosopher Alain de Botton:** Alain de Botton, "Why You Will Marry the Wrong Person," *New York Times*, May 28, 2016, www.nytimes.com/2016/05/29/opinion/sunday/why -you-will-marry-the-wrong-person.html.

138 **"Words are a window into a world":** Jenna Goudreau, "Harvard Psychologist Steven Pinker: The No. 1 Communication Mistake That Even Smart People Make," *CNBC*, February 20, 2018, www.cnbc.com/2018/02/20/harvard-psychologist-steven-pinker-shares-no-1 -communication-mistake.html.

139 **difficult work-related conversation:** Matt Scott, "Top 10 Difficult Conversations: New (Surprising) Research," *Chartered Management Institute*, July 29, 2015, www.managers.org.uk /insights/news/2015/july/the-10-most-difficult-conversations-new-surprising-research.

139 **tempted to just avoid them:** Douglas Stone, Bruce Patton, and Sheila Heen, *Difficult Conversations: How to Discuss What Matters Most* (New York: Penguin, 2010).

140 **"because it will surface anyway":** Holson, "Anger Management."

140 **not ready to have a difficult conversation:** Laura Delizonna, "High-performing Teams Need Psychological Safety. Here's How to Create It," *Harvard Business Review*, August 24, 2017, https://hbr.org/2017/08/high-performing-teams-need-psychological-safety-heres -how-to-create-it.

141 **Ilan's grandfather told him:** Lehman, interview.

141 **In studies of married couples:** Joyce W. Yuan, "Physiological Down-regulation and Positive Emotion in Marital Interaction Emotion," *American Psychological Association* 10, no. 4 (2010): 467–74, www.gruberpeplab.com/teaching/psych231_fall2013/documents/231_Yuan 2010.pdf.

141 **work through issues more quickly:** Yuan, "Physiological Down-regulation."

142 **business school students at Stanford:** Chris Gomes, phone interview with author, February 22, 2018.

142 **Chris Gomes, an alum who now runs a start-up:** Ibid.

142 **"stroll-in-late vibe":** Holson, "Anger Management."

145 **next promotion cycle, the gender gap:** Laszlo Bock, interview with the authors, March 8, 2018.

145 **If they speak with confidence:** Deborah Tannen, *Talking from 9 to 5: Women and Men at Work* (New York: William Morrow, 1991).

145 **whether or not they were in the minority:** Christopher Karpowitz and Tali Mendelberg, *The Silent Sex: Gender, Deliberation, and Institutions* (Princeton, NJ: Princeton University Press, 2014).

146 **conversations by talking over others:** Adrienne B. Hancock and Benjamin A. Rubin, "Influence of Communication Partner's Gender on Language," *Journal of Language and Social Psychology* 34, no. 1 (2015), http://journals.sagepub.com/doi/abs/10.1177/0261927X1453319 7?papetoc=.

146 **faster to deem themselves experts:** Muriel Niederle and Lise Vesterlund, "Do Women Shy Away from Competition? Do Men Compete Too Much?"*Quarterly Journal of Economics* 122, no. 3 (August 1, 2007): 1067–1101, https://doi.org/10.1162/qjec.122.3.1067.

146 **"didn't come forward as experts":** Susan Chira, "Why Women Aren't C.E.O.s, According to Women Who Almost Were," *New York Times*, July 21, 2017, www.nytimes.com/2017/07/21 /sunday-review/women-ceos-glass-ceiling.html.

146 **Obama took note, and began calling:** "The Clever Strategy Obama's Women Staffers Came Up with to Make Sure They Were Being Heard," *Women in the World*, September 14, 2016, http://nytlive.nytimes.com/womenintheworld/2016/09/14/the-clever-strategy-obamas -women-staffers-came-up-with-to-make-sure-they-were-being-heard.

147 **face of discrimination or harassment:** Alexander M. Czopp, "Standing Up for a Change: Reducing Bias through Interpersonal Confrontation," *Journal of Personality and Social Psychology* 90, no. 5 (2006): 784–803, https://pdfs.semanticscholar.org/f3c7/4aa95cb2d4ce04cf ccbf7298290ce3cbb370.pdf.

147 **"hear your thoughts on specific details":** Francesca Gino, "How to Handle Interrupting Colleagues," *Harvard Business Review*, February 22, 2017, https://hbr.org/2017/02/how-to -handle-interrupting-colleagues.

147 **Anne Kreamer, author of** *It's Always Personal***:** Anne Kreamer, phone interview with authors, March 6, 2018.

147 **who can provide emotional support:** Lorna Collier, "Why We Cry," *Monitor on Psychology* 45, no. 2 (February 2014), www.apa.org/monitor/2014/02/cry.aspx.

148 **passion makes others view your tears more favorably:** Elizabeth Baily Wolf, Jooa Julia Lee, Sunita Sah, and Alison Wood Brooks, "Managing Perceptions of Distress at Work: Reframing Emotion as Passion," *Organizational Behavior and Human Decision Processes* 137 (November 2016): 1–12, www.hbs.edu/faculty/Pages/item.aspx?num=51400.

148 **"anyone who had to use the crying room":** Jennifer Palmieri, *Dear Madam President* (Grand Central Publishing: New York, 2018).

148 **"screaming and yelling and getting angry":** Eric Johnson, "Six Things We Can Do Today to Help Women Succeed in the Workplace," *Recode*, March 26, 2018, www.recode.net/2018 /3/26/17162636/six-things-help-women-succeed-workplace-diversity-training-what-she -said-joanne-lipman-recode-decode.

149 **simply another member of the team:** Kisha Richardson, interview with the authors, May 14, 2018.

149 **"not as able to hear each other":** Kira Hudson Banks, "Talking about Race at Work," *Harvard Business Review*, March 3, 2016, https://hbr.org/ideacast/2016/03/talking-about-race -at-work.html.

149 **"offensive to you, in the moment or later":** "Engaging in Conversations about Gender, Race, and Ethnicity in the Workplace," *Catalyst*, 2016, www.catalyst.org/system/files /engaging_in_conversations_about_gender_race_and_ethnicity_in_the_workplace.pdf.

150 **explicitly referencing those groups:** Ian Haney Lopez, *Dog Whistle Politics: How Coded Racial Appeals Have Reinvented Racism and Wrecked the Middle Class* (Oxford: Oxford University Press, 2015).

150 **tend to be more biased:** Victoria C. Plaut, Kecia M. Thomas, and Matt J. Goren, "Is Multi-

culturalism or Color Blindness Better for Minorities?" *Psychological Science* 20, no. 4 (2009): 444–46.

150 **concealing racial discrimination:** Seval Gündemir and Adam D. Galinsky, "Multicolored Blindfolds: How Organizational Multiculturalism Can Conceal Racial Discrimination and Delegitimize Racial Discrimination Claims," *Social Psychological and Personality Science* (August 2017), http://journals.sagepub.com/doi/abs/10.1177/1948550617726830.

150 **Dixon, CEO of Founder Gym:** Mandela SH Dixon, "My White Boss Talked about Race in America and This Is What Happened," *Medium*, July 9, 2016, https://medium.com/kapor -the-bridge/my-white-boss-talked-about-race-in-america-and-this-is-what-happened -fe10f1a00726.

150 **more than doubled since 2000:** Chip Conley, "I Joined Airbnb at 52, and Here's What I Learned about Age, Wisdom, and the Tech Industry," *Harvard Business Review,* April 18, 2017, https://hbr.org/2017/04/i-joined-airbnb-at-52-and-heres-what-i-learned-about-age-wisdom -and-the-tech-industry.

151 **Generation Z, born after 1997:** Jeanne C Meister and Karie Willyerd, "Are You Ready to Manage Five Generations of Workers?" *Harvard Business Review,* October 16, 2009, https://hbr.org/2009/10/are-you-ready-to-manage-five-g.

151 **lamented one grump in 1624:** Jon Seder, "15 Historical Complaints about Young People Ruining Everything," *Mental Floss*, August 15, 2013, http://mentalfloss.com/article/52209 /15-historical-complaints-about-young-people-ruining-everything.

151 **digitally hopeless job-hoggers:** "Generation Stereotypes," *Monitor on Psychology* 36, no. 6 (June 2005): 55, www.apa.org/monitor/jun05/stereotypes.aspx.

151 **"get over themselves as they get older":** Carolyn Baird, "Myths, Exaggerations, and Un-comfortable Truths: The Real Story behind Millennials in the Workplace," IBM Institute for Business Value, accessed April 21, 2017, http://www-935.ibm.com/services/us/gbs/thought leadership/millennialworkplace.

152 **mental horizons and reducing discrimination:** Meister and Willyerd, "Are You Ready . . . ?"

152 **"If you shipped a feature and no one used it":** Conley, "I Joined Airbnb at 52."

152 **peak in our forties and fifties:** Joshua K. Hartshorne and Laura T. Germine, "When Does Cognitive Functioning Peak? The Asynchronous Rise and Fall of Different Cognitive Abilities Across the Life Span," *Psychological Science* 26, no. 4 (April 2015): 433–43, http://journals .sagepub.com/doi/abs/10.1177/0956797614567339.

152 **"spot in a meeting with a lot of people":** Erin Meyer, "Managing Confrontation in Multi-cultural Teams," *Harvard Business Review*, April 6, 2012, https://hbr.org/2012/04/how-to -manage-confrontation-in.

154 **emotions we feel comfortable expressing:** Lydia Itoi, "Distinguished Lecture: How Does Culture Shape Our Feelings?" Stanford Distinguished Lecture by Jeanne Tsai, September 25, 2015, https://bingschool.stanford.edu/news/distinguished-lecture-how-does-culture-shape -our-feelings.

154 **"people think you're depressed":** Itoi, "Distinguished Lecture."

154 **emotional expression tendencies:** Erin Meyer, "Getting to Si, Ja, Oui, Hai, and Da," *Harvard Business Review*, December 2015, https://hbr.org/2015/12/getting-to-si-ja-oui-hai-and-da.

154 **"I don't fully understand your point":** Meyer, "Managing Confrontation."

154 **colleague may not be as outwardly appreciative:** Miriam Eisenstein and Jean W. Bodman, "'I Very Appreciate': Expressions of Gratitude by Native and Non-native Speakers of American English," *Applied Linguistics* 7, no. 2 (July 1, 1986): 167–85, https://academic.oup.com /applij/article-abstract/7/2/167/163718.

155 **extroverts do better when it's noisy:** Russell G. Geen, "Preferred Stimulation Levels in Introverts and Extroverts: Effects on Arousal and Performance," *Journal of Personality and Social Psychology* 46, no. 6 (1984): 1303–12, www.researchgate.net/publication/232469347 _Preferred_stimulation_levels_in_introverts_and_extroverts_Effects_on_arousal_and _performance.

155 **lemon juice than an extrovert:** Susan Cain, *Quiet: The Power of Introverts in a World That Can't Stop Talking* (New York: Broadway Books, 2013).

157 **receiving critical feedback:** "The Perils of Performance Appraisals," Association for Psychological Science, January 9, 2014, www.psychologicalscience.org/news/minds-business /the-perils-of-performance-appraisals.html.

157 **negative than our view of ourselves:** Paul Green Jr. et al., "Shopping for Confirmation: How Disconfirming Feedback Shapes Social Networks," Harvard Business School Working Paper, September 2017, https://hbswk.hbs.edu/item/shopping-for-confirmation-how-dis confirming-feedback-shapes-social-networks.

159 **information they need to get promoted:** Harriet B. Braiker, *The Disease to Please: Curing the People-pleasing Syndrome* (New York: McGraw-Hill Education, 2002).

159 **receive generalized commentary:** Shelley Correll and Caroline Simard, "Research: Vague Feedback Is Holding Women Back," *Harvard Business Review*, April 29, 2016, https://hbr .org/2016/04/research-vague-feedback-is-holding-women-back.

159 **"sometimes your comments miss the mark":** Nora Caplan-Bricker, "In Performance Reviews, Women Get Vague Generalities, While Men Get Specifics," *Slate*, May 2, 2016, www .slate.com/blogs/xx_factor/2016/05/02/stanford_researchers_say_women_get_vague _feedback_in_performance_reviews.html.

159 **ability to bridge that gap:** Cade Massey, interview with authors, October 6, 2017.

160 **"What is your opinion on this":** McCord, interview.

160 **"confident you can reach them":** "The Unexpected Sparks of Creativity, Confrontation and Office Culture," Goop Podcast interview with Adam Grant, March 29, 2018, https://itunes .apple.com/us/podcast/the-goop-podcast-debuts-march-8th/id1352546554?i=10004035319 27&mt=2.

161 **mouth but at the other person's ear:** Kim Scott, phone interview with the authors, January 22, 2018.

161 **feedback so she can immediately make improvements:** Elaine D. Pulakos et al., "Performance Management Can Be Fixed: An On-the-Job Experiential Learning Approach for Complex Behavior Change," *Industrial and Organizational Psychology* 8, no. 1 (March 2015): 51–76, www.cambridge.org/core/services/aop-cambridge-core/content/view/S1754942614000029.

162 **Rabkin, a vice president at Facebook:** Mark Rabkin, "Awkward 1:1s: The Art of Getting Honest Feedback," *Medium*, May 21, 2017, https://medium.com/@mrabkin/awkward-1–1s -the-art-of-getting-honest-feedback-2843078b2880.

163 **trustworthiness and accessibility over expertise:** David A. Hofmann et al., "Seeking Help

in the Shadow of Doubt: The Sensemaking Processes Underlying How Nurses Decide Whom to Ask for Advice," *Journal of Applied Psychology* 94, no. 5 (2009): 1261–74. http://psycnet .apa.org/record/2009-12532-010.

163 **improve only when it comes from an expert:** Arie Nadler, "To Seek or Not to Seek: The Relationship between Help Seeking and Job Performance Evaluations as Moderated by Task-relevant Expertise," *Journal of Applied Social Psychology* 33, no. 1 (July 31, 2006): 91–109, https://onlinelibrary.wiley.com/doi/abs/10.1111/j.1559-1816.2003.tb02075.x.

163 **"don't want to feel uncomfortable":** Ilan Zechory and Tom Lehman, "The Genius ISMs," Genius, October 6, 2014, https://genius.com/Genius-the-genius-isms-annotated.

163 **well-intentioned advice might paint an inaccurate picture:** Rachel Emma Silverman, "Gender Bias at Work Turns Up in Feedback," *Wall Street Journal*, September 30, 2015, www.wsj.com/articles/gender-bias-at-work-turns-up-in-feedback-1443600759.

165 **undermine your professionalism:** Lila MacLellan, "The Smiley Face Emoji Has a 'Dark Side,' Researchers Have Found," *Quartz*, August 28, 2017, https://qz.com/1063726/the -smiley-face-emoji-has-a-dark-side-researchers-have-found.

166 **message as *really* angry:** Rachel Sugar, "Your Email Typos Reveal More about You Than You Realize," *Business Insider*, May 31, 2015, www.businessinsider.com/typos-in-emails -2015-5.

166 **"Everyone puts their hand up":** Brian Fetherstonhaugh, interview with the authors, December 11, 2017.

168 **likely for information to be lost:** Stella Garber, "Tips for Managing a Remote Team," *Trello* (blog), May 13, 2015, https://blog.trello.com/tips-for-managing-a-remote-team.

169 **when you've calmed down:** Lehman, interview.

170 **email asks as untrustworthy and nonurgent:** M. Mahdi Roghanizad and Vanessa K. Bohns, "Ask in Person: You're Less Persuasive Than You Think over Email," *Journal of Experimental Social Psychology* 69 (March 2017): 223–26, www.sciencedirect.com/science /article/pii/S002210311630292X.

170 **job plans, and hometowns before negotiating:** Andrew Brodsky, "The Dos and Don'ts of Work Email, from Emojis to Typos," *Harvard Business Review,* April 23, 2015, https://hbr .org/2015/04/the-dos-and-donts-of-work-email-from-emojis-to-typos.

170 **compared to almost everyone in the second:** Michael Morris, "Schmooze or Lose: Social Friction and Lubrication in E-Mail Negotiations," *Group Dynamics: Theory, Research, and Practice* 6, no. 1 (2002): 89–100, www.law.northwestern.edu/faculty/fulltime/nadler/Morris _Nadler_SchmoozeOrLose.pdf.

170 **parody account AcademicsSay:** Nathan C. Hall (@academicssay), "I am away from the office and checking email intermittently. If your email is not urgent, I'll probably still reply. I have a problem," Twitter, May 4, 2014, https://twitter.com/academicssay/status /463113312709124096.

CHAPTER 7: CULTURE

175 **"pursing of the lips . . . Catastrophe":** "The Devil Wears Prada Quotes," IMDB.com, accessed April 11, 2108, www.imdb.com/title/tt0458352/quotes.

176 **internalize her expressed emotion:** Ella Glikson and Miriam Erez, "Emotion Display Norms in Virtual Teams," *Journal of Personnel Psychology* no. 12 (2013): 22–32, http://econtent.hogrefe.com/doi/full/10.1027/1866-5888/a000078.

176 **message length, punctuation, GIFs, and emoji:** Ibid.

176 **spread to her husband's coworkers:** Winnie Yu, "Workplace Rudeness Has a Ripple Effect," *Scientific American*, January 1, 2012, www.scientificamerican.com/article/ripples-of-rudeness.

176 **write and send his response, and then return:** Anese Cavanaugh, *Contagious Culture: Show Up, Set the Tone, and Intentionally Create an Organization That Thrives* (New York: McGraw-Hill, 2015).

177 **"productivity than if we're all rattled":** Gretchen Rubin, phone interview with the authors, February 23, 2018.

177 **"Tell me a story about something":** Adam Grant, "The One Question You Should Ask about Every New Job," *New York Times*, December 19, 2015, www.nytimes.com/2015/12/20/opinion/sunday/the-one-question-you-should-ask-about-every-new-job.html.

180 **our ability to do work well and on time:** Sigal Barsade, "Balancing Emotional and Cognitive Culture," *Wharton Magazine*, Spring/Summer 2016, http://whartonmagazine.com/issues/spring-2016/balancing-emotional-and-cognitive-culture.

180 **shy away from necessary conflict:** Sigal Barsade and Olivia A. O'Neill, "Manage Your Emotional Culture," *Harvard Business Review*, February 2016, https://hbr.org/2016/01/manage-your-emotional-culture.

180 **gratitude are discouraged tend to have higher turnover rates:** Kim Cameron et al., "Effects of Positive Practices on Organizational Effectiveness," *Journal of Applied Behavioral Science* (January 26, 2011), http://journals.sagepub.com/doi/10.1177/0021886310395514.

180 **less money than their kinder colleagues:** Leanne ten Brinke et al., "Hedge Fund Managers with Psychopathic Tendencies Make for Worse Investors," *Personality and Social Psychology Bulletin*, October 19, 2017, http://journals.sagepub.com/doi/full/10.1177/0146167217733080.

181 **more likely to make bad decisions:** Barry M. Staw et al., "Threat-rigidity Effects in Organizational Behavior: A Multilevel Analysis," *Administrative Science Quarterly 26*, no. 4 (1981): 501–24, www.jstor.org/stable/2392337?seq=1#page_scan_tab_contents.

181 **better able to cope with job stress:** Emily D. Heaphy and Jane E. Dutton, "Positive Social Interactions and the Human Body at Work: Linking Organizations and Physiology," *Academy of Management Review* 22, no. 1 (2008): 137–62, http://webuser.bus.umich.edu/janedut/POS/Heaphy%20and%20Dutton%20amr.pdf.

181 **patience instead of fury, we trust them more:** Kim Cameron, "Leadership through Organizational Forgiveness," University of Michigan Ross School of Business, accessed April 12, 2018, www.bus.umich.edu/facultyresearch/research/TryingTimes/Forgiveness.htm.

181 **influence your entire organization:** James H. Fowler and Nicholas A. Christakis, "Cooperative Behavior Cascades in Human Social Networks," *Proceedings of the National Academy of Science* 107, no. 12 (March 23, 2010): 5334–38, www.pnas.org/content/107/12/5334.full.

181 **"smile today will keep guest complaints away":** Shawn Achor, *Before Happiness* (New York: Crown Business, 2013).

182 **hung copies around his office:** Giles Turnbull, "It's ok to say what's ok," UK Government Blog, https://gds.blog.gov.uk/2016/05/25/its-ok-to-say-whats-ok.

182 **helped new hires absorb the culture quickly and easily:** Giles Turnbull, email interview with authors, March 20, 2017.

182 **workplace happiness and motivation:** Sigal Barsade and Olivia A. O'Neill, "Manage Your Emotional Culture," *Harvard Business Review*, January–February 2016, https://hbr.org/2016/01/manage-your-emotional-culture.

183 **"how we might design a better process":** Douglas Stone et al., *Difficult Conversations* (New York: Penguin, 2010).

183 **"may be better for you to leave":** Sigal Barsade, phone interview with the authors, January 21, 2018.

183 **"Don't make small talk with him":** Paul Kalanithi, *When Breath Becomes Air* (New York: Random House, 2016).

183 **explains Cornell Professor Kevin Kniffin:** Susan Kelley, "Groups That Eat Together Perform Better Together," *Cornell Chronicle*, November 19, 2015, http://news.cornell.edu/stories/2015/11/groups-eat-together-perform-better-together.

184 **$15 million jump a year in productivity gains:** Alex Pentland, *Honest Signals* (Cambridge, MA: MIT Press, 2008).

184 **writes their names on the coffee cups:** Keith Yamashita, interview with the authors, December 19, 2017.

184 **fully paid weeklong trip to anywhere in the world:** "Tory Burch: A Culture of Women's Empowerment," *Business of Fashion*, May 20, 2014, www.businessoffashion.com/articles/careers/tory-burch-culture-womens-empowerment.

185 **resources officer at ServiceNow:** Pat Wadors, phone interview with the authors, December 13, 2017.

188 **"call on everyone else by name":** Yamashita, interview.

190 **strongest predictors of turnover:** Katie Benner, "Slack, an Upstart in Messaging, Now Faces Giant Tech Rivals," *New York Times*, April 16, 2017, www.nytimes.com/2017/04/16/technology/slack-employee-messaging-workplace.html.

190 **"I" to "we" pronouns:** Gabriel Doyle et al., "Alignment at Work: Using Language to Distinguish the Internalization and Self-regulation Components of Cultural Fit in Organizations," *Proceedings of the 55th Annual Meeting of the Association for Computational Linguistics*, July 2017, 603–12, www.aclweb.org/anthology/P17–1056.

191 **"room to learn from their mistakes":** Wadors, interview.

191 **At Warby Parker, employees call new hires:** Krystal Barghelame, "What Maslow's Hierarchy of Needs Can Teach Us About Employee Onboarding," *Gusto*, accessed April 13, 2018, https://gusto.com/framework/hr/what-maslows-hierarchy-of-needs-can-teach-us-employee-onboarding.

191 **productive nine months down the line:** "Inside Google's Culture of Success and Employee Happiness," *Kissmetrics* (blog), accessed April 13, 2018, https://blog.kissmetrics.com/googles-culture-of-success.

192 **sometimes feels isolated and invisible:** Laura Savino, phone interview with the authors, June 15, 2017.

192 **"helps you understand each other":** Courtney Seiter, phone interview with the authors, December 15, 2017.

193 **receive this kind of informal feedback:** Megan Wheeler, phone interview with the authors, January 8, 2018.

193 **explains Kristen Chirco of E Group:** Jon Hainstock, "5 Proven Strategies for Motivating Employees Who Work Remotely," *Hubspot* (blog), January 26, 2017, https://blog.hubstaff .com/motivating-employees-who-work-remotely/#1.

195 **Obama while studying at Princeton:** Thomas Gilovich and Lee Ross, *The Wisest One in the Room: How You Can Benefit from Social Psychology's Most Powerful Insights* (New York: Free Press, 2016).

195 **Although everyone experiences periods of self-doubt:** Gregory M. Walton and Geoffrey L. Cohen, "A Question of Belonging: Race, Social Fit, and Achievement," *Journal of Personality and Social Psychology* 92, no. 1 (2007): 82–96, www.goshen.edu/wp-content/uploads/sites /2/2016/08/WaltonCohen2007.pdf.

196 **"Does my group belong":** Carissa Romero, "Who Belongs in Tech?" *Medium*, January 26, 2016, https://medium.com/inclusion-insights/who-belongs-in-tech-9ef3a8fdd3.

196 **sociologist Adia Harvey Wingfield told us:** Adia Harvey Wingfield, phone interview with the authors, April 18, 2018.

196 **speak without an accent or avoid slang:** Adia Harvey Wingfield, "Being Black—but Not Too Black—in the Workplace," *The Atlantic*, October 14, 2015, www.theatlantic.com/business /archive/2015/10/being-black-work/409990.

196 **underestimate how isolating this can be:** Loran F. Nordgren et al., "Empathy Gaps for Social Pain: Why People Underestimate the Pain of Social Suffering," *Journal of Personality and Social Psychology* 100, no. 1 (2011): 120–28, http://psycnet.apa.org/record/2010 –26912–002.

196 **non-minorities to feel alone:** Sylvia Ann Hewlett et al., "People Suffer at Work When They Can't Discuss the Racial Bias They Face Outside of It," *Harvard Business Review*, July 10, 2017, https://hbr.org/2017/07/people-suffer-at-work-when-they-cant-discuss-the-racial -bias-they-face-outside-of-it.

196 **uninclusive work environments:** Gene H. Brody et al., "Resilience in Adolescence, Health, and Psychosocial Outcomes," *Pediatrics* 138, no. 6 (December 2016); http://pediatrics .aappublications.org/content/138/6/e20161042.

196 **"empathy for the black community wasn't there":** Emily Chang, *Brotopia* (New York: Portfolio, 2018), 125.

197 **"listening when we'd rather yell":** Seth Godin, "Emotional Labor," SethGodin.com, accessed April 8, 2018, http://sethgodin.typepad.com/seths_blog/2017/05/emotional-labor.html.

197 **feel stressed and eventually burn out:** Susan David, "Managing the Hidden Stress of Emotional Labor," *Harvard Business Review*, September 8, 2016, https://hbr.org/2016/09/managing -the-hidden-stress-of-emotional-labor.

197 **lean on them for emotional support:** Julia Carpenter, "The 'Invisible Labor' Still Asked of Women at Work," CNNMoney, October 18, 2017, http://money.cnn.com/2017/10/18/pf /women-emotional-labor/index.html.

197 **"pretending to find him fascinating":** Emilie Friedlander, "The Emotional Labor of

Women in the Workplace," *The Outline*, November 27, 2017, https://theoutline.com/post /2514/the-emotional-labor-of-women-in-the-workplace.

198 **"I'd watch other people say things":** Friedlander, "The Emotional Labor of Women."

198 **wrote CEO Josh James:** Josh James, "CEOs: Building a More Inclusive Culture Should Be at the Top of Your 2018 Plan," LinkedIn, April 4, 2018, www.linkedin.com/pulse/ceos-building -more-inclusive-culture-should-top-your-2018-josh-james.

200 **"everyone gets over it":** Paul Tough, "Who Gets to Graduate?" *New York Times*, May 15, 2014, www.nytimes.com/2014/05/18/magazine/who-gets-to-graduate.html.

200 **part of the intervention group:** Gregory M. Walton and Geoffrey L. Cohen, "A Brief Social-Belonging Intervention Improves Academic and Health Outcomes of Minority Students," *Science* 331, no. 6023 (2011): 1447, http://science.sciencemag.org/content/331/6023/1447.

200 **highly selective engineering program:** Gregory M. Walton et al., "Two Brief Interventions to Mitigate a 'Chilly Climate' Transform Women's Experience, Relationships, and Achievement in Engineering," *Journal of Educational Psychology* 107 (2015): 468–85.

200 **likely to be seen as threatening:** Molly Reynolds, "Should We Talk about Race at Work? PwC Thinks So," *Huffington Post*, August 9, 2016, www.huffingtonpost.com/molly-reynolds /should-we-talk-about-race_b_11333870.html.

200 **"bring their whole selves to work":** Timothy F. Ryan, " 'The Silence Was Deafening'—Why We Need to Talk about Race," LinkedIn, www.linkedin.com/pulse/silence-deafening-why -we-need-talk-race-timothy-f-ryan.

200 **content strategist Cameron:** Cameron Hough, "A Guide for White Allies Confronting Racial Injustice," June 23, 2015, https://drive.google.com/file/d/0B2vDBY9AHUjQN0t JYXlLUmtJUVE/view?pref=2&pli=1.

201 **someone outside of the targeted group:** Alexander M. Czopp et al., "Standing Up for a Change: Reducing Bias Through Interpersonal Confrontation," *Journal of Personality and Social Psychology* 90, no. 5 (2006): 784–803, https://pdfs.semanticscholar.org/f3c7/4aa95cb2 d4ce04cfccbf7298290ce3cbb370.pdf.

201 **"even when they're not in the room":** Pat Wadors, phone interview with authors, December 13, 2017.

201 **"it takes the edge off":** Mellody Hobson, "PwC Talks: Mellody Hobson's Advice on Having Conversations about Race," *PWC*, August 7, 2015, www.youtube.com/watch?v=sXXB4 NHv5hQ.

CHAPTER 8: LEADERSHIP

207 **"breaking an unspoken contract":** Laszlo Bock, interview with the authors, March 7, 2018.

208 **and are kinder to our colleagues:** Richard E. Boyatzis, "Examination of the Neural Substrates Activated in Memories of Experiences with Resonant and Dissonant Leaders," *The Leadership Quarterly* 23 (2012): 259–72, www.criticalcoaching.com/wp-content/uploads /2015/04/Boyatzis_LeadershipQuarterl12.pdf.

208 **leaders when they show emotion:** Peter H. Kim et al., "Power as an Emotional Liability: Implications for Perceived Authenticity and Trust after a Transgression," *Journal of Experimental Psychology* 146, no. 10 (2017): 1379–1401, http://psycnet.apa.org/record/2017-43117-001.

209 **company is doing poorly:** Peter J. Jordan and Dirk Lindebaumb, "A Model of Within Person Variation in Leadership: Emotion Regulation and Scripts as Predictors of Situationally Appropriate Leadership," *The Leadership Quarterly* 26 (2015): 594–605, https://pdfs .semanticscholar.org/0ed1/f04f0b822a611be1ee142e75d32d0323d9b9.pdf.

209 **we don't consciously realize they're angry:** James J. Gross and Robert W. Levenson, "Emotional Suppression: Physiology, Self-report, and Expressive Behavior," *Journal of Personality and Social Psychology* 64, no. 6 (1993): 970–986, http://psycnet.apa.org/record/1993–36668–001.

209 **question your ability to do your job:** Rikki Rogers, "TMI: How to Deal with an Oversharing Boss," *The Muse*, accessed April 21, 2018, www.themuse.com/advice/tmi-how-to-deal -with-an-oversharing-boss.

209 **trigger the same negative response:** Kerry Roberts Gibson, "When Sharing Hurts: How and Why Self-disclosing Weakness Undermines the Task-oriented Relationships of Higher Status Disclosers," *Organizational Behavior and Human Decision Processes* 144 (January 2018): 25–43, www.sciencedirect.com/science/article/pii/S0749597815302521.

210 **"tornado bell goes off in a mall":** Julie Zhou, *The Making of a Manager: What to Do When Everyone Looks to You* (New York: Portfolio, 2018).

210 **"should be coming in earlier":** Grant Packard et al, "(I'm) Happy to Help (You): The Impact of Personal Pronoun Use in Customer-Firm Interactions," *Journal of Marketing Research*, May 2016, http://journals.ama.org/doi/abs/10.1509/jmr.16.0118?code=amma-site.

211 **"What would be helpful to you right now":** Search Inside Yourself Program, authors attended in New York City, November 3, 2017.

211 **suggestions heard when you're not in charge:** Susan Cain, "Not Leadership Material? Good. The World Needs Followers," *New York Times*, March 24, 2017, www.nytimes.com/2017/03/24 /opinion/sunday/not-leadership-material-good-the-world-needs-followers.html.

211 **problems or strong emotions:** Pablo Briñol et al., "The Effects of Message Recipients' Power Before and After Persuasion: A self-validation analysis," *Journal of Personality and Social Psychology* 93, no. 6 (2007): 1040–53, http://psycnet.apa.org/record/2007–17941–009.

211 **"wrong way in their two years":** Bill George, phone interview with the authors, March 2, 2018.

211 **"while great managers play chess":** Marcus Buckingham, "What Great Managers Do," *Harvard Business Review*, March 2005, https://hbr.org/2005/03/what-great-managers-do.

212 **"soothe your own anxieties":** Jerry Colonna, phone interview with the authors, December 12, 2017.

212 **"it's scary and I need your":** Carol Hymowitz, "One Woman Learned to Start Being a Leader," *Wall Street Journal*, March 16, 1999, www.wsj.com/articles/SB921531662347678470.

213 **"how much weight the people around":** Bock, interview.

213 **uplifting and empowering story possible:** Tony Schwartz, "Emotional Contagion Can Take Down Your Whole Team," *Harvard Business Review*, July 11, 2012, https://hbr.org/2012 /07/emotional-contagion-can-ta.

215 **"when you walk in the door":** Kim Scott, *Radical Candor* (New York: St. Martin's, 2017).

215 **didn't know why the manager was mad:** Lukas F. Koning and Gerben A. Van Kleef, "How Leaders' Emotional Displays Shape Followers' Organizational Citizenship Behavior," *The Leadership Quarterly* 26, no. 4 (August 2015): 489–501, www.sciencedirect.com/science /article/pii/S1048984315000296.

215 **stress levels dropped by more than 30 percent:** Jamil Zaki, "How to Soften the Blow of Bad News," *Wall Street Journal*, December 9, 2016, www.wsj.com/articles/how-to-soften-the -blow-of-bad-news-1481319105.

215 **"bad day as a boss is bullshit":** Kim Scott, phone interview with the authors, January 22, 2018.

216 **interrupt him except the president or his wife:** David Leonhardt, "You're Too Busy, You Need A 'Schultz Hour,'" *New York Times*, April 18, 2017.

216 **report feeling alone in their roles:** Thomas J. Saporito, "It's Time to Acknowledge CEO Loneliness," *Harvard Business Review*, February 15, 2012, https://hbr.org/2012/02/its-time -to-acknowledge-ceo-lo.

216 **"help you move on to the next job":** Ilana Gershon, "The Quitting Economy: When Employees Are Treated as Short-term Assets, They Reinvent Themselves as Marketable Goods, Always Ready to Quit," *Aeon*, July 26, 2017, https://aeon.co/essays/how-work-changed-to-make -us-all-passionate-quitters.

216 **great source of new business and referrals:** Lindsay Gellman, "Companies Tap Alumni for New Business and New Workers," *Wall Street Journal*, February 21, 2016, www.wsj.com /articles/companies-tap-alumni-for-new-business-and-new-workers-1456110347.

218 **"professional setting, your boss isn't going to text you":** Julia Byers, phone interview with the authors, October 15, 2017.

218 **boss is bringing you down:** Shawn Achor and Michelle Gielan, "Make Yourself Immune to Secondhand Stress," *Harvard Business Review*, September 2, 2015, https://hbr.org/2015/09 /make-yourself-immune-to-secondhand-stress.

219 **specific personality traits:** Bill George, "True North: Discover Your Authentic Leadership," BillGeorge.com, March 28, 2007, www.billgeorge.org/articles/true-north-discover-your -authentic-leadership.

219 **less friendly or approachable and as more competitive:** Dan Goleman, "Are Women More Emotionally Intelligent Than Men?" *Psychology Today*, April 29, 2011, www.psychologytoday .com/blog/the-brain-and-emotional-intelligence/201104/are-women-more-emotionally -intelligent-men.

220 **"always keep our emotions in check":** Jennifer Palmieri, *Dear Madam President* (New York: Grand Central Publishing, 2018).

221 **tune out emotion and start problem solving:** Goleman, "Are Women More Emotionally Intelligent?"

221 **unsupported in an emotionally trying situation:** Ibid.

221 **a top-performing leader, no matter their gender:** Ibid.

221 **they tend to introduce male doctors:** Julia A. Mayer, "Speaker Introductions at Internal Medicine Grand Rounds: Forms of Address Reveal Gender Bias," *Journal of Women's Health* 26, no. 5 (May 2017), www.liebertpub.com/doi/abs/10.1089/jwh.2016.6044?journal Code=jwh.

222 **didn't want to work for another woman:** Olga Khazan, "Why Do Women Bully Each Other at Work?" *The Atlantic*, September 2017, www.theatlantic.com/magazine/archive/2017/09 /the-queen-bee-in-the-corner-office/534213.

222 **"my abilities and partly being judged":** Ibid.

223 **writes psychologist Laurie Rudman:** Ibid.

223 **people as management material:** Ashleigh Shelby Rosette et al., "The White Standard: Racial Bias in Leader Categorization," *Journal of Applied Psychology* 93, no. 4 (2008): 758–77, www.ncbi.nlm.nih.gov/pubmed/18642982.

223 **absent from the list of Fortune 500 CEOs:** "Asians in America: Unleashing the Potential of the 'Model Minority,'" Center for Talent Innovation, July 1, 2011, www.talentinnovation.org /publication.cfm?publication=1270.

223 **"positions can be an emotional challenge":** Adia Harvey Wingfield, phone interview with the authors, April 18, 2018.

224 **making mistakes in a leadership role:** Robert W. Livingston, "Backlash and the Double Bind," Gender, Race, and Leadership Symposium: An Examination of the Challenges Facing Non-prototypical Leaders (2013), www.hbs.edu/faculty/conferences/2013-w50-research -symposium/Documents/livingston.pdf.

224 **describes a Latina executive:** Sylvia Ann Hewlett et al., "U.S. Latinos Feel They Can't Be Themselves at Work," *Harvard Business Review,* October 11, 2016, https://hbr.org/2016/10 /u-s-latinos-feel-they-cant-be-themselves-at-work.

224 **are least likely to find mentors in large corporations:** Alexandra E. Petri, "When Potential Mentors Are Mostly White and Male," *The Atlantic*, July 7, 2017, www.theatlantic.com /business/archive/2017/07/mentorship-implicit-bias/532953.

224 **CEOs who retired or were forced out:** Gillian B. White, "There Are Currently 4 Black CEOs in the Fortune 500," *The Atlantic*, October 26, 2017, www.theatlantic.com/business/archive /2017/10/black-ceos-fortune-500/543960.

224 **"manage somebody who's older than I am":** Peter Cappelli, "Managing Older Workers," *Harvard Business Review,* September 2010, https://hbr.org/2010/09/managing-older-workers.

225 **became a manager at Facebook:** Julie Zhou, "Managing More Experienced People," *The Looking Glass Email Newsletter,* October 9, 2017.

225 **managers could learn from them:** Kevin Roose, "Executive Mentors Wanted. Only Millennials Need Apply," *New York Times,* October 15, 2017, www.nytimes.com/2017/10/15 /technology/millennial-mentors-executives.html.

225 **meek are just as likely to inherit the world:** Dana Stephens-Craig, "Perception of Introverted Leaders by Mid- to High-level Leaders," *Journal of Marketing and Management* 6, no. 1 (May 2015), www.questia.com/library/journal/1P3–3687239281/perception-of-introverted -leaders-by-mid-to-high-level.

225 **Bill Gates, Warren Buffett, and Larry Page:** Jim Collins, *Good to Great: Why Some Companies Make the Leap—and Others Don't* (New York: Harper Business, 2011).

226 **introverted leaders are tied to higher profits:** Adam M. Grant et al., "Reversing the Extroverted Leadership Advantage: The Role of Employee Proactivity," *Academy of Management Journal* 54, no. 3 (June 1, 2011), http://amj.aom.org/content/54/3/528.short.

226 **were connected to a better bottom line:** Ian D. Gow et al., "CEO Personality and Firm Policies," *National Bureau of Economic Research Working Paper* No. 22435 (July 2016), www.nber.org/papers/w22435.

226 **Susan Cain's book *Quiet*:** Adam M. Grant et al., "The Hidden Advantages of Quiet Bosses," *Harvard Business Review*, December 2010, https://hbr.org/2010/12/the-hidden-advantages -of-quiet-bosses.

227 **"little superficial dances":** Jennifer Kahnweiler, *The Introverted Leader: Building on Your Quiet Strength* (Oakland, CA: Berrett-Koehler Publishers, 2013).

227 **tendency toward MBWA:** Thomas J. Peters, *In Search of Excellence* (New York: Harper Business, 2006).

228 **introverts work best in quiet spaces:** Russell G. Geen, "Preferred Stimulation Levels in Introverts and Extroverts: Effects on Arousal and Performance," *Journal of Personality and Social Psychology* 46, no. 6 (June 1984): 1303–12, www.researchgate.net/publication/232469347 _Preferred_stimulation_levels_in_introverts_and_extroverts_Effects_on_arousal_and _performance.

228 **"best leaders end up operating like ambiverts":** Emma Featherstone, "How Extroverts Are Taking the Top Jobs—and What Introverts Can Do about It," *Guardian*, February 23, 2018, www.theguardian.com/business-to-business/2018/feb/23/how-extroverts-are-taking-the -top-jobs-and-what-introverts-can-do-about-it.

FURTHER RESOURCES ON EMOTIONS

239 **"until asked to give a definition":** Beverley Fehr and James A. Russell, "Concept of Emotion Viewed from a Prototype Perspective," *Journal of Experimental Psychology* 113, no. 3 (1984): 464.

240 **"brain's way of making meaning":** Lisa Feldman Barrett, phone interview with the authors, November 21, 2017.

241 **their broader term *pe'ape'a*:** Lisa Feldman Barrett, *How Emotions Are Made: The Secret Life of the Brain* (New York: Houghton Mifflin Harcourt, 2017).

241 **escape the tyranny of RBF:** Jessica Bennett, "I'm Not Mad. That's Just My RBF," *New York Times*, August 1, 2015, www.nytimes.com/2015/08/02/fashion/im-not-mad-thats-just-my -resting-b-face.html.

241 **"When you see a bitchy face":** Barrett, interview.

241 **handle relationships with empathy:** Andrea Ovans, "How Emotional Intelligence Became a Key Leadership Skill," *Harvard Business Review*, April 28, 2015.

241 **Without emotional intelligence:** "Breakthrough Ideas for Tomorrow's Business Agenda," *Harvard Business Review*, April 2003.

242 **public speaking than we are of dying:** Karen Kangas Dwyer and Marlina M. Davidson, "Is Public Speaking Really More Feared Than Death?" *Communication Research Reports* 29, no. 2 (April 2012): 99–107, www.tandfonline.com/doi/full/10.1080/08824096.2012.667772? src=recsys.

244 **doesn't define your entire mood:** Susan David and Christine Congleton, "Emotional Agility," *Harvard Business Review*, November 2013, https://hbr.org/2013/11/emotional-agility.

244 **called emotional granularity:** Lisa Feldman Barrett, "Are You in Despair? That's Good," *New York Times*, June 3, 2016, www.nytimes.com/2016/06/05/opinion/sunday/are-you-in -despair-thats-good.html.

244 **become vindictive when stressed:** Ibid.

244 **workplace training firm LifeLabs Learning:** LeeAnn Renninger, phone interview with the authors, April 19, 2018.

245 **lesser-known emotion:** Tiffany Watt Smith, *The Book of Human Emotions* (New York: Little, Brown, 2016).

EMOTIONAL TENDENCIES ASSESSMENT

249 **on emotional regulation in chapter 8: "Leadership":** LeeAnn Renninger, phone interview with the authors, April 19, 2018.

250 **add them together with the subtotal:** Amy C. Edmondson, "Team Psychological Safety," *Administrative Science Quarterly* 44, no. 2 (1999): 350–83.

251 **number from 1 to your subtotal:** Bonnie M. Hagerty and Kathleen M. Patusky, "Developing a Measure of Sense of Belonging," *Nursing Research* 44, no. 1 (January 1995): 9–13, www .researchgate.net/publication/15335777_Developing_a_Measure_Of_Sense_of_Belonging.

Index

PENGUIN PARTNERSHIPS

Penguin Partnerships is the Creative Sales and Promotions team at Penguin Random House. We have a long history of working with clients on a wide variety of briefs, specializing in brand promotions, bespoke publishing and retail exclusives, plus corporate, entertainment and media partnerships.

We can respond quickly to briefs and specialize in repurposing books and content for sales promotions, for use as incentives and retail exclusives as well as creating content for new books in collaboration with our partners as part of branded book relationships.

Equally if you'd simply like to buy a bulk quantity of one of our existing books at a special discount, we can help with that too. Our books can make excellent corporate or employee gifts.

Special editions, including personalized covers, excerpts of existing books or books with corporate logos can be created in large quantities for special needs.

We can work within your budget to deliver whatever you want, however you want it.

For more information, please contact
salesenquiries@penguinrandomhouse.co.uk